Let Workers Move

DIRECTIONS IN DEVELOPMENT
Trade

Let Workers Move

Using Bilateral Labor Agreements to Increase Trade in Services

Sebastián Sáez, editor

THE WORLD BANK
Washington, D.C.

Contents

Boxes

Figures

Tables

Foreword

People have moved across borders since ancient times. Historically, migration was explained by many different factors, among them the need to transport goods through trading routes. Today migration is facilitated by declining costs in communications and transportation services. People can move from one continent to another in a matter of hours instead of weeks or months. The decline in transportation costs and other factors have facilitated temporary migration.

Trade in services is one of the most dynamic dimensions of global trade, growing faster than trade in goods. The temporary movement of people is one of the modes by which services are delivered across borders.

Despite significant technological changes that have facilitated cross-border transactions, for a number of activities services delivery still requires the close proximity of the producer and the consumer of services. Most nurses, managers, specialists, tradespeople, and semiskilled and low-skilled workers must be physically present to deliver their services. For developing countries, the temporary movement of people, in particular semiskilled and low-skilled workers, is the basis of their comparative advantage in trade in services.

Unlike the flows of capital and goods, which have been significantly liberalized in recent decades, severe trade barriers continue to impede the temporary movement of people. Although the benefits of even a small liberalization in migration flows are huge, countries have put a large number of instruments in place to manage the flows of people. This book examines how countries can increase trade in services through the movement of people despite these measures.

The entry into force of the World Trade Organization—and more specifically, the General Agreement on Trade in Services—was a significant step toward liberalizing trade in services, including through the temporary movement of people. But after almost 20 years, progress remains slow. Efforts at the regional level have also had limited results. What can developing countries do to increase trade in services?

This book explores the experience of both sending and receiving countries with bilateral labor agreements (BLAs). Although BLAs are not designed with the aim of facilitating the movement of people to deliver services, they can potentially be tailored to achieve these goals, complementing multilateral and regional level efforts to promote services exports.

The book highlights the importance of shared responsibility to ensure temporariness—the most important condition for further liberalizing the movement of people. Temporariness requires close collaboration between sending and receiving countries to create the institutional arrangements and incentives necessary to select, monitor, and ensure that workers covered by the agreements return to their countries. Both sending and receiving countries have an interest in ensuring temporariness, so that schemes remain sustainable over time.

Close collaboration between the private sector and the government in both sending and receiving countries is also critical. In receiving countries, the private sector can help identify the skills required in the labor market. In sending countries, it can help find and select the most appropriate workers demanded in receiving countries. All stakeholders should agree to additional requirements to ensure migrant workers' welfare.

Bilateral agreements are not without shortcomings. Chief among them is their nonbinding nature. Receiving countries prefer flexible agreements, which can be adjusted depending on labor market conditions. This flexibility hurts service providers from sending countries, who assume all the risks of changing economic conditions.

There is no simple solution to this problem. BLAs are a complement to, not a substitute for, both global efforts to build a more liberal international regime and regional initiatives, which may be more relevant for small and medium-size economies.

Liberalization appears to have been stymied by the political sensitivity associated with temporary labor mobility in both receiving and sending countries. This constraint advises for a cautious, gradual, and cooperative approach. Receiving countries must carefully assess the impact of temporary migration flows on domestic labor markets; sending countries should be mindful of the need to mitigate the potential negative impact on domestic development. Policy makers should factor in these dimensions to garner the necessary political support.

The book will be of great interest to policy makers interested in expanding opportunities of services trade, academics in developing countries interested in trade as a development tool, and trade experts involved in trade negotiations. We hope that the questions it raises will motivate new research and guide the analysis of economic policy on service trade and its interaction with the temporary movement of people.

Mona Haddad
Sector Manager
International Trade Department
Poverty Reduction and Economic Management Network
World Bank

Acknowledgments

This book was prepared by a team led by Sebastián Sáez from the World Bank's International Trade Department, Poverty Reduction and Economic Management Network, under the direction of Mona Haddad. The editor would like to thank the authors of the individual chapters who contributed to the project: Antonio Bonet, Arti Grover Goswami, Manjula Luthria, Mai Malaulau, Marion Panizzon, John Paolo R. Rivera, Denise Jannah D. Serrano, Yolanda Stratchan, and Tereso S. Tullao, Jr.

The editor would also like to thank the many individuals who contributed to the project. The original concept note benefited from comments by Michael Engman (World Bank), Antonia Carzaniga (World Trade Organization), and Sherry Stephenson (Organization of American States) that helped direct the project. An early draft benefited from comments by Antonia Carzaniga (World Trade Organization) and Caglar Ozden (World Bank), who kindly agreed to peer-review the book. Rupa Chanda, Michael Engman, Bernard Hoekman, Martin Molinuevo, and Maurice Schiff provided additional comments and suggestions. Ian Gillson, Charles Kunaka, Aaditya Mattoo, Julia Burr Oliver, Sonia Plaza, Jose Guilherme Reis, Jose Daniel Reyes, and Daria Taglioni provided useful suggestions and comments at different stages of the project.

Shienny S. Lie provided excellent administrative assistance and helped format the volume. Amir Alexander Fouad provided support during the book's preparation and coordinated the International Trade Department's publication program. Barbara Karni patiently edited the book, helping significantly to shape its messages.

This project was supported in part by the governments of Finland, Norway, Sweden, and the United Kingdom through the Multidonor Trust Fund for Trade and Development. Neither the project nor the book would have been possible without the continuous support and guidance of the staff of the International Trade Department and its management team, in particular Mona Haddad (Sector Manager) and Bernard Hoekman (Director). The editor would also like to thank the World Bank's Office of the Publisher for the efficient management of the publication process, in particular, Abdia Mohamed, Melody Knight, and Deborah Appel-Barker who provided excellent editorial, design, production, and printing services for this book.

Contributors

Antonio Bonet is the president of ACE International Consultants, Madrid.

Arti Grover Goswami is a consultant in the International Trade Department of the World Bank.

Manjula Luthria is a senior economist in the Middle East and North Africa Social Protection unit of the World Bank.

Mai Malaulau is a consultant to the East Asia Poverty Reduction unit of the World Bank.

Marion Panizzon is an assistant professor of international economic law at the World Trade Institute, University of Bern.

John Paolo R. Rivera is an associate professor in the School of Economics at De La Salle University, in Manila.

Sebastián Sáez is a senior trade economist in the International Trade Department of the World Bank.

Denise Jannah D. Serrano is a lecturer in the School of Economics at De La Salle University, in Manila.

Yolanda Stratchan is a young professional at the Multilateral Investment Fund of the Inter-American Development Bank.

Tereso S. Tullao Jr. is a professor in the School of Economics and director of the Angelo King Institute for Economic and Business Studies at De La Salle University, in Manila.

Abbreviations

AFAS	ASEAN Framework Agreement on Services
AFTA	ASEAN Free Trade Area
ANZCERTA	Australia–New Zealand Closer Economic Relations
APEC	Asia Pacific Economic Cooperation
ASEAN	Association of Southeast Asian Nations
AusAid	Australian Agency for International Development
BLAs	Bilateral labor agreements
CARIFORUM	Caribbean Forum
CARICOM	Caribbean Community
CEFTA	Central European Free Trade Agreement
CEOE	Confederation of Business Organizations
CHED	Commission on Higher Education
CHFO	Catalogue of Hard-to-Fill Occupations
CIGEM	Migration Information and Management Centre in Mali
CMEA	Council for Mutual Economic Assistance
COMESA	Common Market for Eastern and Southern Africa
CSAWP	Canada-Commonwealth Caribbean Seasonal Agricultural Workers Program
CSME	CARICOM Single Market and Economy
DGM	Directorate General for Migration
DOLE	Department of Labor
EEA	European Economic Area
EFTA	European Free Trade Agreement
ENP	European Neighbourhood Policy
ENT	economic needs test
EPA	Economic Partnership Agreement
ESC	Economic and Social Council
EU	European Union
FARMS	Foreign Agricultural Resource Management Services

FIC	Forum Island Country
FTAA	Free Trade Area of the Americas
GAM	global approach to migration
GATS	General Agreement on Trade in Services
GATT	General Agreement on Tariffs and Trade
GDP	gross domestic product
HEART	Human Employment and Resource Training
HRSDC	Human Resources and Skills Development Canada
IAU	inter-agency understanding
ICT	information and communication technology
ILO	International Labour Organization
IMF	International Monetary Fund
INEM	Instituto Nacional de Empleo
IOM	International Organization for Migration
LDC	least developed country
LEAP	Labor and Employment Action Plan
LOE	Ley Orgánica de Extranjeria
LPN	Licensed Practical Nurse
M&E	monitoring and evaluation
MERCOSUR	Southern Common Market Agreement
MFN	most favored nation
MIIINDS	Ministry of Immigration, Integration, National Identity and Solidarity Development
MNP	Movement of Natural Persons
MOA	memorandums of agreement
MOU	memorandum of understanding
MRA	mutual recognition agreement
NAFTA	North American Free Trade Agreement
NRCO	National Reintegration Center for OFWs
NZAID	New Zealand Aid Programme
OECD	The Organisation for Economic Co-operation and Development
OFII	Office Français de l'Immigration et de l'Intégration
OFW	overseas Filipino worker
OWWA	Philippine Overseas Workers Welfare Administration
PIDS	Philippine Institute of Development Studies
POEA	Philippine Overseas Employment Administration
PPP	public-private partnership
PRC	Professional Regulation Commission

PSWPS	Pacific Seasonal Worker Pilot Scheme
PSZ	priority solidarity zone
PTA	preferential trade agreement
ROAME	Répertoire Opérationnel Africain des Métiers et des Emplois
RSE	Recognised Seasonal Employer
SAARC	South Asian Association for Regional Cooperation
SADC	Southern African Development Community
SENA	Servicio Nacional de Aprendizaje
SWP	Seasonal Worker Program
TESDA	Technical Education and Skills Development Authority
TN	Trade NAFTA
UTSTM	Unidad Técnica de Selección de Trabajadores Migratorios
WTO	World Trade Organization

CHAPTER 1

Trade in Services and Bilateral Labor Agreements: Overview

Sebastián Sáez

Unlike the movement of capital, the movement of labor across countries remains highly restricted—despite the huge global returns to international labor mobility. According to one estimate, allowing the temporary migration of skilled and unskilled workers equivalent to 3 percent of the workforces of the world's developed countries would increase global welfare by more than US$156 billion a year (Winters 2008).

If the benefits of temporary labor mobility are so great, why is there not more movement?[1] During the Uruguay Round negotiations under the auspices of the General Agreement on Tariffs and Trade (GATT), negotiators established a rules-based system to regulate and liberalize trade in services, including through the temporary movement of people. The results on the temporary movement of people were disappointing.

Since the entry into force of the World Trade Organization (WTO) in 1995, efforts to liberalize trade in services have continued. Although the Doha Development Round of trade negotiations has discussed the issue and countries have attempted to further liberalize trade in services at the regional and bilateral level, success has remained meager (Hoekman and Ozden 2010; Martin and Mattoo 2011; Stephenson and Hufbauer 2010). The number of categories of people included in the agreements is small, usually covering only business visitors and high-level employees of multinational corporations. Low-skilled workers, a key category of interest for several developing countries, are excluded, and limitations and conditions on access to markets, such as economic needs tests (ENTs) and other regulatory barriers, remain.

Progress appears to have been stymied not by the forum of negotiations but by the political sensitivity associated with even temporary labor mobility.

This chapter benefited from inputs and suggestions from Arti Grover Goswami, Manjula Luthria, Mai Malaulau, Philip Martin, Yolanda Strachan, and Tereso Tullao. Throughout the book, the terms *bilateral labor agreements*, *guest worker programs*, and *memorandum of understanding* are used interchangeably. They may differ in legal status, domestic ratification procedures, and scope.

To circumvent this problem, experts are increasingly proposing the use of bilateral labor agreements (BLAs), which are generally not part of trade agreements (Hoekman and Winters 2009; Mattoo and Payton 2007; Stephenson and Hufbauer 2010).[2] BLAs are cooperation arrangements, legally binding or not, between destination and origin countries to manage labor migration (ILO 2006).

A properly functioning international migration regime, which is not available and is unlikely to be so in the medium term, would be the coherent approach to a more inclusive globalization (Bhagwati 2004; Goldin, Cameron, and Balarajan 2011). Such a comprehensive regime has to address skill and demographic imbalances, family reunification issues, and the costs and benefits of permanent versus temporary migration. Another set of important issues covers family settlement, citizenship rights, and other social benefits, which are crucial for assimilation and efficient long-term outcomes. These broader issues go beyond the focus of this book.

The objective of this book is to identify and discuss possible options for increasing services trade through the temporary movement of people, as a complement, not a substitute, to what can be achieved at the WTO, regional, and bilateral levels through trade agreement. BLAs could play a complementary role provided they are designed with the aim of promoting services trade through the temporary movement of people and fulfill specific requirements, including requirements that ensure temporariness. In general, such agreements have not been designed to promote trade in services; they have traditionally been tailored to facilitate or manage labor migration flows.

The book is divided into two parts. Chapters 1–3 assess what has been achieved so far in trade agreements in terms of the temporary movement of services providers. They also discuss the pros and cons of using BLAs as possible channels for the expansion of trade in services. Chapters 4–8 use case studies to examine the viability and performance of BLAs as a complement to other efforts to liberalize the temporary movement of people. They are based on the experiences of sending and receiving countries in Europe, North America, the Caribbean, and the Pacific.

Several key messages emerge from the analysis:

- BLAs are designed mainly by receiving countries to manage and control the flows of migrants. They are not designed to promote services exports by the sending country—but they can be used to do so. The Philippines' agreements with Spain and the United Kingdom focus on health care services, for example, a sector in which the Philippines has a comparative advantage. BLAs between small island countries and Australia and New Zealand have led to a range of largely positive outcomes.

- Binding trade agreements may be better equipped to address the movement of skilled labor, whereas BLAs may be more appropriate for semiskilled and unskilled labor, because of their greater flexibility and the potentially larger number of migrants involved. Trade agreements can provide rules and disciplines that grant market access for a wide range of activities. In contrast, BLAs can allow countries, especially developing countries, to focus on the temporary movement of very specific categories of workers, such as electricians within the construction sector or computer programmers within the information and communication technology sector, or specific types of medical services required in a country. Because these agreements include no commitment to provide minimum access, receiving countries can adjust access according to market needs and general economic conditions, without having to compensate sending countries. A key challenge is to transform this greater flexibility, which mainly benefits the receiving country, into an advantage for the sending country as well.

- Temporary schemes have little impact on countries' demographic profiles, particularly in the European Union (EU) (Hoekman and Ozden 2010).

- Temporary schemes may limit losses from permanent brain drain for source countries and allow returnees to increase productivity in their native country by bringing back newly acquired human and physical capital. They may also reduce incentives for undocumented migration.

The experiences of some Caribbean countries, the Pacific Islands, and the Philippines illustrate the importance of shared responsibility—at the design, implementation, and institutional levels. At the design level, sending and receiving countries need to agree on a set of objectives and align the design to meet them. At the implementation level, joint and cooperative management effort involving state and nonstate actors on both sides is required. At the institution-building level, needs must be jointly diagnosed, capacity constraints addressed, and, if possible, progress monitored and evaluated.

Why Do People Migrate?

Many factors explain international migration (Goldin, Cameron, and Balarajan 2011; Martin 2011). Income differences encourage people to migrate across national borders. Migration networks facilitate migration. The revolutions in communications and transportation help migrants learn about opportunities abroad and cross national borders; liberal rights regimes in many host countries make it easy for migrants to remain abroad. In the future, climate change will play a significant role in migration flows as well.

Aging and population decline may expand the demand for migrants, in both developed and developing countries. In developed countries, the share of the population 60 and older is projected to rise from 20 percent in 2005 to 33 percent in 2050; in developing countries, the figure is projected to double, from 10 to 20 percent (Martin 2011).

In 2010, the world's 214 million international migrants represented 3.1 percent of the world's 6.9 billion people (table 1.1). They represented 10.3 percent of the population in developed countries and 1.5 percent of the population in developing countries.

Table 1.1 Number of People and International Migrants in World, by Region, 2010

Region	Population (millions) (a)	Number of international migrants (millions) (b)	International migrants as percentage of world population (c)	Percentage of all international migrants (d)	Ratio (d)/(c)
More developed	1,237	128	18	60	3.3
Less developed	5,671	86	82	40	0.5
Africa	1,033	19	15	9	0.6
Asia	4,167	61	60	29	0.5
Europe	733	70	11	33	3.1
Latin America	589	7	9	3	0.4
United States and Canada	352	50	5	23	4.6
Oceania	36	6	1	3	5.4
World	6,909	214	100	100	1.0

Source: Martin 2011.

Have Multilateral and Regional Agreements Increased Opportunities for Labor Migration?

Chapter 2 assesses the success of multilateral and regional agreements in increasing opportunities for the movement of temporary labor in trade-related services. It concludes that the effects have been limited and are likely to remain so at least in the foreseeable future. The rules of the WTO's General Agreement on Trade in Services (GATS) on the temporary movement of people are designed to promote trade in services through the temporary movement of people while allowing members to continue to manage migration flows. Trade agreements at the regional and bilateral level have followed a similar approach. The rules (or lack of rules) are drafted to limit flows of people from traditional sending countries; they do not take into consideration the particular situations of "services providers" from countries not seeking to promote permanent migration.

The GATS does not limit labor mobility to specific categories of services providers according to their skills; it includes both skilled and unskilled workers. In practice, however, negotiations have focused on four main categories of skilled workers, for the benefit of developed countries: business visitors and salespeople, intracorporate transferees, independent professionals, and contractual services suppliers (Stephenson and Hufbauer 2010).

The GATS Mode 4 commitments, which allow for intracorporate transferees, help multinational firms send skilled professionals from their home countries to corporate offices in other countries. They do not address developing countries' interests by, for example, providing clear and substantive rules on the temporary movement of workers. In addition, members have adopted few commitments on the mobility of semiskilled or unskilled workers. Developing countries' greatest interest lies in the categories of independent professionals and suppliers of contractual services rather than employees of multinational corporations. Greater flexibility in these categories would allow most developing countries to send more professionals abroad for temporary employment (Chanda 2009).

Some progress has been made in regional and bilateral agreements in liberalizing the temporary movement of services providers. Indeed, some recent trade agreements have included a wider range of categories, including independent services providers, trainees, and technicians. Most preferential trade agreements, however, do not diverge very far from the GATS. Agreements between the EU and Mexico, between the United States and Jordan, and among Southern Common Market Agreement (MERCOSUR) members, for example, use the GATS model. Most agreements contain similar provisions, with differences reflecting the depth and extent of commitments rather than fundamentally different approaches.

Trade agreements have three main shortcomings in dealing with the temporary movement of people. First, their legally binding provisions may restrain negotiators from committing to obligations that are difficult to change if necessary. Second, the burden of precedence may limit negotiators' ambitiousness. Countries are engaged in different sets of negotiations at the multilateral, regional, and bilateral levels. Typically, results in one agreement are the basis for the next set of negotiations, and countries are expected to exchange the best concessions from the most recently concluded agreement. Although there may be merit to providing full access to workers from a country that is not a migrant-sending country, because of the precedence this concession may set for other trading partners, the receiving country will not grant an ambitious market access concession.

Can BLAs Succeed Where Multilateral and Regional Agreements Have Not?

Chapter 3 identifies the potential advantages of BLAs over trade agreements. Although the largest labor movements between countries take place outside the channel of bilateral agreements, a large number of countries use such agreements, known as employment treaties, labor agreements, recruitment treaties, migration agreements, and agreements for exchange of labor. Such agreements can take the form of intergovernmental agreements, protocols of agreements, memoranda of understanding, memoranda of agreement, and national policy regulations. BLAs set out each country's commitments, which may include quotas and the length of the stay (see ILO 2006; OECD 2004).

Countries may sign such agreements to promote political interests, reflect friendly relations, or reinforce cooperation in managing irregular migration. For receiving countries, BLAs help achieve a labor flow that meets the needs of employers and industry while providing for better management of labor flows and the promotion of cultural ties and exchanges. For sending countries, BLAs ensure continued access to overseas labor markets (ILO 2006; OECD 2004).

Because bilateral agreements involve only two parties and do not require nondiscrimination against third parties, they may restrict market access less than multilateral or regional trade agreements. Bilateral agreements also make it easier to reach consensus toward harmonization of the parties' regulatory frameworks. Unlike trade agreements, BLAs can facilitate the movement of all types of workers, not only professionals and skilled workers. They can also narrowly target the types of workers to whom access is granted. For instance, Canada's memorandum of understanding (MOU) with Mexico and several Caribbean countries governs only the entry of seasonal agricultural workers. Its BLA with Colombia provides access for low-skilled Colombian workers in Canada's food-packing industry.

BLAs can be used to manage migration and ensure that workers remain in the country only temporarily. The return rate among Colombian agricultural workers admitted to harvest fruit in Catalonia under Colombia's BLA with Spain is more than 90 percent, for example (Stephenson and Hufbauer 2010).

In general, BLAs are not as strict as multilateral and regional agreements on trade in services in terms of the legal obligations they entail. Because they work within the confines of the contracting parties' existing legal frameworks, they do not require amendments to laws. Unlike international trade agreements, in which commitments are legally binding, parties to BLAs are permitted to adjust their commitments in response to economic and market changes. This flexibility potentially allows the parties to be more aggressive in making commitments. In multilateral and regional agreements, there is a tendency for contracting parties to be risk averse and conservative in their commitments, because nonimplementation has legal implications and consequences. In contrast, BLAs are subject to approval only by the receiving countries. If they do not want to enter into an MOU, there is nothing a sending country can do.

To date these type of agreements have been used to manage migration flows. However, countries that are not sending countries but may wish to promote their exports of services through the temporary movement of people may complement their trade agreements with BLAs, which can be tailored to specific categories of workers in which the sending country has relative advantages in specific countries without creating precedents for other negotiations.

What Do the Case Studies Show?

Chapters 4–8 present evidence from case studies. The case studies examine the experience of Spain's BLAs with Colombia and Ecuador (chapter 4); France's agreements with countries in West and North Africa and Eastern Europe (chapter 5); the Philippines' experience with BLAs and trade in services (chapter 6); the Pacific Islands' agreements with Australia and New Zealand (chapter 7); and some Caribbean countries' agreements with English-speaking countries (chapter 8). The cases were selected on the basis of the importance of the migration flows as well as the countries' experience with labor agreements. They illustrate the complementarities and differences between labor mobility liberalized in the context of a trade agreement and labor mobility facilitated in a bilateral nontrade agreement.

Spain

Chapter 4 examines Spain's experience with Colombia and Ecuador. It concludes that rather than liberalizing access to the Spanish labor market, Spain's BLAs control the number of permanent and temporary migrant workers. BLAs build on general immigration regulations. The number of migrants entering Spain before the 2008 financial crisis as a result of these agreements has been small, possibly because Spain's general immigration scheme is liberal. Although the government determines how many foreign workers will be admitted and the skills required to gain entry, the private sector determines which workers are granted work permits. Private companies may choose workers from countries that have not signed BLAs. Countries that have signed agreements have an advantage, however, in that provisions of the agreements facilitate the identification and selection of potential candidates.

Colombia and Ecuador could try to improve access for services providers by focusing on semiskilled workers in specific sectors (because of the current economic crisis, this option is probably not politically viable in the short term). Doing so would require better implementation of BLAs, however, in particular regarding the development of training projects and the recognition by Spain of foreign workers' experience abroad.

The extent to which countries can increase temporary migration depends partly on factors beyond their control. Spain's BLAs, for example, are limited by EU laws and regulations (specifically, the Schengen visa, border security regulation, and EU readmission rules) as well as by other commitments, such as WTO/GATS and bilateral agreements negotiated by the EU, including with Colombia.

Given this limitation, Colombia and Ecuador may want to explore BLAs in markets outside the EU. The experience and institutions created in their agreements with Spain are a good basis for starting this process.

France

Chapter 5 examines France's bilateral agreements with developing countries. Apart from seasonal agricultural workers and young professionals, France's bilateral agreements do not liberalize admission in channels reserved exclusively for countries signing bilateral agreements with France. To the contrary, these agreements set quotas on the number of third-country citizens that can be granted entrance into France on a most favored nation (MFN) basis.

To date, the only preference granted to partners to BLAs is that they can attempt to add occupations to the list of shortage occupations open on an MFN basis to all third-party countries. Source countries can thus benefit from BLAs with France only if they possess sufficient leverage to augment France's list of 30 shortage occupations with occupations in which they have an interest in exporting labor. This bargaining power hinges on the source country's access to a regional bloc, such as the European Neighborhood Policy or the Euro-Mediterranean partnership.

In contrast, France stands to gain significant advantages from BLAs. By facilitating first professional experiences of foreign students, admitting young professionals, stimulating the return migration of foreign students, and establishing circulation (reentry) visas for businesspeople, scientists, and artists, the agreements indirectly stimulate French investments in the partner country.

The level of preferential treatment that can be attributed to the French agreements is low in other areas, too. Most types of favorable treatment—such as the one-stop shop for visa and work permit applications and certain forms of migration-specific development aid (return and reintegration support, co-development savings accounts)—are available to certain migrant source countries without migration pacts with France. Other criteria qualify these countries for development aid or facilitated labor market admission.

The limited achievement of bilateral agreements in increasing access to labor markets must be assessed in the context of the EU policy constraints under which they operate. France's pacts neither adjust France's immigration law nor substitute for multilateral solutions to labor migration. Rather, they harmonize the treatment of former colonies in preexisting bilateral regimes. In doing so, they prepare these migrant source countries for an EU–wide regional migration agreement.

The Philippines

Chapter 6 looks at one of the world's largest exporters of labor, the Philippines. In 2009, nearly 10 percent of its 90 million people lived and worked abroad in at least 200 countries.

Given the huge overseas demand for nurses and other health care professionals and the recognition of the quality of Filipino nurses working abroad, Spain and the United Kingdom found it beneficial to enter into MOUs with the Philippines to manage the flow of these professionals. The Philippines has no template for its BLAs. The agreements' contents depend on the economic development, labor needs, and labor market situation in the Philippines and its labor-receiving countries.

Under BLAs, the return of temporary workers is governed by the terms of deployment. Some countries require unskilled and semiskilled temporary workers to return to their home countries after the completion of their contracts. Filipino workers who return to the Philippines can immediately apply for another deployment in another country; workers who want to be redeployed to the same company or the same country must wait for a minimum number of months before reapplying.

The Philippines has shown that bilateral trade agreements can potentially enhance trade in services. It has designed and implemented these agreements as MOUs, which are less binding than commitments made under a regional trade agreement or the GATS. This flexibility allows receiving countries to engage in dialogue with the Philippines' temporary worker program.

The Filipino government may also have inadvertently introduced distortions into the domestic market, however. Engman (2010) studies the case of Filipino nurses working abroad. He identifies problems caused not by the BLAs but rather by domestic policies that promote the migration of nurses. First, the migration of nurses tends to be permanent, contrary to the objectives of services exports through the temporary movement of people. Second, despite bilateral agreements, the movement of nurses to Japan and the United Kingdom has declined over the years or not taken off at all. Third, incentives created in the domestic market have led to the excessive supply of nurses, both by maintaining a light regulatory framework for private tertiary education and by failing to enforce existing rules on quality assurance. Fourth, there has been no diversification toward developing new related industries, such as health tourism, which other countries in the region, such as Malaysia and Thailand, have developed.

McKenzie, Theoharide, and Yang (2012) add another dimension. They assess the negative economic consequences of the Filipino government's efforts to impose wage floors for migrant workers. They conclude that wage floors raise the wages of workers able to secure jobs but reduce the number of jobs available and cause shocks to fall entirely on employment rather than wages.

A policy lesson from the Philippines is that governments need to assess the potential negative impact on the domestic market of policies that aim to export services through the temporary movement of people.

The Pacific Islands

Chapter 7 examines the Pacific region, where BLAs take the form of MOUs between individual Pacific countries and Australia, New Zealand, or both for the supply of seasonal farm workers. The MOUs have had largely positive development impacts, according to Gibson and McKenzie (2010). They raised per capita incomes in the sending countries by 30 percent and increased household ownership of durable goods, home improvements, use of bank accounts, and school attendance.

The MOUs with Australia and New Zealand are nonbinding template agreements that provide flexibility for tailoring, as long as it occurs within the legislative and policy parameters of receiving country schemes. Policy variations are designed to improve the attractiveness of recruiting workers from Pacific Islands that would be more expensive to recruit from if the same formula were applied to all labor-sending countries.

A significant increase in the number of workers or the diversification of markets and sectors, including into more semiskilled sectors, will call for more sophisticated responses from capacity-constrained Pacific Island governments, however. Except in Papua New Guinea, the capacity of domestic private recruiting agents is weak. Existing BLAs have a strong development focus and provide a vehicle for building the capacity needed. They provide a useful model for managing labor migration adopted elsewhere in the world.

The Caribbean

Chapter 8 examines the Caribbean, a region endowed with a well-educated English-speaking population with strong cultural and historical ties to the United States, Canada, and the United Kingdom. Jamaica and Trinidad and Tobago are already strong exporters of skilled labor, particularly teachers, nurses, and other health professionals. These countries view temporary labor migration as a mechanism for taking advantage of opportunities abroad, managing domestic unemployment, enhancing professional skills and experience, and encouraging skills transfer to local industries.

For decades, Caribbean countries have been sending a constant flow of people to Canada, the United States, and the United Kingdom. According to a 2009 World Bank study, the number of English-speaking nurses trained in the Caribbean Community (CARICOM) that were working in these countries was roughly three times the number working in the English-speaking CARICOM. The report estimates that among CARICOM–trained nurses, 750 were living in Canada, 4,750 in the United Kingdom, and 15,500 in the United States. In order to stem the brain drain of qualified and experienced nurses from the Caribbean, a managed approach to nurse migration seeks to balance the needs and labor demands of developed countries while allowing Caribbean countries to ensure the sustainability and quality of their domestic health and health education sectors.

As the World Bank has highlighted, challenges remain. Significant among them is the need to address current and future nurse shortages and to protect countries against a large outflow of nurses while at the same time recognizing individuals' right to freedom of movement and to access to health services. Policies that strengthen supply-side responses, manage migration policies, and improve monitoring and evaluation of the nurse and education markets can help countries achieve both goals.

Can BLAs Expand Exports of Services?

BLAs have the potential to expand services exports, but such expansion is not automatic. Three components are necessary to ensure the promotion of services exports through the temporary movement of people: the identification of opportunities, agreement between host and source countries on the terms and conditions the temporary movement of people will take place, and implementation and monitoring of the agreement.

The first step involves close collaboration between the public sector, the private sector, and other stakeholders. The experience analyzed suggests that countries seeking to explore potential new ways to promote services exports should make the following efforts:

- Work with the private sector to identify potential services activities that could benefit from BLAs. Identify key stakeholders among economic sectors, firms, workers, and government officials. For example, services providers, through their associations, could identify supply and demand.
- Conduct analytical work to create awareness and inform policy makers, stakeholders, and the public in general about the impacts of facilitating temporary labor mobility.
- Maintain permanent and open dialogue with stakeholders to promote ownership and facilitate the design of future initiatives, including a pilot case.

- Undertake a proactive initiative to seize the momentum and quickly identify a potential project once opportunities are identified and a constructive dialogue has been initiated to move the agenda forward.
- Observe firsthand some of the challenges faced in recruitment (such as verification of educational qualifications or health records), in order to improve systems at the local and national level in real time.
- Engage with trading partners as well as the private sector in receiving counties to match supply and demand and establish the institutional arrangements required to support the temporary movement of workers.

Policy makers also need to work closely with employers and employees to assess and understand the following:

- The challenges of cost sharing (how much is fair, feasible, and likely to reduce the chances of overstaying)
- The challenges of finding work that matches the duration of the visa to the importance of complementary issues, such as access to basic health coverage, tax obligations, and an effective circularity visa system to prevent overstaying
- How long it takes workers to become fully operational and productive (which allows the training period and costs to be defined)
- Average savings (which allows the duration to be fine-tuned)
- How to stay compatible with the WTO

The second step requires a flexible approach. Depending on the types of workers and their skills level, agreements will need to be signed. Amin and Mattoo (2007) propose obligations for both host and source countries that should be included in a "model agreement" for migration of unskilled and skilled labor (see also Chanda 2009) (table 1.2).

Success requires strong collaboration between the governments of host and source countries; institutional mechanisms to ensure the effective management of the flows and conditions for migrant workers; and a system, including incentives and sanctions, that works to keep migration temporary. The International Labour Organization (ILO) has identified several other basic elements that must be included in BLAs, including medical examinations, transportation, conflict-resolution mechanisms, social security, and working conditions, all of which are critical to workers' welfare (ILO 2006).

The experience of the Pacific Islands with Australia and New Zealand shows that even small states can effectively manage the process if adequate support is provided. At the same time, the case study shows that small countries must be careful in engaging selectively with specific countries, because of the potential costs associated with administering a large number of agreements.

In many cases, existing agreements lack the necessary indicators to monitor success and impact. The Australian and New Zealand MOUs support formal monitoring and evaluation of the temporary labor schemes. Gathering data on

Table 1.2 Basic Elements of Model Agreement for Temporary Migration

Type of country	Unskilled labor	Skilled labor
Host country	• Indicate the number of guest workers needed.	• Submit to the source country a list of vacancies, with details on required qualifications, the duration of employment, working conditions, the rights of migrants, and a copy of the contract between the employer and the prospective migrant.
	• Before the migrant arrives, prepare the work contract, which specifies the duration of stay, the wage rate, working hours and working conditions, other benefits, and the basic rights to which the migrant will be entitled. Build effective channels of communication with future employers to facilitate the migration process.	• Ban employers who violated contracts in the past from participating in the program.
	• Facilitate the processing of contracts and visas.	• Ban visa overstayers from taking part in the program.
	• Give preference to workers who returned on time in the past.	• Extend the initial duration of employment when it involves the migrant spending at least three years in the source country from a termination date of the initial contract.
	• Seek employers' cooperation in monitoring timely return and compliance with the terms of the contract. Ban employers who violated contracts in the past from participating in the program.	• Facilitate the temporary movement of professionals in areas with strong on-the-job learning opportunities, subject to vacancies and labor market tests that may be in place.
Source country	• Set up an agency to which prospective migrants can submit their applications.	• Establish an agency in which prospective migrants can submit their applications. Maintain a database with all relevant information, and ensure that it is accessible to employers in the host country.
	• Provide help with screening, selection, recruitment, and predeparture orientation of migrants.	• Disseminate information on the qualifications required to work in the host country and other information to facilitate flows in the future.
	• Position a liaison officer in the receiving country to monitor migrants and the fulfillment of the terms of the contract.	• Facilitate the process of recruiting and screening applicants, obtaining security clearance and visa and other travel documents, and providing predeparture orientation.
	• Ensure the timely return of migrants, through monitoring, incentives, reintegration programs, and other measures.	• Extend an ex ante commitment to rehire migrants currently working in the private sector on their return.

Source: Adapted from Amin and Mattoo 2007.

participants and control groups over time allowed both countries to create rich panel data sets, which allowed robust econometric estimates of the development benefits of such temporary movement of people to be made. These econometric findings helped fine-tune the schemes so they better met their commercial and development goals.

Other complementary policies may be required as well. In some cases, depending on skills and sectors, these agreements will not solve all problems. Mattoo and Mishra (2009) study the case of Indian professionals working in the United States. They assess the qualifications and licensing requirement costs that these professionals face in accessing this market. They suggest that to facilitate access for professionals, the highest priorities are immigration quotas and visa procedures. Both issues could be addressed in the context of BLAs. Other impediments, such as nonrecognition of qualifications, costly examinations, and additional course and other training requirements, are not necessarily parts of these agreements. Regarding these impediments, the Philippines' experience with Spain and the United Kingdom, as well as the Caribbean countries' experience in Canada and the United States, provide options for addressing these issues. These experiences show that a more comprehensive, sectoral approach covering the different barriers is required, involving a larger set of stakeholders. Such an approach may also determine the most convenient strategy for a country.

Conclusion

The economic benefits of freer movement of people, including migration, are well known. In an ideal world, the temporary movement of people to provide services would benefit from a level of openness similar to that governing the movement of capital. Political constraints have significantly limited these flows and will continue to do so, at least in the medium term. The flow of the temporary movement of people confronts the same constraints and restrictions that confront migration flows, with particularly strong effects on many developing countries, whose comparative advantages heavily depend on labor, in particular, low-skilled labor.

The WTO/GATS negotiations represent an extremely important opportunity, especially for developing countries, to further liberalize the movement of people. Doing so has proven difficult in the context of the current round of the Doha negotiations, however, in terms of both the results themselves and the length of time it has taken to achieve them. Developing countries may explore additional avenues, including regional and bilateral trade agreements, as well.

BLAs could be added to the existing set of trade policy tools. To date, such agreements have been used primarily as a means of regulating bilateral migratory flows of less skilled workers (although some developing countries have included services providers such as nurses and other health care workers in their agreements). However, nothing prevents these agreements from being used to open up the market for other categories of workers in services, particularly in highly restrictive markets.

BLAs can be an attractive option for middle-income countries whose migratory flows are relatively small and do not generate fears in receiving countries. Source country governments should make credible commitments to ensure the temporary nature of these flows. In conjunction with the private sector, they should establish mechanisms for selecting the sectors to promote in target markets.

For the world's poorest countries, BLAs could help limit the negative impact of brain drain on development. Although these agreements can be expensive to implement, the experience of the Pacific Islands suggests that even countries with very weak capacity can benefit from BLAs if both parties to the agreement have the political will to cooperate.

Notes

1. For a review of the welfare gains of liberalization of labor mobility, see Hatton and Williamson (2005); Rodrik (2011); Winters (2008); and Stephenson and Hufbauer (2010).
2. Other experts believe that temporary immigration programs, such as BLAs, will not allow liberalization objectives to be met (Hatton and Williamson 2005).

References

Amin, M., and A. Mattoo. 2007. "Migration from Zambia: Ensuring Temporariness through Cooperation." In *Services Trade and Development: The Experience of Zambia*, edited by A. Mattoo and L. Payton, 259–91. Washington, DC: World Bank.

Bhagwati, J. 2004. *In Defense of Globalization*. Oxford, U.K.: Oxford University Press.

Chanda, R. 2009. "Mobility of Less-Skilled Workers under Bilateral Agreements: Lessons for the GATS." *Journal of World Trade* 43 (3): 479–506.

Engman, M. 2010. "A Tale of Three Markets: How Government Policy Creates Winners and Losers in the Philippines Health Sector." Working Paper, Group d'Economie Mondiale, Sciences Po, Paris.

Gibson, J., and D. McKenzie. 2010. "The Development Impact of a Best Practice Seasonal Worker Policy." Policy Research Working Paper 5488, World Bank, Washington, DC.

Goldin, I., G. Cameron, and M. Balarajan. 2011. *Exceptional People: How Migration Shaped Our World and Will Define Our Future*. Princeton, NJ: Princeton University Press.

Hatton, T. J., and J. G. Williamson. 2005. *Global Migration and the World Economy: Two Centuries of Policy and Performance*. Cambridge, MA: MIT Press.

Hoekman, B., and C. Ozden. 2010. "The Euro-Mediterranean Partnership: Trade in Services as an Alternative to Migration?" *Journal of Common Market Studies* 48 (4): 835–57.

Hoekman, B., and A. Winters. 2009. "Multilateralizing Preferential Trade Agreements: A Developing Country Perspective." In *Multilateralizing Regionalism: Challenges for the Global Trading System*, edited by R. Baldwin and P. Low, 636–680. Cambridge, U.K.: Cambridge University Press.

ILO (International Labour Organization). 2006. *Handbook on Establishing Effective Labour Migration Polices in Countries of Origin and Destination*. Geneva ILO. http://www.ilo .org/public/english/protection/migrant/download/osce_handbook_06.pdf.

Martin, P. 2011. "The 2008–09 Recession: Implications for International Labor Migration." In *Managing Openness: Trade and Outward-Oriented Growth After the Crisis*, edited by M. Haddad and B. Shephard, 287–98. Washington, DC: World Bank.

Martin, W., and A. Mattoo. 2011. *Unfinished Business? The WTO's Doha Agenda*. Washington, DC: World Bank.

Mattoo, A., and D. Mishra. 2009. "Foreign Professionals in the United States: Regulatory Impediments to Trade." *Journal of International Economic Law* 12 (2): 435–56.

Mattoo, A., and L. Payton. 2007. *Services Trade and Development: The Experience of Zambia*. Washington, DC: World Bank.

McKenzie, D., C. Theoharide, and D. Yang. 2012. "Distortions in the International Migrant Labor Market Evidence from Filipino Migration and Wage Responses to Destination Country Economic Shocks." Policy Research Working Paper 6041, World Bank, Washington, DC. https://openknowledge.worldbank.org/handle/10986/6044.

OECD (Organisation for Economic Co-operation and Development). 2004. *Migration for Employment: Bilateral Agreements at a Crossroads*. Paris: OECD.

Rodrik, D. 2011. *The Globalization Paradox: Democracy and the Future of the World Economy*. New York: W. W. Norton & Company.

Stephenson, S., and G. H. Hufbauer. 2010. "Increasing Labor Mobility: Options for Developing Countries." In *International Trade in Services: New Trends and Opportunities for Developing Countries*, edited by O. Cattaneo, M. Engman, S. Sáez, and R. M. Stern, 29–66. Washington, DC: World Bank.

Winters, L. A. 2008. "The Temporary Movement of Workers to Provide Services. GATS Mode 4." In *A Handbook of International Trade in Services*, edited by A. Mattoo, R. M. Stern, and G. Zanini, 480–541. Oxford, U.K.: Oxford University Press.

World Bank. 2009. "The Nurse Labor and Education Markets in the English-Speaking CARICOM: Issues and Options for Reform." Report 48988-LAC, World Bank, Washington, DC.

CHAPTER 2

How Well Have Trade Agreements Facilitated Temporary Mobility?

Arti Grover Goswami and Sebastián Sáez

Trade theory suggests that the free movement of goods is equivalent to the movement of factors of production and thus precludes the need for movement of factors, specifically labor. However, traditional trade theory disregards the fact that some services require proximity between the supplier and the consumer and therefore necessitate the movement of labor. Temporary mobility of labor from labor-abundant developing countries to labor-scarce developed countries can potentially yield large returns. This chapter reviews the restrictions on and gains from temporary labor mobility. It also evaluates the performance of the General Agreement on Trade in Services (GATS) and preferential trade agreements (PTAs) in promoting services trade.

Negotiations on the temporary movement of people, defined as Mode 4 of supplying services under the GATS, began with the Uruguay Round of trade negotiations (1986–93). Because these negotiations were the first multilateral negotiations among 124 participants on the relatively new and politically sensitive topic of trade in services, they met with little success. The results of the negotiations focused primarily on facilitating business visits and the movement of high-level personnel—usually intracorporate transferees—within multinational corporations. The lack of commitments for semiskilled and low-skilled workers in the Uruguay Round has been very disappointing for developing countries, which are rich in low-skilled labor. The GATS has also thwarted the interests of some multinational corporations, which would have liked to see more scope for international movement of their personnel.

The main concern about the temporary movement of services providers relates to the competitive challenge to less skilled local workers. Because mass migration of less skilled workers raises fears in developed countries of the decline in relative wages, restrictions are often placed on the movement of labor, including restrictions on nationality requirements, visa restrictions, financial restrictions on obtaining visas, and nonrecognition of professional qualifications. These sorts of restrictions are not new to trade theory. They are similar to the import quotas and import substitution policies of the 1960s and 1970s. The challenge posed by the temporary movement of services providers is similar to the problems faced by such workers by imports of labor-intensive goods from developing countries. As in the case of trade in labor-intensive goods, greater openness in low-skilled labor mobility must be accompanied by policies to ease adjustment among less skilled local workers in developed countries.

The empirical literature suggests that the returns to even relatively small movements of labor are huge. Winters (2008), for example, estimates that an increase in developed countries' quotas on the inward movement of both skilled and unskilled temporary workers equivalent to 3 percent of their workforces would generate an increase in world welfare of more than $156 billion. Aging populations in industrial countries as well as shortages of skilled and low-skilled labor suggest that industrial countries would benefit from the temporary movement of services providers. Yet significant restrictions on movement limit the potential gains from trade in services via Mode 4. Given the sizable gains from the temporary movement of people for providing services and the underperformance of GATS in achieving it, there is an urgent need to evaluate alternatives for negotiating greater openness in the temporary movement of people for providing services.

This chapter is organized as follows. The first two sections discuss the extent of and barriers to labor mobility. The third section discusses the arrangements in the GATS for encouraging Mode 4 services exports and highlights the main problems in implementing temporary mobility with the GATS. The fourth section explores the depth of PTA in solving the labor mobility issues left unresolved in the GATS by analyzing various PTAs around the world. The last section draws conclusions about the performance of agreements with respect to temporary mobility.

Extent of Temporary Mobility

The revolution in information and communication technology (ICT) has had a profound impact on the nature, productivity, and tradability of services (Ghani and Kharas 2010). It has resulted in the rapid expansion of modern services, such as business-processing services, accounting, business consulting, education, remote access services, medical-record transcription, entertainment, production services, and design and marketing services. Unlike traditional services, these services require little close interaction between the producer and the consumer. They can be stored and traded digitally and are not subject to many of the trade barriers that physical exports must overcome.

For services, trade is possible via four modes of supply:

- Mode 1 covers cross-border transactions, such as telemedicine.
- Mode 2 covers services provided to customers who are tourists or students travelling abroad.

- Mode 3 covers the establishment of a commercial presence abroad to deliver services.
- Mode 4 covers managers, specialists, and professionals who move across borders on a temporary labor base to deliver services.

Trade in services conceptualizes labor mobility as the temporary movement of natural persons (Mode 4), which the World Trade Organization (WTO) GATS defines as the supply of a service "by a service supplier of one Member, through presence of natural persons of a Member in the territory of any other Member" (Article I.2 [d]). A natural person of another member is defined as "a natural person who resides in the territory of that other Member or any other Member, and who under the law of that other Member: (a) is a national of that other Member; or (b) has the right of permanent residence in that other Member" (Article XVIII [k]).

An important issue in measuring Mode 4 services trade is that there is a thin line between employment and services contracts, especially for self-employed workers and labor services provided through employment agencies. For services provided through employment agencies, it is not always easy to define what actually constitutes a service. Should, for instance, fruit pickers be categorized as temporary agricultural workers (outside the scope of Mode 4 and hence the GATS) or as suppliers of fruit-picking services (covered by Mode 4)? The answer depends partly on how broadly WTO members interpret the scope of the category "services incidental to agriculture" in the services sectoral classification list. However, even where a service sector is indicated, it may not correspond to the categories used by many WTO members in making their GATS commitments (Nielson and Cattaneo 2003; WTO and OECD 2005).

The Organisation for Economic Co-operation and Development (OECD) identifies a number of issues with respect to measuring Mode 4 trade in services (OECD 2010, 31). It states that "some movements, for example those involving cross-border service providers, may not be explicitly identified" and that "in still other cases, work assignments are short and the movements may escape recording entirely." In addition, it shows that "in some countries, movements what appear … as temporary are classified as permanent because the migrants in question, for example intracorporate transfers, are granted a status that essentially places them on a permanent migration track."

The WTO (2009) finds that Mode 4 has remained economically small compared with other modes of supply.[1] Its small share in services trade—less than 5 percent—may be attributed not only to geographic, cultural, and similar barriers but also to severe restrictions on market access. Commitments are often confined to the temporary presence of professional experts and specialists, who move among multinational companies. Moreover, the definitional scope of Mode 4 under Article I:2 (d) of the GATS is essentially limited to self-employed foreign services professionals and foreign employees of foreign-owned or -controlled companies that provide services in a host country.

Remittances are probably the closest approximation of capturing services exports through Mode 4. They are measured in the balance of payment statistics in the "transfers and payments" category. According to appendix 5 of the 2008 International Monetary Fund *Balance of Payments and International Investment Position Manual*, "remittances" comprise mainly "compensation of employees" and "personal transfers." Transactions are recorded in the balance of payments when money is paid by residents to nonresidents or vice versa. However, even remittances cannot accurately capture the share of Mode 4, because they are made by both temporary and permanent migrants. Additionally, transfers and payments are made by migrants who are working not only in the services sector but also in manufacturing and agriculture. Furthermore, statistics do not capture payments to undocumented foreign workers (of which there are an estimated 12 million in the United States alone) when spent in the destination countries. Even though the balance of payments records compensation paid to nonresident employees and remittances do not really correspond to trade in services through Mode 4, they are the only indicators available for measuring the magnitude of international labor movement.

As a theoretical alternative, one could look at the volume rather than the value of migrant flows. However, this alternative is no better, because the same degree of imprecision applies. The data are far from a perfect match for Mode 4—undocumented workers are still not captured, for instance. The scope of migration may differ from one country to another. Moreover, such data are available only for a subgroup of OECD member countries.[2]

Karsenty (2000) finds that compensation of employees, the closest official measure for Mode 4, accounts for just 1.4 percent of total services earnings. Walmsley and Winters (2002) estimate that there were 7.2 million skilled and 34.2 million less skilled temporary migrants in the world economy in 1997. These numbers are rather small and reflect the importance of the restrictions on the movement of labor.

Very little information is available on bilateral flows of labor. Nielson and Cattaneo (2003) find that other developed countries provide most foreign workers in the United States, in both skilled and low-skilled categories, although India and China are the largest providers of specialty occupations. "Exchange visitors," which include many cultural and educational exchanges but may also include workers, are also provided mainly by developed countries in Europe. The only potentially unskilled flows of workers—mainly nonagricultural workers, largely from North America—are officially capped at 65,000 a year. A breakdown of H1-B visa beneficiaries by occupation, age, qualifications, and wages suggests that the relatively high levels of skills involved in temporary movement is attributed to the dominance of the ICT industries. Nielson and Cattaneo suggest that relative to the size of its population, the Philippines is a major supplier of temporary labor—perhaps the world's largest. Some Gulf states, of which Saudi Arabia stands out, are also enjoying gains from services trade through Mode 4.

Barriers to Temporary Mobility

The GATS has tried to liberalize the movement of workers. Most of the liberalization pertains to skilled workers, however, and even for this category, liberalization has been narrow in scope. Why is the global economy not open to the movement of low-skilled labor? Temporary migration is seen with as much suspicion as permanent migration. The movement of low-skilled services providers from developing to developed countries increases competition for indigenous low-skilled workers. Winters (2008) notes that qualitatively, such competition is similar to the competition from imports of labor-intensive goods from the developing world; it produces the same aggregate gains and distributional consequences (losses for the low-skilled, gains for everyone else; see box 2.1). Several countries have adopted barriers that restrict Mode 4 services trade.[3]

In order to protect domestic markets and consumers, most countries impose restrictions on the flows of temporary workers. Examples of such restrictions are described below.

Quantitative Restrictions

Countries often maintain labor market regulations that limit the percentage of foreign workers firms may employ. For example, a country may require that at least 80 percent of the workers employed by a firm be nationals of that country. In addition, immigration regimes may establish quota systems for accessing the market.

Residency and Nationality Requirements

The movement of labor is limited by policies on nationality and residency or visa requirements. In many instances, such restrictions prohibit trade (Hoekman and Braga 1997). Several destination countries require that activities such as legal, insurance, educational, surveying, or investment advisory services be provided by citizens or residents of the host country.

Price-Based Measures

Receiving countries may impose fees that limit entry. Such fees include entry and exit taxes, visa fees, discriminatory airline landing fees, and port taxes. In addition, to gain entrance, some countries require individuals to show proof that they have sufficient resources to finance themselves while in the host country.

Technical Standards and Licensing

Professional qualifications, licenses, and training attained in the home country are usually not recognized in destination countries; when they are, the rules are often burdensome and lack transparency, especially in the legal, accountancy, and medical professions. Regulation has also been used to restrict the entry of foreigners, by, for example, requiring the attainment of higher education degrees and the passing of qualifying exams for certain professions. Foreign suppliers are often required to meet standards that are stricter and

Box 2.1 Benefits of Mode 4 Liberalization

The temporary movement of services providers from surplus to deficit locations can generate large gains in income. Although the movements entail distributional consequences, which can be managed with prudent redistributional policies, they present an opportunity for overall economic development.

Income Gains

Using a computable general equilibrium model and 1977 data, Hamilton and Whalley (1984) estimate the income gains from the complete elimination of all immigration restrictions. Their results suggest that the potential gains are enormous: 60–204 percent of world gross domestic product (GDP) in 1977. Income gains result from the movement of workers in developing countries to countries with higher salaries, which reflect greater productivity, as a result of better institutions and more capital. The reallocation of workers from low-productivity to high-productivity jobs results in large gains.

These results were corroborated in later studies. Iregui (1999), who used more precise measures of elasticities and population characteristics, finds aggregate income gains for the world as a whole to be 15–67 percent of world GDP. She finds that most of the gains come from the movement of unskilled labor. The gains from the movement of skilled workers are much smaller (3–11 percent of world GDP) than the gains from the movement of all workers (13–59 percent).

Moses and Letnes (2004) used more precise values of productivity. They find gains of 4.3–111 percent of world GDP in 1977 and 5.6–155 percent in 1998. The large differences in estimates, both within and between studies, can be explained by different modeling frameworks (partial versus general equilibrium) and assumed values of the parameters.

Even with less than complete liberalization of Mode 4, Moses and Letnes (2004) find that income gains are still large. They find that the gains from eliminating 10 percent of the wage inequality between countries would yield income gains of about 2.2 percent of world GDP. Walmsley and Winters (2002) confirm this finding by estimating the gain from a 3 percent increase in the developed country workforce. Their estimates suggest that partial liberalization of the movement of labor would have yielded a gain of $156 billion in 2002, representing 0.6 percent of the world GDP. Like Iregui (1999), they also show that most of the gains in aggregate income emanate from the movement of unskilled workers ($110 billion, or 70 percent of the total gains) rather than skilled labor.

Winner and Losers

As in the case of trade in goods, trade in services (through Mode 4) creates winners and losers. Most studies suggest that the gain outweighs the loss. However, political forces tend to focus on the groups that lose. The distributional effects of migration can be theoretically assessed by modeling the movement of people as an increase in the supply of labor in developed countries.

In developed countries, the liberalization of labor mobility benefits firms and hurts domestic workers, because the number of worked hours increases while hourly wages decline.

box continues next page

Box 2.1 Benefits of Mode 4 Liberalization *(continued)*

Winters (2008) finds that the gain for firm owners is larger than the loss for domestic workers, suggesting that liberalization of Mode 4 leads to an overall gain.

The impact of liberalization of Mode 4 services trade on developing countries is the exact opposite: nonmigrant capitalists lose while workers gain, with the effect on nonmigrant capitalists larger than the effect on workers. If remittances are ignored, income in developing countries declines. Moses and Letnes (2004) find that reducing wage inequality between developed and developing countries by 10 percent leads to an 11.4 percent increase in the wages of nonmigrant workers and a 21 percent decline in the return to capital in the sending countries. Walmsley and Winters (2002) estimate that a 3 percent increase in the workforce in developed countries would cause GDP to fall $7 billion in Brazil and $2 billion in China.

The gains for migrants from developing countries are much larger than the losses to their home country (because of the increase in productivity). Walmsley and Winters (2002) find that migrants actually account for more than the total gain from increased labor mobility ($171 billion compared with $156 billion of total gain). Total gains are smaller than the gains to migrants because the sending countries incur losses. Winters's (2008) estimates suggest that remittances could easily offset the small decline in output in the home country. This would be the case in India, for example, which would experience a net gain of $16 billion.

For developed countries, unskilled worker's wages decline as a result of increased competition from migrants. Borjas (1999) finds that the immigration wave to the United States from 1980 to 1998 resulted in a decrease in domestic wages equivalent to 1.9 percent of GDP, primarily as a result of wage declines for low-skilled workers. The wages of high school dropouts declined 8.9 percent. In contrast, skilled workers and capital owners benefited from immigration. The net gain from immigration was 0.1 percent of U.S. GDP, or $8 billion a year, over the 1980–98 period, equivalent to about 5 percent of U.S. economic growth in this period. Moses and Letnes (2004) and Walmsley and Winters (2002) confirm these findings.

Poverty Reduction

Even though migrants are not likely to be from the poorest segments of society, the poor are likely to gain from migration. They gain because they move into the jobs vacated by migrants or because opportunities to migrate to better jobs abroad encourage them to invest in education. This result would be true as long as opportunities for migration do not drain a large proportion of skilled or entrepreneurial workers from the sectors employing the poor.

Remittances present an alternative channel for poverty alleviation. Ratha and Mohapatra (2007) find that remittances are also associated with increased household investments in education, entrepreneurship, and health, all of which have high social return in most circumstances. Children in remittance-receiving households have lower school dropout rates, and their households spend more on private tuition for their children. Children in remittance-receiving households also have higher birth weight, suggesting that remittances enable households to afford better nourishment. Remittances also provide capital to entrepreneurs, reduce credit constraints, and boost entrepreneurship, especially in countries with good investment climates. Orozco (2007) reports that one-third of the remittances in Latin American and Caribbean communities are sent to semirural and rural areas, where incomes are far below national averages.

Let Workers Move • http://dx.doi.org/10.1596/978-0-8213-9915-6

more costly to meet than the standards applied to domestic providers of similar services (Hoekman and Braga 1997). For instance, the Nursing and Midwifery Council in the United Kingdom sets standards for the length and content of the program for foreign nurses (Engman 2010). Foreign nurses with education and practice experiences that closely match U.K. requirements still need to complete several months of learning modules in the United Kingdom. Nurses from developing countries, such as the Philippines, are also required to participate in three to six months of supervised practice.

Discriminatory Access to Information Channels and Distribution Networks

The absence of market information restricts foreign suppliers of services from gaining access to local markets. This discrimination takes the form of barring access to information channels and distribution networks. The lack of transparency and predictability in government measures such as immigration legislation, procedures, and practices is another major barrier to market access for developing countries.

Government Procurement and Sourcing Policies

In order to protect their national interests as well as local markets, governments give preference to local suppliers when awarding contracts. Government contracts account for a large share of the market for a number of services. Discriminatory procurement policies may thus have detrimental effect on trade in services (Tullao 2003).

Administrative and Procedural Blocks

The absence of clarity in schedules of commitments included in trade agreements, especially in terminologies and definitions, blocks the movement of labor, deterring trade in services through Mode 4.

Economic Needs Tests

In order to limit the entry of foreign suppliers of service, most countries use an economic needs tests (ENTs), which requires employers to prove the need for a foreign supplier. In some cases, this test is operationalized by essentially arbitrary decisions of immigration officials. In most cases, potential employers must go through extensive bureaucratic processes to prove their needs, making temporary movement unattractive except in case of the greatest need (Chaudhuri, Mattoo, and Self 2004; Winters 2008).

Visa and Employment Permits

Virtually all counties require visas from foreign suppliers of service, whether temporary or permanent. Visa applications for temporary migrants are typically screened very carefully, as they are for potential permanent migrants. Host countries use visa and entry to limit the entry of foreign suppliers of services, in order to protect the local industry. Trade agreements, including the GATS, do not usually address issues related to visa requirements for services suppliers (Chaudhuri, Mattoo, and Self 2004).

Wage Parity Conditions

The requirement that wages paid to foreign workers be similar to the wages paid to nationals in a particular profession is intended to create a nondiscriminatory environment. In fact, it erodes the cost advantage of hiring foreigners and works like a de facto quota (Chaudhuri, Mattoo, and Self 2004).

Contribution of the GATS

WTO agreements do not include provisions on labor mobility. However, Mode 4 of the GATS covers the movement of individuals as services suppliers. The GATS annex on the movement of natural persons supplying services is limited to temporary movement, although the interpretation of "temporary" is left undefined, leading members to adopt various time periods. Although GATS Mode 4 covers services suppliers of all skill levels, in practice, the main beneficiaries of commitments have been skilled workers. According to Chanda (2008), only 17 percent of the commitments adopted by WTO members cover low-skilled workers. Because countries have privileged adopting similar commitments for all the sectors under Mode 4 ("horizontal commitments," in GATS jargon), sectors that heavily depend on the temporary movement of people did not receive any specific liberalization advantage (Chanda 2008). Generally, members' commitments have normally been adopted for the following categories of labor for the purpose of scheduling commitments under Mode 4:

- *Business visitors and salespersons*: foreign nationals traveling abroad to negotiate a sale of a service or explore the possibility of establishing commercial presence (Mode 3) for their company in the destination country. Their main purpose is to facilitate future transactions rather than actually carry out the transactions.
- *Intracorporate transferees*: employees of a foreign services firm that has set up a commercial presence in another country and that transfers them to this location.
- *Independent professionals*: self-employed persons supplying a service to a company or an individual in a foreign country.
- *Contractual services suppliers*: employees of a foreign services firm that does not have a local or commercial presence in the host country. The employees are contracted to provide the service to another firm based in the host country.

GATS commitments on Mode 4 favored the liberalization of Mode 3—that is, the establishment of a commercial presence, which was of particular interest to developed countries. While establishing subsidiaries in developing countries, multinational firms were constrained by the lack of skilled professionals in the host country as well as by the regulatory barriers to bringing their own skilled professionals from abroad. Commitments under the GATS that allowed for intracorporate transferees helped multinational firms bring skilled professionals from their home countries. The mutually supportive approach adopted by WTO members when scheduling commitments under Modes 3 and 4 partially explains why GATS Mode 4 commitments have been limited to skilled professionals. Although the focus has been on facilitating the entry of skilled labor, GATS Mode 4 may not necessarily lead to brain drain from developing countries as long as ample commitments are in place to maintain temporariness (box 2.2).

Developing countries' interests were not quite addressed in the GATS, and no commitments were made with respect to the mobility of semiskilled and unskilled workers. The fact that developing countries' commitments under Mode 4 do not differ significantly from the commitments of developed countries suggests that the complex political economy nature of the topic is not related to the level of development (Carzaniga 2003).

Countries became more open after the mid-1990s. Chaudhuri, Mattoo, and Self (2004) find that countries that acceded to the WTO after 1995 have been more willing to make commitments for "contract suppliers" (that is, employees of a foreign enterprise that has concluded a contract to supply a service in a country but does not have a commercial presence in that market).

Carzaniga (2003) finds that the levels of commitments vary across modes of supply. Within a given sector, commitments under Mode 4 tend to be significantly more restrictive than regulations for other modes. No developed country has scheduled a "none" entry for its Mode 4 commitments, and only 1 percent of market access commitments undertaken by developing countries are fully liberal. This record lies in contrast to Mode 2 commitments, half of which are full commitments. Horizontal limitations on Mode 4 also apply across all sectors: there are five times as many such limitations scheduled for Mode 4 than for Mode 2. An overview of members' horizontal commitments reveals that the majority of the entries—almost 280 out of a total 400—were executives, managers, or specialists. About 170 entries were explicitly related to intracorporate transferees.

Box 2.2 Temporary Worker Programs and Brain Drain

Conventional wisdom suggests that international migration of the highly skilled from poor to rich countries ("brain drain") threatens development. A 2007 report by the OECD finds that a disproportionately large number of low-income countries' nationals with a university degree are residing in OECD countries. In parts of Sub-Saharan Africa and Central America, for example, more than half of all university graduates migrate to OECD countries, with potentially serious consequences for critical sectors such as education, health, and engineering.

The report suggests that developing countries could benefit from high-skilled migration provided the receiving and sending countries partner in encouraging the repatriation of skills and knowledge ("brain circulation"). This sort of partnership can be found in temporary worker programs, which could potentially benefit both receiving and sending countries. (For a survey of the brain drain literature, see Commander, Kangasniemi, and Winters 2004.)

One of the most recurrent restrictions in GATS commitments in allowing access to foreign labor markets relates to "preemployment," usually of one year; numerical quotas and ENTs rank next in the frequency of limitations (Carzaniga 2003). Although quotas usually relate to the total staff of a firm, some members also reserve the right to operate quotas based on parameters such as senior staff or wages. The GATS leaves significant administrative discretion to its member countries by the frequent scheduling of ENTs without indicating the criteria on which they are based.

Experts emphasize that WTO/GATS provisions on the temporary movement of people do not apply to measures affecting individuals seeking access to the employment market "nor shall [they] apply to measures regarding citizenship, residence or employment on a permanent basis" (GATS Annex on the Movement of Natural Persons). However, Chanda (2008) points out two important structural problems of the GATS: the lack of separation between temporary and permanent labor and the fact that most limitations relate to general immigration legislation and labor market regulations pertaining to permanent migration.

Problems Implementing Temporary Mobility through the GATS

Several problems hinder use of the GATS as an effective tool for promoting services exports through Mode 4 (Amin and Mattoo 2005). First, most existing commitments are related to Mode 3 services trade; most commitments relate to business travelers and intracorporate transferees. Such commitments are of limited interest to developing countries, which do not have significant investments in developed countries. Moreover, GATS commitments are often qualified by other restrictions relating to prior employment, quotas, ENTs, or residency requirements.

Second, the commitments made under the GATS are legally binding. Winters and others (2002) point out that although several European countries have programs for less skilled workers (such as seasonal workers in agriculture, tourism, and the hotel trade and workers in construction), members prefer not to include them in their GATS commitments because doing so could deprive them of the flexibility with which they currently implement the schemes. For this reason, these programs are usually implemented on a bilateral basis. Chaudhuri, Mattoo, and Self (2004) note that WTO members' Mode 4 commitments generally do not even reflect prevailing entry conditions, because members have committed to less than the access granted in practice (Colombia, Mexico, and República Bolivariana de Venezuela). This means that despite their more liberal access regime, countries have retained discretion to restrict market access without violating their international commitments under the WTO.

Third, although the GATS deals with temporary labor migration, even the meaning of *temporary* is left undefined in the GATS schedule (Chanda 2008). The distinction between services providers and individuals entering the labor market in a country is not very clear. Because temporary entry under GATS commitments can last for up to three years (in some cases even longer), services providers in effect enter the local labor market, even though they are not applying for permanent residence or citizenship, as they are providing a service that a local person could probably perform. For instance, Japan allows foreign business travelers to stay for a maximum of 90 days, but certain categories of intracorporate transferees can stay as long as five years. Similarly, the skills and occupations that are committed to facilitated entry under the GATS are also not explicitly defined. Without clear definitions, regulatory authorities have broad discretion in deciding what constitutes a specialist (and presumably in changing the definition according to political and labor market pressures). These problems reduce the transparency and credibility of commitments and ultimately discourage countries from negotiating in this area (Carzaniga 2003).

Fourth, although flexibility in the definition of *temporary* may sometimes work as an advantage, it leads to a deeper problem, because an open-ended notion of *temporary* blurs the distinction between Mode 4 and migration—a distinction that could have provided significant political reassurance. Without assurances that the commitments made in the GATS actually pertain to temporary labor movement, it is hard to convince immigration officials that Mode 4 does not undermine border integrity or labor officials that it does not undermine labor law or local job markets.

Fifth, most developed countries collect social security contributions from temporary workers, but most workers do not establish entitlements to social security benefits in return. Such "excessive" social security taxes are effectively tariffs on the provision of services provided through Mode 4, which are usually dealt with bilaterally and are therefore candidates for liberalization at a multilateral level (Chanda 2008). However, Winters (2008) believes that such tariffs are more transparent than nontariff barriers, such as numerical quotas and worker licensing procedures. Experience in the goods market suggests that nontariff barriers are more costly than tariff barriers and hence should be given higher priorities for liberalization. In fact, even the ENT, which inhibits temporary movement not only per se but also through lack of definitional clarity, also works like an import quota. The effective liberalization of temporary movement of people requires that members agree to develop a common code of practice for ENTs (as suggested under the European Union [EU] proposal in the current Doha negotiations), with the objective of rendering them specific, transparent, and nondiscriminatory and defining their application criteria.

Sixth, the GATS is not very clear on the types of contracts covered.[4] The WTO Secretariat (2005, 2009) reports the debate among WTO members and among experts about whether natural persons from member A (the sending territory) employed by a services firm of member B (the receiving territory)—not owned or controlled by member A—should also be covered by GATS Mode 4. This debate is based on the text of the GATS Annex on Movement of Natural Person Supplying Services under the Agreement, which applies to "measures affecting natural persons who are service suppliers of a Member, and natural persons of a Member who are employed by a service supplier of a Member, in respect of the supply of a service." The first category is clear: "natural persons who are service suppliers of a Member" covers self-employed or independent services suppliers who obtain their remuneration directly from customers. There is some debate about who is covered by the second category ("natural persons of a Member who are employed by a service supplier of a Member"). GATS Article I.2 (d) seems to cover only foreign employees of foreign firms established in another member. The Secretariat background note suggests that foreigners working for host country companies fall under GATS Mode 4 if they work on a contractual basis as independent suppliers for a locally owned firm but are not necessarily covered if they are employees of that firm. It is not clear, for example, whether the GATS covers an Irish software professional employed by a domestic firm in the United States.

Performance of PTAs

This section explores the coverage and treatment of labor mobility in PTAs. It compares them with the GATS commitments under Mode 4 services trade.

PTAs affect labor mobility in a variety of ways. They are much broader in scope than GATS coverage, potentially covering all aspects of trade and labor mobility. Unlike the GATS, some PTAs are not confined to temporary movement (Nielson 2003; WTO and OECD 2005). Moreover, even though the GATS can, in principle, cover all types of skills, it has been the practice of its member to cover mainly skilled workers. By contrast, some PTAs cover workers at all skill levels (Nielson 2003).

Types of PTAs

Trade agreements are diverse. Some PTAs offer close to full labor mobility. Examples include the European Union, the Agreement on the European Economic Area (EEA), the European Free Trade Association (EFTA), the Common Market for Eastern and Southern Africa (COMESA), and Australia–New Zealand Closer Economic Relations (ANZCERTA). Free movement of labor is usually allowed among countries at similar levels of development.

When countries differ slightly in the level of development or there are gains from movement of only special kinds of labor, PTAs can provide market access for certain groups or include a separate chapter on mobility. Examples include the Caribbean Community (CARICOM), the North American Free Trade Agreement (NAFTA), the Canada-Chile agreement, agreements between the European Union and Eastern European countries, the Japan-Singapore Free Trade Agreement, and the Group of Three (Colombia, Mexico, and República Bolivariana de Venezuela).

Many agreements use the GATS model with some additional elements without making deeper commitments. Examples include the U.S.–Jordan Free Trade Agreement, the EU–Mexico Free Trade Agreement, the Association of Southeast Asian Nations (ASEAN) Free Trade Area (AFTA), the Euro-Mediterranean Association Agreements (Morocco and Tunisia), and the New Zealand–Singapore Closer Economic Partnership. Additional elements may include visa commitments for both independent traders and people linked to investment beyond services suppliers. Under the U.S.–Jordan Free Trade Agreement, for example, Jordanian nationals are eligible for U.S. treaty-trader (E-1) and treaty-investor (E-2) visas, and similar treatment is guaranteed for U.S. nationals seeking entry to Jordan. In contrast, the EU–Mexico PTA, like the GATS, does not include access to the labor market; unlike in the GATS, receiving countries maintain their right to regulate the entry and stay of individual. Some services sectors, such as audiovisual, air transport services, and maritime cabotage, are specifically excluded from the scope of the negotiations.

Some agreements replicate the GATS model. Examples include the Southern Common Market Agreement (MERCOSUR), Asia Pacific Economic Cooperation (APEC), and the South Asian Association for Regional Cooperation (SAARC).

Some PTAs include no provisions for facilitating labor mobility. Examples include the Central European Free Trade Agreement (CEFTA) and the Southern African Development Community (SADC).

PTAs between countries that are geographically close or at similar levels of development can afford to be more liberal toward labor mobility, as demonstrated by the European Union, EFTA, the Agreement on the EEA, and the Trans-Tasman Travel Arrangement. PTAs among geographically or economically distant countries include the APEC forum and the U.S.–Jordan Free Trade Agreement. There are exceptions to this trend, as exemplified by the SAARC, which grants significant market access despite the geographical and economic distance among member countries.

Categories of Labor Included

PTAs differ in their coverage of skills. Most PTAs facilitate the entry of highly skilled professionals; some also allow for easy entry of low-skilled workers. NAFTA, for instance, covers traders and investors, business visitors, intracorporate transferees, and professionals, specifically targeting professional services suppliers. In contrast, Canada's trade agreements increase access not only for professionals but also for semiskilled foreign workers. Its trade agreements with Columbia (signed in 2008) and Peru (signed in 2009), for example, facilitate entry for 50 types of technicians, including mechanics, construction inspectors, food and beverage supervisors, chefs, plumbers, and oil and gas well drillers (Stephenson and Hufbauer 2010).

Japan's PTAs essentially replicate Japan's GATS commitments, except that they include a category of investors not necessarily confined to Mode 4 and personal contract suppliers engaged with public or private organizations to perform engineering-related services. In its agreement with Mexico, the personal contract suppliers category includes specialists in the humanities and international services. Its PTAs with Indonesia and the Philippines augment the personal contract suppliers category to include nurses and caregivers. In its agreement with Thailand, personal contract suppliers include instructors of Thai music, dance, cuisine, boxing, language, and spa services (Carzaniga 2008).

The European Commission does not have negotiating authority from EU member states in all services. It has therefore adopted the GATS model for granting market access for Mode 4 services trade. The categories of workers included in Mode 4 commitments include the four that are traditional for PTAs (traders and investors, business visitors, ICT professionals, and independent professionals). The recent EU–CARIFORUM (Forum of the Caribbean Group of African, Caribbean, and Pacific States) Economic Partnership Agreement follows a similar structure. However, for the first time, the European Union expanded coverage of workers to three additional categories (contractual services suppliers, independent professionals, and graduate trainees), at the strong request of the CARIFORUM members (Stephenson and Hufbauer 2010).

The labor mobility chapter of New Zealand's agreement with China includes an additional category of workers, "installers." This category is carried over in the agreement between ASEAN and Australia and New Zealand. The contractual services suppliers category in the Chinese agreement with New Zealand includes Chinese theater professionals, teachers of Mandarin, and Chinese medical specialists (Stephenson and Hufbauer 2010).

Commitments beyond the GATS

PTAs can increase access to the labor market. Some PTAs, such as ANZCERTA, offer full national treatment and market access for services suppliers. PTAs such as NAFTA are not as liberal as some other agreements, but they facilitate entry through specific commitments on visas. The "trade NAFTA" (TN) visa is a special visa for facilitating the entry of skilled workers from Canada and Mexico.[5] Upon demonstrating proof of a job offer, it permits employment for one year, with unlimited renewal. The conditions for obtaining the TN visa are quite relaxed for Canadians, so much so that the visa can be obtained at the port of entry once required documents are provided.

The U.S. agreement with Australia created a special category of E-3 visas for Australian nationals hired by U.S.–based firms.[6] In its agreements with Chile and Singapore, the United States created a special category of visa (H-1B1) for professional workers.[7] Although in principle these visas should go toward fulfilling the 65,000 quota for H-1B visas, in practice they are set aside from the H-1B cap (Carzaniga 2008).

The Canada-Chile agreement includes no provisions for facilitated entry. However, it imposes no numerical restrictions on the temporary entry of any category. Similarly, the United States' agreement with Jordan is quite conservative, following a GATS–like positive list approach to scheduling commitments.

Agreements such as CARICOM, NAFTA, the Canada-Chile agreement, the European agreements, APEC, and the U.S.–Jordan agreement provide special market access or facilitated access for certain groups, including individuals who are not suppliers of services. CARICOM, for instance, allows for free mobility of university graduates; NAFTA, the Canada-Chile trade agreement, and the European agreements include people involved in activities related to agriculture and manufacturing. Work permits are required for traders and investors, intracorporate transferees, and professionals but not business visitors; labor certification or labor market assessment/tests are removed for all four groups. Although visas are still required, fees for processing applications are limited to the cost of services rendered (Nielson 2003).

The Canada-Chile agreement is similar in spirit to NAFTA in terms of coverage of skills, but it places no numerical limits on the 72 categories of professional labor included in the agreement (Stephenson and Hufbauer 2010). Although APEC includes no special market access provision, it facilitates the entry of business visitors under its business travel card scheme, which allows multiple short-term business visits, with stays of two or three months per arrival. The U.S.–Jordan agreement includes specific visa commitments (Article 8) for both independent traders (Article 8.1) and people linked to investment (Article 8.2), not just services suppliers (Nielson 2003).

Some agreements, such as the Japan-Singapore agreement, deal with all temporary movement, including movement related to investment or to trade in goods or investment (as in the case of the Group of Three). Some PTAs encourages mobility of key personnel based on Mode 3 (commercial presence of multinational firms in another country) by including provisions on firms' needs to bring in key personnel in their investment chapter. For instance, the ASEAN Investment Framework Agreement calls for the promotion of freer movement of skilled labor and professionals, the U.S.–Jordan agreement includes visa commitments for investors, and the EU–Mexico agreement section on financial services includes provisions on the nationality of key personnel. Most PTAs, including the Group of Three, the Japan-Singapore agreement, and some bilateral agreements in Latin America, cover the temporary movement of business people, intracorporate transferees, and services suppliers and investors in a separate chapter on movement of business people. Although such provisions go beyond the GATS in specifying the treatment of key personnel, they nevertheless reflect the reality of WTO members' GATS commitments to providing better access for Mode 4 services trade linked to Mode 3. Thus, in principle, a PTA can encourage greater mobility of labor with respect to the GATS or, in a worst-case scenario, simply reflect a country's existing GATS commitments. One exception is the Australia-Singapore agreement, where the GATS offer actually surpasses commitments made under the PTA, which mentions only four of the several varieties of services supplied by contractual services suppliers (Carzaniga 2008).

Remaining Restrictions

In general, access to the labor market does not automatically grant the right to practice a certain profession. Over and above entry regulations are regulations for licensing and recognition of qualifications or nationality requirements. For instance, although the European Union provides a general right to work anywhere in the European Union, there are nationality requirement for certain jobs in public services. Countries in the European Union do not offer liberal access for the movement of labor from developing countries with respect to their GATS commitments. In fact, their agreements follow the GATS–type positive list approach (Carzaniga 2008). Similarly, some agreements—such as NAFTA; the Group of Three; and agreements between Canada and Chile, the European Union and Mexico, Japan and Singapore, and the United States and Jordan—provide broad labor mobility but exclude certain sectors for entry of foreign labor. PTAs also do not impinge on the right of receiving countries to regulate the entry and stay of individuals, as long as such regulations do not nullify or impair specific commitments undertaken. Some agreements (for example, the EU–Mexico agreement and a proposal in the Free Trade Area of the Americas [FTAA]) also design a slightly broader regulatory right for receiving countries, including regulations related to work, labor conditions, and the presence of natural persons, in the general formulation of measures that members can apply, provided that they do not nullify or impair specific commitments undertaken.

The agreement within the European Union is perhaps the most liberal. Most other agreements provide only special access or facilitate existing access within existing immigration arrangements. In most PTAs, labor mobility does not supersede general migration legislation; participating countries retain broad discretion to grant, refuse, and administer residence permits and visas. Some agreements, such as the Euro-Mediterranean Partnership (between Europe and Morocco and Tunisia), specify that liberalizing provisions cannot be used to challenge immigration decisions refusing entry or that dispute settlement under the agreement can be invoked only in cases in which the matter involves a pattern of practice and local remedies have been exhausted (this is the case in NAFTA and the Canada-Chile agreement) (Nielson 2003).

The EU agreement grants a general level of free mobility with very few restrictions; the agreements concluded by the European Union with countries at a slightly lower level of development, such as countries in Eastern Europe and the Baltics, do not grant such free movement for workers.[8] Temporary entry is allowed for individuals providing services and representatives of firms negotiating the sale of services, provided they are not engaged in direct sales to the public or supplying services themselves. A horizontal transition period of 10 years applies.

Even agreements that have a very liberal regime, such as the European Union, make exceptions to free movement on grounds of public policy, public security, or public health. Within the European Union, however, any restrictions on labor mobility need to be justified as serious threats to a fundamental interest of society or as protection of human rights and fundamental freedoms and the proportionality principle. They should not be invoked simply to serve economic ends.

As PTAs move from higher to lower degrees of mobility, restrictions are added to the existing regime. For instance, the EU treaty on free labor mobility has expanded to include the EFTA–EEA states (Switzerland, Iceland, Liechtenstein, and Norway), allowing EEA nationals essentially the same rights to work in the EU area as nationals of EU member states Although there are no restrictions on the freedom to provide services and temporary services providers receive national treatment, special conditions apply to transport, financial, audiovisual, and telecommunications services, and the number of days is limited to 90 a year. Although no visas are required, some limits apply. For example, transition periods apply to Swiss nationals, and special rules govern border workers, public service and public authority activities, and the acquisition of real estate in Switzerland. Similar rules apply within CARICOM, where, in principle, free movement is allowed for university graduates, other professionals and skilled persons, and a few selected occupations.

In conclusion, most PTAs do not diverge very far from the GATS, as evident even in the language chosen to define labor mobility. NAFTA provided the model for temporary mobility in the GATS language by including the negative definition of "temporary." The EU–Mexico, U.S.–Jordan, and MERCOSUR agreements use the GATS model and sometimes also refer to the GATS (U.S.–Jordan). Because existing PTAs also influence prospective PTAs—as they did in the Canada-Chile

Figure 2.1 Facilitation of Labor Market Access Provided by Selected Preferential Trade Agreements

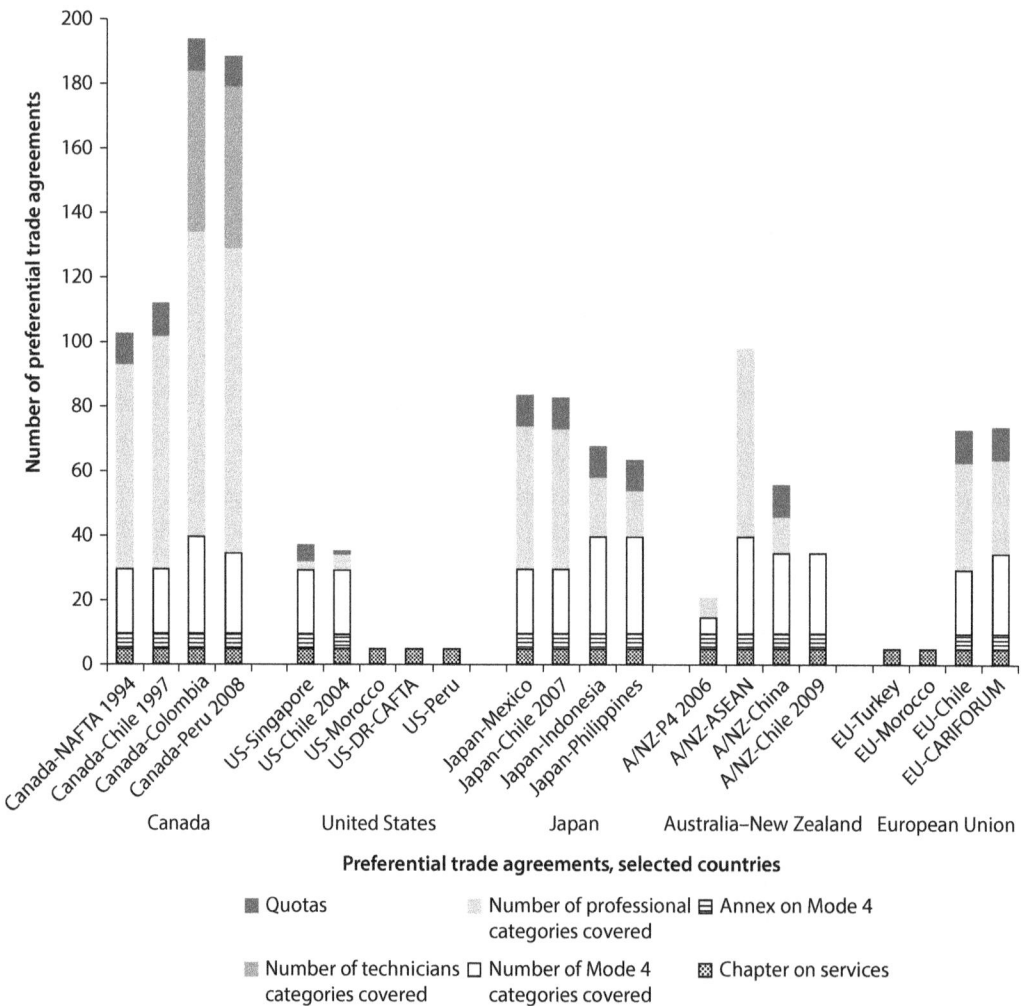

Source: Stephenson and Hufbauer 2010.
Note: A/NZ = Australia–New Zealand; CARIFORUM = Forum of the Caribbean Group of African, Caribbean and Pacific States; DR-CAFTA = Dominican Republic–Central America Free Trade Agreement; EU = European Union; NAFTA = North America Free Trade Agreement.

agreement, which was heavily motivated by the NAFTA model—they limit the extent of liberalization of Mode 4 services trade. In fact, most agreements generally contain similar provisions, with differences reflecting the depth and extent of commitments rather than fundamentally different approaches. For instance, Australia's PTA with Singapore was based on the GATS template, with improvement only in the duration of stay for ICT workers (Carzaniga 2008).

Stephenson and Hufbauer (2010) graphically summarize the PTAs negotiated by Australia, Canada, the European Union, Japan, New Zealand, and the United States (figure 2.1). The height of each bar indicates the degree to which each agreement facilitates labor market access.

The assessment of PTAs suggests that such agreements have adopted an open and liberal stand only when negotiated by countries with similar levels of development. Even when countries are geographically close but at different levels of development, PTAs tend to be restrictive (examples include NAFTA and the European Union's agreements with Eastern European countries). PTAs among developed and developing countries that are geographically distant (such as the EU–Chile agreement) are even more restrictive. PTAs between developed and developing countries usually focus on skilled professionals, as the GATS does; they usually exclude self-employed, unskilled, and semiskilled workers.

Conclusion

Most studies that estimate the gains from the movement of labor suggest that the gains from the reallocation of workers from low- to high-productivity jobs are large and stem largely from the movement of unskilled workers. From the perspective of a developing country, there are larger gains from the movement of unskilled workers because even though skilled temporary migrants earn higher wages by moving abroad, their movement also has a negative effect on their home economies. From the perspective of a developed country, allowing larger numbers of unskilled foreign workers in is more beneficial in terms of welfare because they are usually in short supply in the developed region.[9]

The GATS has played a very limited role in promoting labor mobility, especially for low-skilled workers. Most commitments are related to Mode 3, which is of limited interest to developing countries. The GATS is very rigid; the commitments made under it are legally binding; and its terminology is not very clear, especially with regard to the definition of *temporary*, the coverage of contracts, and even what constitutes a service. However, even for skilled temporary migration, the commitments under Mode 4 are more stringent than the actual restrictions in place.

PTAs have also met with limited success in promoting low-skilled labor temporary work programs. Some agreements have designed a slightly broader regulatory right for receiving countries, including regulations related to work, labor conditions, and the presence of natural persons related to measures that members can apply, provided that they do not nullify or impair specific commitments undertaken. Most PTAs do not diverge very far from the

GATS, as evident even in the language chosen to define labor mobility. Although the number of trade agreements covering services is growing rapidly, services trade commitments through Mode 4 remain limited.

Notes

1. The WTO (2009) background sectoral note on the Presence of Natural Persons (Mode 4) also presents the measurement challenges of this mode of supply. See also Maurer and Magdeleine (2008).

2. The OECD collects information on the number of temporary foreign workers in surveys of firms, visas, border crossings, and so forth. These data cover intracorporate transferees and other temporary workers. See OECD (2007) for details.

3. This list covers more measures than Article XVI (Market Access) of the GATS.

4. According to Carzaniga (2008), foreigners working for a host-country company as independent service suppliers on a contractual basis are covered by the GATS. However, foreigners employed by that company are not covered by the GATS.

5. The visa was uncapped for Canadians in 1994 and for Mexicans in 2004.

6. The quota, of 10,500, has not been fully utilized: only 2,100 Australians used the visa in 2006 (Carzaniga 2008).

7. The visa provided for an initial stay of 18 months with unlimited extensions. An annual quota of 1,800 visas for professionals from Chile and 5,400 visas for professionals from Singapore was granted, in addition to the fixed total of H-1B visas from all countries.

8. The countries include Bulgaria, the Czech Republic, Estonia, Hungary, Latvia, Lithuania, Poland, Romania, the Slovak Republic, and Slovenia.

9. The distinction between the net benefits of skilled and unskilled mobility should not be overemphasized. Estimation models such as the Walmsley and Winters (2002) model are very simple and ignore all of the potential subtleties associated with the brain drain or costs related directly to the number of people who move, such as transportations, subsistence, and racial discrimination.

References

Amin, M., and A. Mattoo. 2005. "Does Temporary Migration Have to Be Permanent?" Policy Research Working Paper 3582, World Bank, Washington, DC.

Borjas, G. 1999. *Heaven's Doors: Immigration Policy and the American Economy*. Princeton, NJ: Princeton University Press.

Carzaniga, A. 2003. "The GATS, Mode 4, and Pattern of Commitments." In *Moving People to Deliver Services*, edited by A. Mattoo and A. Carzaniga, 21–6. Washington, DC: World Bank.

———. 2008. "A Warmer Welcome? Access for Natural Persons under Preferential Trade Agreements." In *Opening Markets for Trade in Services Countries and Sectors in Bilateral and WTO Negotiations*, edited by J. A. Marchetti and M. Roy, 475–502. Cambridge, U.K.: Cambridge University Press.

Chanda, R. 2008. "Low-Skilled Workers and Bilateral, Regional, and Unilateral Initiatives: Lessons for the GATS Mode 4 Negotiations and Other Agreements." Report, United Nations Development Programme, Geneva, Switzerland.

Chaudhuri, S., A. Mattoo, and R. Self. 2004. "Moving People to Deliver Services: How Can the WTO Help?" *Journal of World Trade* 38 (3): 363–93.

Commander, S., M. Kangasniemi, and L. A. Winters. 2004. "The Brain Drain: Curse or Boon? A Survey of the Literature." In *Challenges to Globalization: Analyzing the Economics*, edited by R. Baldwin and A. Winters, 235–78. Chicago, IL: University of Chicago Press. http://www.nber.org/chapters/c9540.pdf.

Engman, M. 2010. "A Tale of Three Markets: How Government Policy Creates Winners and Losers in the Philippine Health Sector." Working Paper, Group d'Economie Mondiale, Sciences Po, Paris.

Ghani, E., and H. Kharas. 2010. "Overview." In *The Service Revolution in South Asia*, edited by E. Ghani, 1–34. Oxford, U.K.: Oxford University Press.

Hamilton, C., and J. Whalley. 1984. "Efficiency and Distributional Implications of Global Restrictions on Labor Mobility: Calculations and Policy Implications." *Journal of Development Economics* 14 (1, 2): 61–75.

Hoekman, B., and C. Braga. 1997. "Protection and Trade in Services." Policy Research Working Paper 1747, World Bank, International Economics Department, Washington, DC.

IMF (International Monetary Fund). 2008. *Balance of Payments and International Investment Position Manual*, 6th edition. Washington, DC: IMF. http://www.imf.org/external/pubs/ft/bop/2007/pdf/appx5.pdf.

Iregui, A. 1999. "Efficiency Gains from the Elimination of Global Restrictions on Labor Mobility: An Analysis Using a Multiregional CGE model." Report No. 146, Estudios Económicos, Banco de la República, Bogotá, Colombia.

Karsenty, G. 2000. "Assessing Trade in Services by Mode of Supply." In *GATS 2000: New Directions in Services Trade Liberalization*, edited by P. Sauve and R. M. Stern, 33–56. Washington, DC: Brookings Institution Press.

Maurer, A., and J. Magdeleine. 2008. "Measuring GATS Mode 4 Trade Flows." Working Paper ERSD-2008-05, World Trade Organization (WTO), Geneva, Switzerland.

Moses, J., and B. Letnes. 2004. "The Economic Cost to International Labor Restrictions: Revisiting the Empirical Discussion." *World Development* 32 (10): 1609–26.

Nielson, J. 2003. "Labour Mobility in Regional Trade Agreements." In *Moving People to Deliver Services*, edited by A. Mattoo and A. Carzaniga, 92–111. Washington, DC: World Bank.

Nielson, J., and O. Cattaneo. 2003. "Current Regimes for the Temporary Movement of Service Providers: Case Studies of Australia and United States." In *Moving People to Deliver Services*, edited by A. Mattoo and A. Carzaniga, 113–56. Washington, DC: World Bank.

OECD (Organisation for Economic Co-operation and Development). 2007. *Gaining from Migration: Towards a New Mobility System*. Paris: OECD.

———. 2010. *International Migration Outlook SOPEMI*. Paris: OECD.

Orozco, M. 2007. "The Role of Remittances in Leveraging Sustainable Development in Latin America and the Caribbean." March 6, Inter-American Dialogue, Washington, DC.

Ratha, D., and S. Mohapatra. 2007. *Increasing the Macroeconomic Impact of Remittances on Development*. Washington, DC: World Bank.

Stephenson, S., and G. H. Hufbauer. 2010. "Increasing Labor Mobility: Options for Developing Countries." In *International Trade in Services: New Trends and Opportunities for Developing Countries*, edited by O. Cattaneo, M. Engman, S. Sáez, and R.M. Stern, 29–66. Washington, DC: World Bank.

Tullao, T. S. 2003. "Movement of Natural Persons and Human Development." UNDP Discussion Paper, United Nations Development Programme, New York.

Walmsley, T. L., and L. A. Winters. 2002. "An Analysis of the Removal of Restrictions on the Temporary Movement of Natural Persons." CEPR Discussion Paper 3719, Centre for Economic Policy Research, London.

Winters, L. A. 2008. "The Temporary Movement of Workers to Provide Services: GATS Mode 4." In *A Handbook of International Trade in Services*, edited by A. Mattoo, R. M. Stern, and G. Zanini, 482–541. Oxford, U.K.: Oxford University Press.

Winters, L. A., T. L. Walmsley, Z. K. Wang, and R. Grynberg. 2002. "Liberalising Labour Mobility under the GATS." Economic Paper 53, Commonwealth Secretariat, London.

WTO (World Trade Organization). 2009. "Presence of Natural Persons. Mode 4." Background Note, WTO Secretariat, S/C/W/301, Geneva Switzerland.

WTO (World Trade Organization) and OECD (Organisation for Economic Co-operation and Development). 2005. "A Background Note on GATS Mode 4 and Its Information Needs." Paper presented at the meeting of the Technical Subgroup on Movement of Natural Persons (Mode 4) organized by United Nations, Department of Economic and Social Affairs, Paris, January 31–February 1.

CHAPTER 3

When and Why Should Bilateral Labor Agreements Be Used?

Arti Grover Goswami, Manjula Luthria, Mai Malaulau,
and Sebastián Sáez

The flow of temporary movement of workers is estimated to represent about 5 percent of world trade in services (WTO 2010).[1] Increasing the number of temporary workers admitted to work in developed economies by 3 percent would yield estimated annual gains of hundreds of billions of dollars ($156 billion according to Winters and others 2003; $356 billion according to the World Bank 2006; see also the review of empirical studies in Stephenson and Hufbauer 2010). Given the potentially large gains associated with liberalizing labor markets, why has it been so difficult to corral the economic and political forces to support Mode 4 liberalization? The reasons lie in the very nature of labor mobility, which butts head to head with several tenets of multilateral negotiations.

First, the most favored nation (MFN) principle implies that once access is negotiated, it must be granted on an unconditional basis to all nations. Granting unconditional access to labor markets to all World Trade Organization (WTO) members does not sit well with most countries, which feel compelled to balance the liberalization of labor markets with domestic economic or social concerns.

Second, small countries with little bargaining power benefit from the multilateral rules that protect them against more economically powerful trading partners, in particular, through MFN obligations. In practice, however, they are in a weak position to influence market access negotiations. Countries usually exchange concessions with larger trading partners and extend benefits to smaller countries through the unconditional application of MFN obligations. In the context of a bilateral negotiation, with a more limited scope in terms of services sectors, or subsectors, smaller countries could attempt to have greater access for a targeted activity. Of course, in order for this attempt to be successful, any bilateral agreement would need to avoid overlap with commitments made to the WTO or under the General Agreement on Trade in Services (GATS).

Third, because trade agreement provisions are internationally legally binding obligations and disciplines that cannot be unilaterally modified or adjusted according to changes in market conditions, countries tend to be cautious when assuming liberalization commitments.

Fourth, a tenet of trade negotiations is reciprocity; a reciprocal interest is necessary for countries to make market-opening commitments. The fact that exporters and importers of labor are usually distinct groups of countries, with developed countries viewing the export of labor as a "one-way street," makes it difficult for them to reach consensus.

A way forward is to replace the rigidity of MFN and trade provisions with flexibility and to replace reciprocity with provisions that create mutual interest—something that cannot be done without a new mechanism. Bilateral labor agreements (BLAs) seem to provide a way out of the gridlock in multilateral negotiations while also being the instrument of choice for instituting temporary labor mobility programs for the poor. This chapter evaluates BLAs, the policy option most often recommended to substitute or complement the GATS (Amin and Mattoo 2007; Mattoo and Stern 2008; Stephenson and Hufbauer 2010). It draws on the case studies of BLAs with two popular destination countries, Spain (chapter 4) and France (chapter 5), and looks at the experience of one source country, the Philippines (chapter 6).

The chapter is organized as follows. The first two sections examine the potential advantages and disadvantages of BLAs. The third section discusses best practice in BLAs for the poor. The last section summarizes the chapter's main conclusions and provides policy recommendations on when BLAs should be used.

Potential Advantages of BLAs

Although not specifically designed to promote the services exports through the temporary movement of people, BLAs can serve as an alternative or complement to multilateral and regional agreements on trade in services (box 3.1). Because BLAs involve only two parties and the principle of nondiscrimination against third parties is not present, the limitations on market access and national treatment are less restrictive than they are in multilateral and regional agreements. In addition, it is easier for two parties to reach consensus on harmonization of their regulatory frameworks.

BLAs can be an important tool for facilitating temporary labor migration. For receiving countries, the primary objective is to address skill gaps in the domestic labor market, including shortages of seasonal, low-skilled, and higher-skilled workers in various sectors.

Skills Coverage

BLAs may cover all types of workers, from unskilled to skilled professionals. They can address not only the manpower requirements of firms establishing a commercial presence (Mode 3) but all firms, domestic and foreign, in all types of industries. BLAs address both the requirements of developed countries that need to facilitate the movement of skilled professionals and the needs of developing countries to deploy their excess labor overseas.

Box 3.1 Historical Perspective: Old Wine in New Bottle

BLAs have been used as a means of employing seasonal and low- or semiskilled foreign labor on a temporary basis. In most cases, destination countries designed bilateral agreements that helped regulate migration from geographically close countries.

The popularity of BLAs fell in the 1970s and 1980s, when stagflation afflicted some industrial countries. Western European countries and the United States began withdrawing from temporary worker programs. By the turn of the 21st century, several developed countries had entered into second-generation BLAs, which tended to be in the form of Memorandums of Understanding (MOUs) rather than more formal contractual arrangements.

BLAs are increasingly being signed by countries in all regions of the world. Canada has been very active in developing bilateral temporary worker programs, concluding agreements with Barbados, Colombia, Jamaica, Mexico, Trinidad and Tobago, and the countries of the Eastern Caribbean. France, Germany, Italy, Spain, and the United Kingdom have signed BLAs with developing countries around the world. South Africa has entered into BLAs, mainly with neighboring countries. China and the Philippines have concluded BLAs with several developed and developing country partners.

Some developing countries have signed MOUs on migratory and labor cooperation with each other. Examples include agreements between Peru and Chile (2006), Peru and Ecuador (2006), and Peru and Mexico (2002). These agreements seek to exchange information and protect the rights of migrant workers, in particular under the UN International Convention on the Protection of the Rights of Migrant Workers and their Relatives. However, these MOUs do not include provisions to promote labor mobility. The Philippines has signed bilateral MOUs with many destination countries to cover the flows, rights, and obligations of its temporary workers. A reciprocal temporary worker program between Argentina and Bolivia includes many of these protections.

Source: Stephenson and Hufbauer 2010.

Although BLAs can open avenues to the temporary migration of mid- and low-skilled workers, at best they have been used only partially for such broad skill movements. France's pacts, for example, have exacerbated skill-selective migration policies (CIMADE 2008, 2009; Salcedo 2008).

Sectoral Coverage

The GATS and regional trade agreements focus mainly on the services sector. Although this sector has become the leading economic sector in many developed countries, other sectors still make significant contributions to the economy. Multilateral and regional agreements on trade in services do not cover global transfer of workers to nonservices sectors in receiving countries. In contrast, temporary labor migration in a BLA covers all sectors except those restricted by the receiving countries. The agricultural sector of some U.S. states draw workers from neighboring countries, such as Mexico; industries in Taiwan, China, and the

Republic of Korea employ Filipino workers in factories.[2] Canada's MOU with Mexico and several Caribbean countries is exclusively for facilitating the entry of seasonal agricultural workers (see chapter 8). This program has been very successful in facilitating the entry of farm workers: in 2000, 7,300 of the total 16,900 workers admitted were from Mexico. The Canadian BLA with Colombia is targeted to providing low-skilled workers for the food-packing industry. Greece has signed BLAs with Albania and Bulgaria to temporarily meet the demand for seasonal agricultural workers; its agreement with the Arab Republic of Egypt facilitates the entry of workers into the fisheries sector. South Africa's BLAs with Botswana, Lesotho, Malawi, Mozambique, and Swaziland were designed to aid the flow of workers in the mining and agricultural sectors. As a result of these agreements, the share of foreigners in the mining workforce rose from 47 percent in 1990 to 60 percent in 2000, (Stephenson and Hufbauer 2010).

China's BLAs cover diverse sectors. Chinese workers in the United Arab Emirates work in construction, factories, and medical care centers and on ships. Chinese workers in Australia work in nursing and other sectors. A BLA with Jordan concerns the textiles and construction sectors.

Sector-specific coverage of the Philippines' BLAs is quite comprehensive. All industries are covered except industries restricted by the receiving countries. The international movement of workers in agriculture, industry, and the service sectors is a clear example. For instance, several sectors from Taiwan, China, and the Republic of Korea have employed Filipino factory workers. Filipino domestic helpers, caregivers, and nurses all over the world are part of the temporary movement of labor in the services sector.[3]

The case studies reveal that most bilateral agreements were not designed to complement the sectoral surpluses and shortages of workers in partnering countries. However, some progress is evident in coverage across sectors. For instance, France maintains two lists of shortage occupations, one with 30 occupations, which applies to all countries, and another with 150 occupations, applicable to new member states of the European Union (EU). The French migration pacts modify the list of 30 occupations in two ways. First, all of the agreements except the one with Mauritius incorporate the list of 30 but widen the scope to all of metropolitan France. Second, the pacts add additional occupations to the list of 30. By creating occupational shortage lists and thus relaxing an important barrier to market access through the GATS (Article XVI), France is complying with demands by developing country WTO members to reduce the number of occupations regulated by economic needs tests (ENTs).

Occupational shortage lists have the advantage over market access commitments of the type listed in WTO members' GATS schedules in that they indicate more precisely the skill level and type of occupation admitted into the foreign labor market. Given that most GATS Mode 4 commitments and replicas in regional trade agreements are horizontally listed and thus apply across the board to all services sectors without specifying sector-specific skills and competencies, the benefit of shortage occupation lists is considerable.

Ensuring Temporariness

The GATS and regional trade agreements make commitments for temporary deployment of skilled workers in services sector overseas. However, migrants can change their immigration status and seek permanent residency under the sponsorship of the host company. Many Indians work in the United States in the information and communication technology (ICT) sector on a temporary H1-B visa, which is valid for three years, with the possibility of a one-time renewal for another three years. Before the end of this six-year period, these professionals are eligible to apply for permanent resident status. Such a route can lead to brain drain, the permanent loss of highly skilled workers to a developed country.

BLAs can be used as an effective tool for managing migration and ensuring that workers return. Under Colombia's BLA with Spain, for example, more than 90 percent of the agricultural workers hired to harvest fruit in the Catalonia region return to Colombia.

Certain institutional requirements must be in place to achieve this goal. To determine the legality of workers, both sides can jointly monitor the agreements, rather than placing the entire burden on the host country (Stephenson and Hufbauer 2010). Private parties can be required to provide guarantees in the form of bonds, or they can be fined for noncompliance. In addition, compliance is more likely if incentives to return to the host country are built into the agreement. The fact that the agreement can be terminated unilaterally without compensation by the host country may also create an incentive for the sending country to establish credible domestic arrangements to ensure temporariness.

Spain has created a dual mechanism to reward the fulfillment of the commitment to return made by agricultural workers when the season ends: complying workers can be hired in successive seasons without going through the selection process, and being hired for four seasons makes it easier for the migrant to obtain the authorization to reside in a stable way. Foreign workers who do not return to their country of origin upon the finalization of a contract are forbidden from accessing any employment offers in Spain for three years.

Under the GATS, only the host country assumes obligations regarding access of temporary workers (Mattoo and Payton 2007). In contrast, obligations by source countries are a key element for BLAs that have, to a limited extent, improved access for unskilled workers. According to Mattoo (2006, 172), source-country obligations "include premovement screening and selection, accepting and facilitating return, and commitments to combat illegal migration. In effect, such cooperation can help address security concerns, ensure temporariness, and prevent illegal labor flows in a way that the host is incapable of accomplishing alone—thus conferring benefits for which the host may be willing to pay in the form of increased access."

In theory, it should be possible to include such an obligation as part of the WTO/GATS negotiations. Considering the difficulties encountered in the Doha Round of negotiations, however, doing so seems be unlikely in the short term.

Flexibility

BLAs differ from multilateral and regional arrangements on trade in services. They generally provide broader sectoral and skill coverage and more flexibility in enhancing trade in services. BLAs can easily include provisions on regulatory framework and recognition requirements that suit the needs and requirements of contracting parties. BLAs also provide more flexibility with respect to the number and skill types of workers covered, as well as the type of activities workers can perform, which can be altered in light of changes and developments in the economy and the labor market (Stephenson and Hufbauer 2010).

Each contracting party respects the other party's laws and regulations on the deployment and employment of foreign workers. Where there are wide gaps in the recognition of skills and professions, parties to a BLA can provide assistance with human resource development, consult with stakeholders, and establish bilateral mutual recognition agreements (MRAs).

Receiving countries can target specific sending countries for specific services, especially where language, culture, or qualifications are concerned (for example, Germany provides green cards for Indian information technology specialists and the United Kingdom has a preference for nurses from the Philippines) or the country seeks to offer preferences, such as the training worker schemes available to workers from the former Council for Mutual Economic Assistance (CMEA) countries (Bulgaria, Cuba, Czechoslovakia, the Democratic Republic of Germany, Hungary, Mongolia, Poland, Romania, the Soviet Union, and Vietnam). The GATS limits both these features by requiring binding (that is, nonreversible) commitments and the application of the MFN clause (that is, no discrimination among sources) (box 3.2). In such a situation, a bilateral contract offers a more pragmatic alternative.

BLAs can also include provisions for terms of employment, safeguard mechanisms, arbitration, and the return of temporary workers. For instance, the MOU between the Philippines and Qatar includes a model employment contract that specifies the requirements of the Filipino workers to be deployed as well as the obligations and responsibilities of the Qatari employers. Arbitration on the interpretation of the agreement and the employment contract is specified, with the involvement of stakeholders from both the sending and receiving countries.

Although each contracting party has obligations, compliance with BLAs is not as strict as it is for multilateral and regional agreements on trade in services. In multilateral and regional agreements, there is a tendency for contracting parties to be risk averse and conservative in their commitments, because nonimplementation has legal implications and consequences. BLAs are very flexible in accommodating changes in responses to economic or labor market developments. They are subject to the approval of the receiving countries: if they do not want to enter into an MOU, there is nothing a sending country can do.

The case study of the Philippines reveals flexibility in the agreements across partnering countries. There is no template for a BLA, because its content varies depending on the environment, economic development, manpower needs, and labor market situation in sending and receiving countries. If the employment and

Box 3.2 Are BLAs Compatible with the MFN Clause?

The MFN clause is a general obligation under the GATS. It provides that with "respect to any measure covered by this Agreement, each Member shall accord immediately and unconditionally to services and service suppliers of any other Member treatment no less favorable than that it accords to like services and service suppliers of any other country."

There are a few exceptions to this clause. First, when WTO members negotiated the GATS, they agreed that they would be allowed to exempt the application of this obligation before the entry into force of the agreements. WTO members were therefore allowed to adopt exemptions contained in country-specific lists. Their duration must not exceed 10 years in principle. New members of the WTO have also been allowed to adopt a limited number of exemptions during their accession negotiations. Second, MRAs are exempt from the MFN clause. Third, the MFN obligation does not apply when WTO members negotiate preferential trade agreements among themselves (Article V of the GATS).

Do BLAs fall within the Article V exception? It is not possible to fully answer this question, which is essentially a legal question. But countries wishing to negotiate BLAs must carefully consider the likely MFN implications. There are two possible considerations. If BLAs are a practical measure to implement and facilitate the temporary movement of service providers as part of a wider trade agreement, they could be considered as following within the Article V MFN provisions. But what happens if the BLAs are not part of trade agreements? One option is to consider whether the category of workers falling within the BLA is covered by the GATS provisions. There is debate over whether service providers covered by a BLA are actually covered by the GATS and therefore the MFN obligation. According to Mattoo (2003), Carzaniga (2008), and UN (2005), the debate centers on whether natural persons from a sending country employed by a service firm of a receiving country that is not owned or controlled by the firm should be covered by GATS Mode 4.

The GATS Annex on Movement of Natural Persons applies to "measures affecting natural persons who are service suppliers of a Member, and natural persons of a Member who are employed by a service supplier of a Member, in respect of the supply of a service." The United Nations (2005) argues that under the first category "natural persons who are service suppliers of a Member" covers self-employed or independent service suppliers who obtain their remuneration directly from customers. There is some debate about who is covered by the second category ("natural persons of a Member who are employed by a service supplier of a Member"). GATS Article I.2(d) would seem to cover only foreign employees of foreign firms established in another member. However, in "Presence of Natural Persons (Mode 4), Background Note by the WTO Secretariat," (S/C/W/75, 1998), the WTO Secretariat suggests "that foreigners working for host country companies would fall under GATS Mode 4 if they worked on a contractual basis as independent suppliers for a locally-owned firm, but would not necessarily seem to be covered if they were employees of that firm" (UN 2005, 8).

Independently of the potential economic distortions this differential treatment based on contractual relationships may create (Mattoo 2003), insofar as workers covered by BLAs are considered employees of the host country, it would seem that they are not "service suppliers"

box continues next page

Box 3.2 Are BLAs Compatible with the MFN Clause? *(continued)*

under the WTO/GATS. Therefore, measures affecting these workers would not be subject to the WTO/GATS disciplines.

There is an alternative in the case of least developed countries (LDCs). On December 2011, WTO members approved the LDC services waiver, allowing preferential treatment to services and services providers from LDCs. The waiver allows all WTO members, including developed and developing countries as well as other LDCs, to provide better conditions of "market access" to services from LDCs than to like services from non–LDCs. Such preferences may be limited in time; may concern only certain sectors, subsectors, or modes of supply; and may not discriminate between services and services providers of other LDCs: MFN treatment is thus guaranteed to LDC services in any conditions. The waiver covers only measures such as quantitative restrictions and ENTs that fall under the "market access" provision of the GATS (Article XVI). Other types of preferences, including positive discrimination, such as specific incentives to services providers from LDCs, can be introduced only if authorized by the WTO Council of Trade in Services. The nature of the waiver offers valuable opportunities to LDC services providers, in particular with regard to the presence of natural persons. The waiver's broad scope allows WTO members to offer preferential access in areas not currently covered by specific commitments, including the movement of low-skilled or unskilled labor.

Sources: Based on Carzaniga 2008; Mattoo 2003; UN 2005; and WTO 2011.

labor protection measures in receiving countries do not meet the Philippines' requirements, the contents of the BLA are very detailed and specific, as in the case of the MOU with Qatar. In contrast, if the receiving country is highly developed and implements a very progressive and proactive policy for labor protection, the focus of the BLAs shifts to recognition requirements.

The BLAs established by the Philippines have helped lower the cost of migration by reducing the risks of migration and enhancing the intermediation and facilitation processes. The MOU with Qatar includes a template for employment contracts that includes specific provisions on the deployment and employment of overseas Filipino workers, up to the provision of safe and potable water. The specific provisions of the agreement imply that problems encountered in the past are being addressed. These provisions suggest that the market power of the Philippines is increasing. It may emanate from the quality of the workers that have been deployed in Qatar in the past.

The French case lies in contrast to the Filipino case. Although theoretically, BLAs can be more flexible and designed in accordance with partnering countries, this has not been the case for French agreements. France does not negotiate its pacts from scratch but uses a predesigned, generic template, which it minimally modifies during treaty negotiations with the partner country. France first tested its pilot with Gabon, which is not a representative country in terms of emigration flows to France. Subsequently, France "sold" the template to other West African countries and Tunisia. De facto the French migration pacts thus resemble more of a package deal of different "tactical issue linkages" imposed on a source country rather than the negotiated result of a mutually beneficial exchange of interests in light of the principle of shared responsibility.

The case studies of Spain's BLAs with Ecuador and Colombia reveal that they have not been tailored by the specific characteristics of the partnering country. Both agreements have similar orientation, structure, and contents. The introductory chapter identifies the signatory parties and defines "migrant workers"; chapter 1 focuses on the communication processes for job offers; chapter 2 examines the "valuation of professional requirements, travel and reception of migrant workers"; chapter 3 looks at "rights and work and social conditions of migrant workers"; chapter 4 contains "special provisions for seasonal workers"; chapter 5 concerns the "return of migrant workers"; and chapter 6 deals with the "rules of application and coordination" of the agreement. Thus, in practice, destination countries do not introduce flexibility when contracting bilaterally.

Simplicity

Because BLAs are agreements between two countries, there is no need to make a list of exceptions or limitations on market access and national treatment. The contracting parties simply agree to honor existing laws, regulations, and policies on market access and national treatment on both the sending and receiving country. Market access is shaped largely by the labor needs of the receiving country. Countries acceding to the multilateral and regional agreements on trade in services have to state a specific list of limitations on market access and national treatment, because conditions for market access and national treatment are very specific in the agreement and apply to all contracting parties. In practice, not all BLAs embody simplicity. In Spain, for example, job offers are made through a yearly quota. The quota of non–EU foreign workers establishes the number of jobs to be offered to third-country nationals. It can be annually approved by agreement of the council of ministers. Every year, the government publishes a list, with input from autonomous communities (the first-level political and administrative division of Spain), business organizations, and trade unions. This list enables the government to make stable and seasonal job offers and to grant visas to search for employment.

The quota is complex and rigid.[4] Many firms are leery of signing contracts without having had previous direct contact with workers but find it difficult to travel abroad. The lack of adequate information for businesses and direct contact with the national selection or decision-making bodies has led many companies to reduce their hiring of foreign workers.

The quota procedure is complicated. It could be improved by simplifying and streamlining procedures, creating or strengthening job offer management units in countries of origin, strengthening direct and personal contact with businesses, and increasing the autonomy of enterprises in the selection process.

Recognition of Qualifications

Because only two parties are involved and occupational coverage is limited and specific, MRAs are more likely than multiparty multilateral or regional agreements to result in regulatory convergence. For example, the U.K.–Spain agreement provides for recognition of Spanish nursing skills in the United Kingdom. The United Kingdom has also signed BLAs with India and the Philippines to temporarily meet its demand for nurses and other health care professionals.

Under Article VII GATS, WTO members are allowed, but not required, to mutually recognize one another's systems of education and vocational and professional training or to accredit one another's licenses, certifications, and professional qualifications. In practice, similarly situated WTO members, mostly industrial countries, conclude MRAs, which, for the most part, exclude developing countries. The lack of an MRA is an important barrier to market access.

A difficulty inherent in liberalizing market access for low-skilled labor is that the paperwork documenting nonformal, artisanal training is usually unavailable in low-income countries. MRAs cannot remedy this problem. For these jobs, "actual demonstration of work quality" may be the only means of judging competence (Varma 2009), even if skill testing is more costly than concluding an MRA (Chanda 2004).

Bilateral migration agreements have been experimenting with skill testing as an alternative to mutual recognition. Spain's cooperation agreement on migration with Ecuador has set up a Technical Unit for the Selection of Migrant Workers (UTSTM), run jointly with the government of Ecuador and the regional office of the International Organization for Migration in Ecuador (Chanda 2008; Friedman and Ahmed 2008; Pinyol 2009). Similarly, the Migration Information and Management Centre in Mali (CIGEM), cofunded by the European Union, provides skill testing, training, and predeparture information, with a view to facilitating the movement of workers within African countries and to the European Union.

As an alternative to individualized ad hoc skill testing, the EU Répertoire Opérationnel Africain des Métiers et des Emplois (ROAME) requires West African countries to standardize their nomenclature for professions. This repertory may eventually be approximated to EU job descriptions, thereby becoming the nucleus of a future MRA. Occupational shortage lists, which eliminate ENTs, have the further advantage of standardizing the nomenclature for occupations. Such lists, like the ones France is using and incorporating into its bilateral migration agreements, have the effect of approximating qualifications, even if they fall short of mutually recognizing them. Drawing on France's experience, the Partnership for Managing Professional Migration between the European Union and Benin, Cameroon, Mali, and Senegal facilitates the establishment of a common nomenclature for African professions and occupations (the ROAME).

Even if such lists are a first step toward a common nomenclature of service providers and mutual recognition of qualifications, listing shortage occupations is a time-consuming endeavor, and such lists carry the risk of being out of date by the time they enter into force. In France, ensuring that a worker's skills match the occupation that needs to be filled is the responsibility of employers and professional organizations. The Ministry of Immigration, Integration, National Identity and Solidarity Development (MIIINDS) relies on French consulates to recognize educational qualifications, such as master's and Ph.D. degrees. The Office Français de l'Immigration et de l'Intégration (OFII) runs professional training courses, during which skill levels are assessed (EMN and MIIINDS 2010). The French migration pacts could, however, set a precedent by "extending professional training programs and setting up more partnerships with the universities between the country of origin and the host country" in order to facilitate the process of joint awarding of qualifications and joint certification (EMN and MIIINDS 2010, 37).

In the Philippines, there are plans for some progression on MRAs for Filipino nurses in the United Kingdom. Article 3 of the MOU between the Philippines and United Kingdom suggests that the implementing agencies will undertake a recruitment project for the Philippines and the U.K. Department of Health. The project will be carried out with a view to sustainably recruiting and employing nurses and other health care professionals from the Philippines, through policy dialogue on the development of the nursing workforce, implementation of best practices for service delivery, and the involvement of professional staff and health care managers in recruitment.

Efficient Labor Market Management

Differences in training, skills, qualifications, and standards may impede the international flow of labor. Recognizing this potential impediment, contracting parties to a BLA can agree to establish recognition agreement. The labor-receiving country can also offer to provide technical assistance to upgrade the skills and qualifications of workers in the sending country. Consultations with stakeholders can also be useful in ironing out differences that impede the free flow of workers across border.

As a whole, BLAs facilitate the process of overseas employment from recruitment to deployment. These restrictions are beyond the domestic regulations that are normally permitted as rights of sovereign states. These agreements result from the marketing efforts of government agencies in sending countries in exploring potential overseas markets for their excess manpower. BLAs serve as an assurance and commitment on the part of a specific destination country that it needs specific workers and skills in the medium term. For the sending country, a BLA can enhance its manpower planning process and overseas labor market information mechanisms for its workers and stakeholders.

BLAs enable receiving countries to manage the inflows of foreign laborers to suit the employment needs of their growing economies. For a country with labor shortages, the ability to sustain economic growth will hinge on the continued inflow of foreign laborers. BLAs ensure that needed workers will be available, especially workers such as nurses, for whom global demand is high. Receiving countries can also use BLAs to monitor the entry of foreign workers and manage foreign workers with irregular immigration and employment status.

The French pacts are driven only partially by the need to meet labor market demand in France. France maintains two lists of shortage occupations, both of which are biased toward skilled jobs. One list, which contains 150 occupations, applies to new EU member states undergoing transition. The other, which contains 30 occupations, applies to all countries. Of these occupations, only 6 are in national shortage; shortages of the other 24 are regionally determined, unless the list is integrated into a migration pact. The list of shortage occupations applies to only two categories of admissions for labor migrants: employees (professionals staying 12 months and longer in France) and temporary workers (professionals staying less than 12 months). But the primary goal of the pacts is to contain certain kinds of labor migration, as evident from the fact that the largest number of labor migrants come from Mali and Morocco, the very countries that are refusing to sign BLAs with France (EMN and MIIINDS 2010).

France's strategy of using BLAs to control illegal migration may also be misplaced. Amin and Mattoo (2006) suggest that guest worker programs have not been successful in inducing cooperation for limiting illegal migration, which tends to reduce their attractiveness to source countries. In fact, the theoretical model Amin and Matoo develop suggests that such programs increase total (legal and illegal) migration, making them a costly compensating device for the host country. Amin and Mattoo recommend that countries willing to use transfers and other forms of economic assistance to induce source countries to cooperate can afford to provide relatively liberal treatment of illegal immigrants.

In Spain, where job offers for vacant posts can be offered through the yearly quota, employment is offered mainly, although not exclusively, to countries with which Spain has signed bilateral agreements for regulating and planning migration flows (Law 4/2000, in accordance with Law 14/2003, Article 39). Despite the fact that the Ley Orgánica de Extranjería (LOE) provides that "job offers made will preferably be addressed to those countries who signed with Spain agreements focused on the regulation of migration flows," employers can request workers from a particular country. The Spanish system does not allow quotas to be established by country. Job offers may be subject to quotas per territory or profession, however.

Spain's policy is based not on predetermined quotas but on the permanent analysis of needs in the labor market. It seeks to ensure that available jobs are offered to Spanish or foreign legal resident workers before being offered abroad. The two basic instruments through which the national situation of employment is defined are (a) the yearly labor quota system (*contingente*) of foreign workers and (b) the Catalogue of Hard-to-Fill Occupations (CHFO), the list of occupations that are difficult to fill with national workers or foreigners legally residing in Spain.

Developmental Impact

Although BLAs are meant as facilitative measures, they can also be used to promote the welfare of deployed workers. Foreign workers are sometimes subjected to abuse, maltreatment, and nonimplementation of contracts. BLAs can address these issues. For instance, under the Spain–Philippines BLA, nurses and other Filipino workers who work in Spain are afforded the same protections as Spanish nationals.

The developmental impact of BLAs is not very clear. In principle, these agreements can promote the acquisition or enhancement of migrants' professional skills and qualifications; remittances, technology transfers, and increases in human capital can foster development in sending countries. BLAs may also have negative impact however, causing brain drain in sending countries (OECD 2004; OSCE, IOM, and ILO 2006).

Examination of the French BLAs suggests that they fail to deliver on the developmental dimension. In terms of thematic coherence, the pacts' main deficiency lies in the discrepancy between goals of development and the categories of labor the pacts admit to the French market. If development were truly a concern, the labor migration component would have to be opened much more widely to lawful entry of low-skilled workers, including seasonal agricultural workers, domestic workers, cleaners, and servers, categories so included in only in the minority of the pacts (Secrétariat Général du Comité Interministériel de Contrôle de l'Immigration 2009).

The performance of signatory countries in providing development aid has been modest at best. For instance, the discretionary space of the new French BLAs is determined by the European Union through the Schengen visa and border security regulation, EU readmission rules, and the financing tools of the European Neighbourhood Policy (ENP). If a migrant-sending country that happens to be eligible for ENP funding concludes a migration pact with France, it may obtain more development aid from France, which would be obliged to match the EU Commission's ENP funding. Migrant-sending countries that have concluded EU–wide readmission agreements are exempt from subscribing to a readmission obligation in a migration pact with France. Consequently, the French migration pact with a labor-sending country will consist of only two rather than three prongs. In cases such as these, the treaty architecture of the French migration pact is lighter, as it does not include a chapter on readmissions and border securitizations.

Development aid is also watered down by the fact that return migrants benefiting from it are not those who require assistance to reintegrate; instead, assistance goes to highly skilled migrants who wish to build a business in their country of origin as a subsidiary enterprise to their primary profession. The employment-generating effect of individualized reintegration support from France varies widely depending on the level of education of the migrant. In Mali, up to 90 percent of men receive voluntary return aid. Despite not having signed a pact on concerted migration management, Mali benefits most from the reintegration program.[5] Another way of measuring developmental impact is through remittances. There are no data on the remittances sent by third-country nationals in France or Spain, however, and estimating their value is difficult.

Remittances from Ecuadorians in Spain do not appear to have helped reduce poverty in Ecuador (Olivié, Ponce, and Onofa 2008). In contrast, in the Philippines, temporary labor migration has generated sizable welfare gains through remittances (Ratha and Mohapatra 2007). Remittance inflows reached more than \$20 billion in 2010 and \$22 billion in 2011 (BSP 2013), stimulating the economy and improving the well-being of migrants' household members through enhanced expenditures on housing, education, medical care, and consumer durables (Tullao, Conchada, and Rivera 2010). The Filipino experience also shows that poorly designed policies can have a negative consequence for the domestic market and that temporary migration policy has a limited impact if not embedded in a wider development strategy (box 3.3).

Potential Disadvantages of BLAs

BLAs have several possible drawbacks. Commitments to supply workers may involve preparing and training workers in the sending country. Failure to place them abroad—as a result of a changed environment in the host country—may result in significant social, educational, and training costs. Committing workers to specific destinations may not reflect global economic and labor conditions. Sending countries may find it difficult to deploy workers to destinations that offer better opportunities and incentives if they have commitments with a particular host country under a BLA. In addition, although the agreement may be intended for temporary migration, the real outcome may be permanent migration. Agreements that allow for the movement of skilled workers may result in brain drain for the sending country.

Receiving countries may not be able to absorb the number of workers they have committed to hire, because of labor market and economic developments in both sending and receiving countries. Depending on the type of BLA, it can also lock a receiving country into hiring workers from a specific sending country, preventing it from forging ties with other potential labor-exporting countries.

Another weakness of BLAs is that, unlike regional trade agreements, they are single-issue instruments (Stephenson and Hufbauer 2010). As a result, they provide developing country partners no scope for trading off their interests in labor mobility against the interests of the developed country trading partners (exchanging concessions on market access on goods or services against greater access to labor markets, for example).

Finally, trade agreements aim to provide a set of rules that secure the terms and conditions under which trade can take place; these rules are guaranteed through legally binding dispute settlement procedures. Unlike commitments made under a regional trade agreement or the GATS, BLAs are nonbinding. They are thus subject to approval by the receiving countries. If receiving countries do not want to enter into an MOU, there is nothing a sending country can do. BLAs thus require sending countries to accept greater uncertainty in exchange for potentially greater access.

Best Practice in BLAs for the Poor

BLAs have had a mixed past, which has generally not inspired confidence in their ability to deliver without creating significant sociopolitical costs. Programs geared to low-skilled migrants, such as seasonal migration programs, have been

Box 3.3 Downsides of the Philippines' Policy of Promoting the Export of Health Care Services Workers

A number of shortcomings have emerged from the policies adopted almost four decades ago to promote the export of health care services through the temporary movement of nurses. First, demand in foreign labor markets is highly volatile: despite the agreement between the United Kingdom and the Philippines, during much of the 1990s, the United Kingdom recruited very few Filipino nurses; in 2000–02, it hired more than 10,000 nurses; as demand dropped again, it hired almost no Filipino nurses in 2008.

Second, the Philippine government helped create an excess supply of nurses, both by maintaining a light regulatory framework for private tertiary education and by not enforcing rules on quality assurance. Enrollment rose from 28,000 in 2000/01 to 454,000 in 2006/07, reducing the chances of obtaining employment abroad (Philippine Overseas Employment Administration deployed an annual average of 9,667 nurses abroad in 2005–08) and at home (Engman 2010).

Third, exporting nurses creates several externalities including (a) the permanent, not temporary, outflow of medical doctors, who requalify as registered nurses in order to emigrate to the United States; (b) the migration of experienced nurses and nurse specialists, leaving the domestic market with inexperienced nurses; and (c) the opportunity cost of educating nurses whose numbers far exceed domestic and foreign demand (Engman 2010).

Fourth, highly restrictive regulations on imports of health care services have impeded the development of an export-oriented health care industry based on foreign direct investment and medical tourism (Engman 2010). In Engman's view, although the government has been active, it has been unsuccessful in opening up foreign markets through trade negotiations. He suggests that policies seeking bilateral and regional agreements on recruitment procedures and recognition of academic credentials and licenses will continue to be ineffective unless the government is willing to exchange greater market access at home for greater market access of its nurses abroad.

Fifth, the government regulates labor contracts to ensure that the wages paid are above occupation-specific minimums. These policies lead to higher wages for workers able to secure jobs but reduce the number of jobs available and place the burden of adjustment to economic shocks in destination countries entirely on the employment rather than the wage margin. Mckenzie, Theoharide, and Yang (2012) conclude that although migrant source countries such as the Philippines are for the most part powerless to change regulations setting minimum wages for migrants in destination countries, they can change their own regulatory practices on migrant labor. In their view, setting minimum wages for migrants by source country has negative economic consequences for migrant workers.

particularly controversial, as witnessed by the policy debate in the United States over a new guest worker program and continued debate in Western Europe about the role of seasonal workers. Some critics of such programs raise concerns that workers will overstay their visa or reduce the wages of native workers (Borjas 2007). Others raise concerns about the possible exploitation of workers.

To be sure, there have been problems with previous temporary schemes. As attractive and mutually beneficial as a temporary movement of labor sounds in theory, in practice the adage "there is nothing more permanent than a temporary worker" seems to capture the general suspicion with which the temporary movement of workers is viewed.

If any progress is going to be made on expanding labor market access for the poor, this popular perception will need to be better understood and reversed. With this goal in mind, this section offers some thoughts on how BLAs can be made to work well globally. The main message is that emphasis needs to shift from liberalization of labor markets, which puts the onus on receiving countries to open up, to management of labor mobility, which puts the onus on both sending and receiving countries to mitigate risks and enhance benefits. Labor mobility is no longer a unilateral decision but rather a bilateral decision-making process, in which the actions of both sending and receiving countries are critical to success.

BLAs involve recognition of at least two fundamental realities. The first is that there is likely to be excess demand for work in the sending country. As a result, some rationing procedures will need to be devised that can be administered and enforced in a credible, if imperfect, manner. The second is that there are significant information market failures that prevent market access from translating into market entry. Government and nongovernment stakeholders in both countries need to work together to reduce the effects of these market failures. "Shared responsibility" becomes the cornerstone of bilateral temporary movement of people schemes.

Invoking the principle of shared responsibility allows some context-specific measures to emerge that reassure host countries that liberalizing labor markets will not automatically lead to the outcomes most feared to be economically or politically costly. This principle affects the design, implementation, and institution-building components of BLAs (Luthria 2011).

Design

The design of a BLA must ensure that the scheme's incentives are compatible with the outcomes desired. Four aspects of basic design—the four Cs—are important.

1. *Cost.* The high fixed cost of movement for the poor usually affects how long migrants need to stay overseas to recover their substantial investment in getting there. The higher the cost borne by the migrant, the longer they need to stay abroad—and the longer they stay abroad, the less likely they are to return. Cost-sharing with employers reduces this burden and enables migrants to accumulate savings more quickly. Imposing some cost on employers in developed countries also solves the problem of foreign workers being used (or being perceived to be used) to undercut local wages, which makes such schemes domestically difficult in developed countries.

2. *Choice of workers.* The qualifications of workers matter greatly. Educated and skilled workers in sending countries often apply for semiskilled or unskilled work abroad. If overqualified workers are selected to perform unskilled jobs, they tend to use temporary schemes as a stepping stone rather than the restricted employment opportunity they are meant to provide. Hiring overqualified workers can undermine a scheme. To prevent this from happening, policy makers need to pay greater attention to recruitment practices in sending countries. (Of course, the expansion of channels for semiskilled and skilled workers to access overseas labor markets—through mutual skills accreditation and recognition—would help take some of this pressure off.)

3. *Circularity.* Access to the international labor market needs to be repeated rather than treated as a one-time event (that is, workers should be able to return year after year). Well-intentioned policy makers in developed countries often try to limit the number of times a single worker can have access to overseas employment. In game theory terms, making temporary employment abroad a repeated rather than a one-shot game changes behavior and aligns it with the intended consequences.

4. *Commercial viability.* Even in times of labor shortages, destination countries can be reluctant to enter into arrangements with developing countries to import unskilled labor because of the fear that when labor market conditions change for the worse and local unemployment rises, they will continue to be bound to a specific intake of foreign workers. Sending countries do not help their cause when they insist on having quotas written into bilateral agreements or MOUs, with a view to providing certainty of access. Instead, the emphasis needs to be on maintaining the commercial viability of temporary labor schemes by putting the private sector's needs front and center and allowing the scheme to adjust to domestic labor market conditions.

Another way to reinforce the temporary character of migration is through contract-based movement, which focuses on tasks (services) that need to be contracted by firms instead of workers or individuals. For example, computing programming or auditing are tasks that firms can temporarily outsource (Hoekman and Ozden 2010). The rational for such a scheme is that from the point of view of a firm, what matters are the services (tasks) demanded or required rather than who performs them. Once the demand for the task is identified, the task could be performed by an individual hired by the firm or by a foreign firm (established or not in the host country) that hires or sends a worker to perform the task. This movement is performed under a contract that establishes the terms, conditions, and stay in the country required to perform the task, after which the service provider returns home.

Contract-based movement has several advantages, according to Hoekman and Ozden (2010). First, it helps make temporariness more credible, as contracts are time bound. Second, although contracts may be recurrent, once the worker reaches the maximum length of stay, he or she must be rotated. Third, contract-based movement allows internalization of some objectives that otherwise require regulations (such as the recognition of licenses and professional qualifications). Under contract-based movement, the firm purchasing the services must assess whether foreign suppliers meet prevailing quality and related performance standards. Such a system is less cumbersome, costly, and time consuming than recertification or the negotiation of (mutual) recognition agreements. Finally, contract-based movement can be designed to generate incentives to encourage workers to return.

Implementation/Management

Good design is often not followed by active management of the risks inherent to the system. As a result, the scheme operates suboptimally or, worse, erodes the goodwill and political capital that are necessary to get a temporary labor scheme to work.

The main reason why active management of all stakeholders is critical is the time inconsistency problem (Amin and Mattoo 2005, 2006). The cost of identifying, sorting, selecting, recruiting, and training is incurred largely in this first stage and is hence treated as a sunk cost. The benefits accrue in the next stage. However, although firms may initially participate in such programs, accepting the temporary nature of the arrangements in time period $t + 1$, such an arrangement may not be in their interest in time period $t + 2$. This may be the case, for example, when the social cost of migration is below a critical level relative to the benefits of keeping trained migrants. The result is too much permanent migration and too little temporary migration—as has happened with numerous temporary labor programs. Particularly for unskilled workers, the social costs are generally perceived to be greater than the private training costs incurred by firms, potentially creating a sizable wedge between private and socially desirable policy.

Table 3.1 identifies the possible scenarios that emerge based on different levels of private fixed costs and social costs. When the fixed costs of selecting, recruiting, transporting, and training workers is high, employers in the host country will try to keep these workers permanently. Conversely, if these costs are low, employers will have a higher tolerance for using them for a finite period and letting them go at the end of a season or cycle, in the expectation of incurring some of these (small) costs in the next cycle. If real or perceived social costs to host countries of having migrants is high (as it usually is for unskilled workers), host governments are keen to ensure temporariness; if the cost is low (as it usually is for skilled workers), they may have a higher tolerance for allowing temporary workers to become permanent.

The least problematic case occurs when the fixed and social costs are low (cell D). In this case, a spectrum of outcomes is tolerable to all three parties: source governments, host governments, and host country firms. Where fixed costs are low but social costs are high (cell B), host governments want temporary migration whereas source governments may prefer permanent migration, creating a conflict of interest between the two governments. However, because fixed costs are low, firms in the host country can be coopted by their governments to

Table 3.1 Effects of Fixed and Social Cost of Migration on Attitudes toward Migration by Host and Source Countries and Firms

	Fixed cost is high	Fixed cost is low	Policy emphasis required to make temporary labor scheme work
Social cost is high	A • Employers in host country want permanent migration. • Source country government probably wants permanent migration. • Host country government wants temporary migration. Problem: Domestically and internationally, firms and home country governments want different outcomes.	B • Firms can accept temporary migration. • Source country government probably wants permanent migration. • Home country government wants temporary migration. Problem: Source country and host country governments want different outcomes, but domestic cooperation is possible because interests of firms and home country governments are aligned.	Burden is on source country government to actively screen, regulate, and repatriate workers. Mechanisms are needed to ensure cooperation of source country government.
Social cost is low	C • Firms want permanent migration. • Source country government wants temporary migration. • Host country government wants permanent migration. Problem: If home country governments and firms collude, a commitment problem will emerge.	D Firms, source countries, and host countries are willing to accept any outcome.	Under scenarios A and C, when fixed costs are high, firms want to keep worker; firms therefore need to be "policed"—something that is expected to be easier under scenario A than under scenario C. Burden is on host country government. Mechanisms are needed to ensure commitment and cooperation of host country government.

Source: Based on Amin and Mattoo 2005 and Luthria 2011.

keep workers only temporarily, as occurs in temporary labor schemes in Australia and New Zealand (see chapter 7).

In a high fixed cost and low social cost scenario (cell C), firms lean toward permanence, and tacit collusion between host governments and employers may run counter to the source country's desires. The most difficult scenario is perhaps scenario A, where both fixed and social costs are high (imagine poor workers from distant lands with high travel and training costs). Under these circumstances, employers will not want to incur high fixed costs repeatedly. They will therefore lean toward keeping workers permanently. The source country may also be willing to let these workers stay permanently. The host government, however, will strongly favor temporariness, because of the high social cost associated with these migrants. In this situation, not only host and source government intentions but also the intentions of host governments and their own employers are at odds.

Overall, in high fixed cost scenarios, governments should scrutinize employers' behavior and actions during implementation. Where social costs are high, the focus needs to be on getting source governments to perform certain due diligence functions properly and offering capacity-building assistance. When social costs

Let Workers Move • http://dx.doi.org/10.1596/978-0-8213-9915-6

are low, the host country government needs to show commitment to returning workers whom the source country wants back. The implications if this scenario on recruitment management practices (public versus private), management of the vetting process for firms that enter into the program, and the determination and enforcement of penalties are not yet fully understood.

Capacity Building

Both receiving and sending countries have adopted hands-off approaches on the assumption that "stroke-of-the-pen" reform will automatically lead to institutional reforms that support temporary labor schemes. This assumption is usually incorrect, because widespread market failures exist in labor markets, particularly in international labor markets. Inadequate information about the existence or quality of labor supply or employment opportunities and coordination market failures (between hiring contractors, government agencies, private employers, unions, and nongovernmental organizations, domestically as well as across borders) can bring even a well-designed system to a halt.

Exacerbating these market failures is the reality of international labor markets, in which the capacity endowments of receiving and sending countries are very dissimilar. Receiving countries need to assist labor-sending countries in reducing information and coordination asymmetries especially if the success of the scheme is perceived to have some additional noneconomic advantage such as institutional building in the source country (box 3.4). Addressing capacity constraints between sending and receiving countries—some separately, some jointly—represents a major step in building trust in the mechanisms that shape the temporary movement of persons.

Regional dialogue and cooperation frameworks (such as the charter of the Association of Southeast Asian Nations [ASEAN]) can play a role. It is common for advocacy for freer trade to be accompanied by aid for trade and "behind-the-border" interventions, such as technical assistance and funding assistance, to ensure that the benefits of freer trade are shared more equally. It is time that similar steps be taken for the temporary movement of labor. Regional charters and institutions could work to put in place capacity-building measures for source country governments to prepare, manage, and coordinate across a variety of domestic and international actors. Without such advice and support, source countries are likely to find themselves ill-equipped to address the various types of market failures in international labor markets.

Monitoring and Evaluation

A second role for regional cooperative frameworks (such as ASEAN) is the mainstreaming of monitoring and evaluation (M&E) of the development impact of temporary labor programs. Credible information on the development impact could reduce the cynicism that prevails among stakeholders and help broker dialogue between sending and receiving countries.

To date, the only scheme that has conducted baseline surveys of participants, tracked workers year after year, and provided credible counterfactuals of what

Box 3.4 Capacity-Building Measures for Labor-Exporting Countries

Most labor-sending countries require advice and funding to establish sound frameworks of policies and practices to facilitate the export of labor. Such assistance should begin with a thorough assessment of the goals, capacities, and governing responsibilities of the relevant public and private actors in the source country, whose active participation is necessary for a successful program.

Some Tangibles: The Must Haves

Legal Framework. Review of existing employment acts to ensure that they include provisions for hiring under a temporary movement of persons program is a necessary first step. The depth of the review depends on how the hiring is expected to be performed: directly by foreign employers, by their locally based agents, or through existing government programs.

Policy Outcomes and Objectives. Having expectations disseminated in sending and receiving countries will focus standards of recruitment and direct the monitoring and evaluation of both the positive and adverse impacts of labor migration by comparing expected outcomes and objectives with results.

Costs. Some countries have set up revolving funds to provide workers with financial support to cover the upfront costs of participating in temporary labor programs. Governments need advice on how best to operate these funds. Assistance with reforming the remittance infrastructure is also often warranted, so that workers can send money home without paying high fees and gain access to financial services.

Some Intangibles that Have Been Indispensable

Education and Training. Structuring and delivering information on temporary labor programs requires training programs at the preapplication, postselection, and predeparture stages. The content of each stage of training varies and needs to be customized to suit the receiving as well as the source country. A domestic awareness campaign can help manage expectations and prevent abuse by illegitimate actors.

Organizational Capacity. Various government departments and ministries may have to work together to facilitate a program. Clarity on the processes of coordination, oversight, and service delivery at each stage is critical to avoid bureaucratic delays. Some trial and error is inevitable, but external help can streamline the various private and public roles. Identifying the leadership, staffing, skills, operational procedures, and training needs of each department to fulfill its mandate is often overlooked and ends up compromising the credibility of the program. It is also important to have good databases that contain detailed information on the workers leaving, ranging from basic demographic data to detailed contractual information regarding the overseas employment. Some minimum data and reporting standards have emerged; source countries may require assistance in instituting and sustaining systems to meet these standards. These systems also generally need to be coordinated, integrated, and technically supported across various government agencies.

Marketing Tools. Source countries often benefit from a "branding" strategy to help enter new markets or sectors. Assistance in devising a realistic strategy and following it up with good

box continues next page

Box 3.4 Capacity-Building Measures for Labor-Exporting Countries *(continued)*

communication and dissemination tools—Web sites, advertising, and focused marketing missions—and sustained marketing relationships can deliver results if well targeted and designed. Branding is most effective if it signals the presence of quality-enhancing measures in the source country, such as comprehensive predeparture training and higher competence in service delivery by public and private sector actors.

---

would have happened in the absence of migration is the one between New Zealand and the Pacific Island countries (see chapter 7). Such evidence has played an important role in maintaining widespread domestic and international support for the program. It also helped get a similar scheme off the ground in Australia. Given the large public good nature of M&E and its high cost, regional attention is warranted to support such efforts more widely.

Conclusion

Given their potential positive and negative effects, when should countries use BLAs? To answer this question, it is necessary to recall that the objective of this analysis is to identify and discuss possible options for increasing services trade through the temporary movement of people as a complement, not a substitute, to what can be achieved through trade agreements. As analyzed in this chapter, BLAs are designed to manage migration flows, not to promote services exports.

WTO/GATS negotiations—and trade negotiations more broadly—are bound by the "precedent burden." To illustrate, for a "big" country, giving a trade concession to a "small" country may have little domestic impact. In a multilateral context such as the WTO, however, doing so requires extending the concession unconditionally to all its members, which may have a significant impact on the domestic economy and induce a negative political reaction. As a result, "big" countries will be more willing to grant concessions to other "big" countries, indirectly benefiting "small" countries through the unconditional application of the MFN clause. This practice may not coincide with small countries' interests, however, which may go unmet. Countries could use BLAs as complementary tools to overcome this limitation. The biggest advantage would still be potential gains from the mutual cooperation to ensure temporariness.

As an alternative, a small country may aim at, through a regional trade agreement, achieving greater market concessions. In practice, although regional or bilateral negotiations affect only the parties involved, countries will be normally mindful of the precedent that the negotiations outcome may imply to other negotiations as well. For example, the concessions on temporary movement of people in the bilateral negotiations of the European Union or the United States are relatively similar among their trading partners or with their WTO concessions. A BLA may provide a complementary avenue to improve these concessions in selective sectors where a country may have a particular offensive interest. In this context, the BLAs would not be part of a strategy to manage migration flows, but would be part of a country strategy to promote services exports through the temporary movement of a particular category of services providers. But this will require a different approach than the one follow until now.

As was mentioned in this chapter, the theoretical advantages of BLAs notwithstanding, however, their effectiveness has been limited. A variety of factors may explain their lack of impact. First, employers have hired fewer workers than expected (partly because of the large number of undocumented immigrants). Second, administrative complexities and bureaucratic delays have plagued the system. Firms are required to present their needs months in advance—something that is not always feasible for them. Third, countries have shown a preference for hiring seasonal migrants from countries closer to home (for whom travel costs are lower).

The French and Spanish BLAs do not represent real options for service exports. They are instruments for importing temporary workers, regulating the inflows of migrants, and improving the working and living conditions of foreign workers in destination countries.

The Philippines has had a somewhat successful experience with BLAs, partially because of the institutions it has in place to facilitate large-scale temporary migration (Agunias 2008). The success of these institutions has been made possible by the cooperation of several levels of government in both the Philippines and the host country. Even in the Philippines, however, shortcomings remain.

There is no easy way to find ways to address international labor mobility. In the words of Stephenson and Hufbauer (2010, 62), increased labor mobility for services providers demands "a long, persistent, and patient search for niches in the labor markets of developed countries where greater entry of migrants is not only tolerated, but welcomed."

Notes

1. In contrast, 55–60 percent of global services are delivered through Mode 3 (commercial presence), 25–30 percent through Mode 1 (cross-border trade), and 10–15 percent through Mode 2 (consumption abroad).

2. Defining what a service encompasses is not always easy, according to a background note prepared by the secretariats of the WTO and the Organisation for Economic Co-operation and Development (OECD). In the case of temporary workers (as well as other service providers), for instance, should an agreement classify a natural person supplying services incidental to agriculture as a service provider or an agricultural worker? A similar problem occurs for categories under "Other business services" of the WTO services sectoral classification list GNS/W/120, such as services incidental to fishery, mining, manufacturing, and other sectors (UN 2005).

3. The BLA also attempts to curb the high fees charged by recruitment agencies that hire migrants by using government offices.

4. The number of forms to fill out and the data that need to be provided may act as an impediment to the use of the quota. The annexes of Order TIN/3498/2009, by which

the quota of 2010 is regulated, illustrates this problem. See http://extranjeros.empleo.gob.es/es/normativajurisprudencia/Nacional/RegimenExtranjeria/RegimenGeneral/documentos/ContratacionesOrigen2010.pdf.

5. In 2007, the number of return aid projects was 153 in Mali, 90 in Romania, and 28 in Senegal. In 2008, France sponsored 132 projects in Mali, 85 in Romania, 55 in Senegal, and 31 in Bosnia-Herzegovina.

References

Agunias, D. R. 2008. "Managing Temporary Labor Migration: Lessons from the Philippine Model." Insight (October), Migration Policy Institute, Washington, DC.

Amin, M., and A. Mattoo. 2005. "Does Temporary Migration Have to Be Permanent?" Policy Research Working Paper 3582, World Bank, Washington, DC.

———. 2006. "Can Guest Worker Schemes Reduce Illegal Migration?" Policy Research Paper 3828, World Bank, Washington, DC.

———. 2007. "Migration from Zambia: Ensuring Temporariness through Cooperation." In Services Trade and Development: The Experience of Zambia, edited by A. Mattoo and L. Payton, 259–91. Washington, DC: World Bank.

Borjas, G. 2007. "A Lemon in the Senate." National Review. http://www.nationalreview.com/articles/220991/lemon-senate/george-j-borjas.

BSP (Bangko Sentral ng Pilinipas). 2013. Overseas Filipinos' (OF) Remittances. Manila: BSP. http://www.bsp.gov.ph/publications/tables/2013_01/news-01152013a1.htm.

Carzaniga, A. 2008. "A Warmer Welcome? Access for Natural Persons under PTA." In Opening Markets for Trade in Services: Countries and Sectors in Bilateral and WTO Negotiations, edited by J. A. Marchetti and M. Roy, 475–502. Cambridge, U.K.: Cambridge University Press.

Chanda, R. 2004. "Movement and Presence of Natural Persons and Developing Countries: Issues and Proposals for the GATS Negotiations." TRADE Working Paper 19, Trade-Related Agenda, Development and Equity, South Centre, Geneva, Switzerland.

———. 2008. Low-Skilled Workers and Bilateral, Regional, and Unilateral Initiatives: Lessons for the GATS Mode 4 Negotiations and Other Agreements. Geneva, Switzerland: United Nations Development Programme.

CIMADE (Comité Inter-Mouvements auprès des Evacués). 2008. Les Accords Relatifs à la Gestion Concertée des Flux Migratoires et au Co-développment, Document d'Analyse, Paris, November.

———. 2009. Document d'analyse: les accords relatifs a la gestion concertée des flux migratoires et au co-développment. http://www.lacimade.org/uploads/File/solidarites-internationales/Documents/accords%20bilateraux/DOC%20ANALYSE%20La%20Cimade%20-%20note%20accords%20gestion%20concert%C3%A9e%20-%20jan09.pdf. English version: http://www.aprodev.eu/files/Development_policy/Dev-migration/Cimade%20paper%20on%20readmission%20agr%20-%20eng-May%2009.pdf.

EMN (European Migration Network) and MIINDS (Ministry of Immigration, Integration, National Identity and Solidarity Development). 2010. Satisfying Labor Demand through Migration Report. Brussels: EMN.

Engman, M. 2010. "A Tale of Three Markets: How Government Policy Creates Winners and Losers in the Philippines Health Sector." Working Paper, Group d'Economie Mondiale, Sciences Po, Paris.

Friedman, U., and D. Z. Ahmed. 2008. "Ensuring Temporariness: Mechanisms to Incentivise Return Migration in the Context of GATS Mode 4 and Least Developed Country Interests." Global Economic Issues Publication, Quaker United Nations, Geneva, Switzerland.

Hoekman, B., and C. Ozden. 2010. "The Euro-Mediterranean Partnership: Trade in Services as an Alternative to Migration?" *Journal of Common Market Studies* 48 (4): 835–57.

Luthria, M. 2011. *Labor Mobility for the Poor: Is It Really Possible?* Economic Premise 45 (January), World Bank, Washington, DC. http://siteresources.worldbank.org/INTPREMNET/Resources/EP45.pdf.

Mattoo, A. 2003. "Introduction and Overview." In *Moving People to Deliver Services*, edited by A. Mattoo and A. Carzaniga, 1–20. Washington, DC: World Bank.

———. 2006. "Services in a Development Round: Proposals for Overcoming Inertia." In *Trade, Doha, and Development: A Window into the Issues*, edited by R. Newfarmer, 161–74. Washington, DC: World Bank.

Mattoo, A., and L. Payton. 2007. *Services Trade and Development: The Experience of Zambia.* Washington, DC: World Bank.

Mattoo, A., and R. M. Stern. 2008. "Overview." In *A Handbook of International Trade in Services*, edited by A. Mattoo, R. M. Stern, and G. Zanini, 3–47. Oxford, U.K.: Oxford University Press.

Mckenzie, D., C. Theoharide, and D. Yang. 2012. "Distortions in the International Migrant Labor Market: Evidence from Filipino Migration and Wage Responses to Destination Country Economic Shocks." Policy Research Working Paper 6041, World Bank, Washington, DC.

OECD (Organisation for Economic Co-operation and Development). 2004. *Migration for Employment: Bilateral Agreements at a Crossroads.* Paris: OECD.

Olivié, I., J. Ponce, and M. Onofa. 2008. *Remesas, pobreza y desigualdad: el caso de Ecuador.* Madrid: Real Instituto Elcano. http://www.realinstitutoelcano.org/wps/wcm/connect/5e0931004f834e2389c6bd6c295fd59b/Estudio_Elcano_1_Olivie_Ponce_Onofa_remesas_Ecuador.pdf?MOD=AJPERES.

OSCE (Organisation for Security and Co-operation in Europe), IOM (International Organization on Migration), and ILO (International Labour Organization). 2006. *Handbook on Establishing Effective Labour Migration Policies in Countries of Origin and Destination.* Geneva, Switzerland: OSCE.

Pinyol, G. 2009. "Labour Agreements for Managing Migration: The Spanish Experience." Paper presented at the Barcelona Center for International Affairs (CIDOB) Foundation Workshop on, "Establishing Labour Migration Policies in Countries of Origin and Destination and Inter-State Collaboration in the Western Balkans," International Organization for Migration, Tirana, February 9–10.

Ratha, D. and S. Mohaptra. 2007. *Increasing the Macroeconomic Impact of Remittances on Development.* Washington, D.C.: World Bank.

Salcedo, P. L. 2008. "Les accords de gestion concertée des flux migratoires et de développement solidaire: un instrument de la nouvelle politique migratoire de la

France au service de l'approche globale des migrations." Mémoire de master en science politique, Université Paris 1.

Secrétariat Général du Comité Interministériel de Contrôle de l'Immigration. 2009. *Rapport au Parlement: les orientations de la politique de l'immigration.* Paris.

Stephenson, S., and G. H. Hufbauer. 2010. "Increasing Labor Mobility: Options for Developing Countries." In *International Trade in Services: New Trends and Opportunities for Developing Countries,* edited by O. Cattaneo, M. Engman, S. Sáez, and R. M. Stern, 29–66. Washington, DC: World Bank.

Tullao, T. S., M. I. P Conchada, and J. P. R. Rivera. 2010. "The Labor Migration Industry for Health and Educational Services: Regulatory and Governance Structures and Implications for National Development." World Bank, Washington, DC.

UN (United Nations). 2005. "Background Note on GATS Mode 4 and Its Information Needs." Meeting of the Technical Subgroup on Movement of Natural Persons (Mode 4), Department of Economic and Social Affairs, Statistics Division, United Nations, Paris, January 31–February 1.

Varma, S. 2009. "Facilitating Temporary Labor Mobility in African LDCs: Addressing Mode 4 Related Supply Side Constraints." ICTSD Dialogue, International Centre for Trade and Sustainable Development, Geneva, Switzerland, February 26.

Winters, L. A., T. L. Walmsley, Z. K. Wang, and R. Grynberg. 2003. "Liberalizing Temporary Movement of Natural Persons: An Agenda for the Development Round." *World Economy* 26 (8): 1137–61.

World Bank. 2006. *Global Economic Prospects.* Washington, DC: World Bank.

WTO (World Trade Organization). 2010. "Presence of Natural Persons. Mode 4." Background Note, WTO Secretariat, S/C/W/301, Geneva, Switzerland.

———. 2011. "Preferential Treatment to Services and Service Suppliers of Least-Developed Countries." Decision of December 17, WT/L/847, Geneva, Switzerland.

CHAPTER 4

Can Bilateral Labor Agreements Help Colombia and Ecuador Increase Their Service Exports to Spain?

Antonio Bonet and Sebastián Sáez

This chapter describes general migratory trends and mechanisms for accessing the Spanish labor market. It assesses the importance of service providers' access to that market through Spain's commitments as a member of the European Union (EU) under the World Trade Agreement (WTO)/General Agreement on Trade in Services (GATS) agreements. It concludes that the number of foreign workers that access the Spanish market under the GATS is small, especially compared with other mechanisms, including bilateral labor agreements (BLAs).

The chapter is organized as follows. The first section describes Spain's transition toward a labor-importing country and explains how it regulates the flow of temporary workers. The second section examines the exporting of services to Spain through GATS Mode 4. The third section looks at the BLAs with Colombia and Ecuador and assesses their main results. The last section describes way these agreements could be improved.

Spain's Immigration Policy Framework

This section describes Spain's transition toward a labor-importing country. It then identifies the pillars of Spain's immigration policy and explains how Spain regulates the flow of temporary workers.

From Supplier to Recipient of Foreign Workers: Migration in Spain since 1985

Spain's transition from supplier to recipient of foreign workers occurred in three stages (Cachón 2009). Until 1985 (phase 1), immigration flows to Spain were small, and most immigrants (65 percent) were European; only 18 percent were from Latin America, and just 10 percent were from Africa or Asia. Most of these non-European immigrants came to Spain for political reasons. From 1975 to 1985, the increase in foreign residents in Spain averaged 2.2 percent a year.

From 1986 to 1999 (phase 2), Spain increasingly became a country of destination. Social changes in Spain and the country's entry into the European Union gave rise to an influx of economically motivated migrants. Labor market restructuring in Spain during the second half of the 1980s, along with a marked change in the labor preferences of local workers, resulted in a significant mismatch between labor supply and demand. As a result, from 1992 to 2000, the number of foreigners from developing countries increased by an average rate of 214 percent a year, compared with the 60 percent increase in the number of foreigners from industrial countries.

Since 1999 (phase 3), even larger increases in immigration flows have led to problems of social inclusion. The challenges of multiculturalism have become a matter of public debate, with the "institutionalization" of immigration in Spain viewed by some as a social problem. In 2000, 920,000 immigrants—2.3 percent of Spain's population—were on the municipal rolls. By 2009, this number had soared to 5.6 million, a 12 percent of the population, remaining stable since (figure 4.1).[1]

This surge is partly explained by Spain's accession to the euro area, together with economic crises in several Latin American countries and long-standing decline in Africa. Another factor is the large decline in real interest rates following the adoption of the euro, which benefited sectors with long maturities and large investments like construction, which requires much unskilled labor. The progressive incorporation of women into the labor market increased demand for household services, which migrants were happy to provide at wages low by Spanish standards (yet high in purchasing power in the migrants' countries of

Figure 4.1 Foreigners as a Share of Spain's Population, 1981–2012

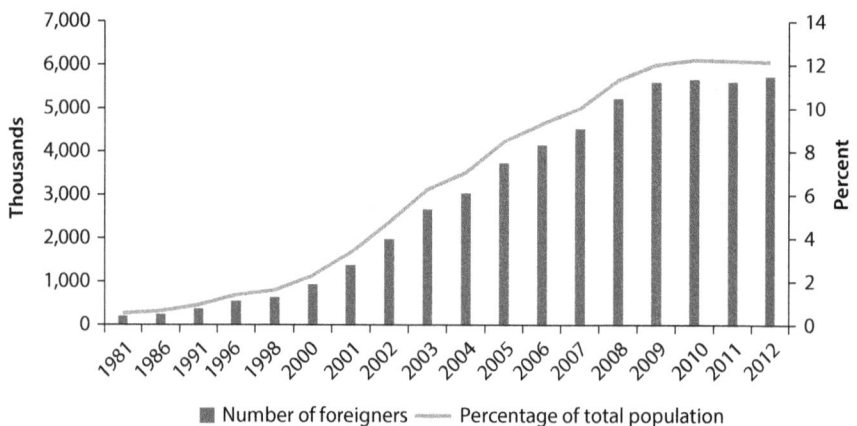

■ Number of foreigners ——— Percentage of total population

Source: Instituto Nacional de Estadística n.d.
Note: Foreigners are defined as residents recorded by the municipal register. Everyone who lives in Spain must be inscribed in the register of the municipality in which he or she usually resides. In Spain, immigrants and natives alike may register in their municipality of residence to gain access to health care and social protection, regardless of their legal status. However, a number of immigrants are not registered because they are unaware of the process, they fear enforcement authorities' access to the database, or their municipal government rejects their registration.

origin). These effects, together with network effects, attracted a burgeoning number of migrants.

Over the years, the immigrant population has grown, in part through family reunification programs; the second generation of immigrants is now attracting further immigration. In addition, the deep restructuring of labor markets, which is linked to the significant presence of immigrants in certain branches of activity and regions, has attracted labor from other countries (Geromini, Cachón, and Texidó 2004).[2]

The Pillars of Spanish Immigration Policy

Spain's immigration policy rests on four pillars (Cachón 2009; EMN 2010):

- Orderly management of legal migration flows, which are directly linked to labor market needs
- Cooperation with other countries (to contribute to the economic and social development of origin and transit countries)
- Social integration of legal immigrants
- The fight against illegal immigration

This chapter focuses on the orderly management of labor migration, which is based on the link between immigration policy and employment. The aim of this policy is to ensure that available jobs are offered to Spanish citizens or foreign legal residents before they are offered to foreign workers.

Spanish immigration legislation distinguishes between foreigners subject to the European Community regime and foreigners subject to general immigration rules. Foreigners subject to the first regime include citizens of EU member states or countries that are a party to the Agreement on the European Economic Area (Iceland, Liechtenstein, Norway, and Switzerland) and their families. These citizens are free to enter, leave, travel, and live in Spain; they may also engage in any economic activity, either as paid employees or self-employed workers, service providers, or students, under the same conditions as Spanish citizens.

Foreigners not qualifying for the European Community regime require authorization to live and work in Spain as well as a special work visa (Geromini, Cachón, and Texidó 2004). Employers wishing to hire non–EU nationals must obtain prior administrative authorization. However, lack of a work authorization does not invalidate an employment contract with regard to the foreign worker's rights or prevent the foreign worker from obtaining any benefits to which he or she may be entitled.

The Contingente (Quota)

Spanish legislation on migration specifically addresses the need to recruit temporary workers. In addition to temporary residence and work authorizations granted through the so-called general regime, the government may annually approve a *contingente* (quota) of foreign workers from non–EU countries (see Cachón 2009; EMN 2010; Geromini, Cachón, and Texidó 2004). In theory, the quota covers general employment offers; all BLAs signed by Spain state that the signatory country may benefit in a preferential way from the quota. However, the Spanish system does not allow for the establishment of per country quotas. Thus, in practice, countries with which Spain has signed BLAs have not enjoyed any type of preference (Geromini, Cachón, and Texidó 2004).

In 2011, 5.3 million foreigners had registration certificates or valid residence cards, of which 2.7 million were non–EU citizens (44 percent from Latin America and 38 percent from Africa, as shown in table 4.1). (Most of the statistics in this chapter are from the Ministry of Labor and Immigration. In 2011, the ministry changed its name. It is now the Ministry of Employment and Social Security.)

Migration to Spain must be arranged from the country of origin to fill the needs of the labor market. The two basic instruments for determining the internal labor market situation are the yearly foreign worker quota system and the Catalogue of Hard-to-Fill Occupations (CHFO), the list of occupations (by province, autonomous community, city, and island) that are difficult to supply with national workers or foreigners legally residing in Spain. These occupations are mainly in the labor-intensive and seasonal work sectors—especially agriculture, hotels, and services—and are typically filled by low- or medium-skilled workers.

Updated quarterly, the CHFO is the main tool for proving that no workers in Spain can fill a job position, which can then be offered to a third-country national through the general regime. Spanish enterprises use the CHFO to request posting of positions for which they wish to apply for residency and work authorizations for foreign workers residing outside Spain. Once a job appears on the CHFO, the employer can apply for that authorization. If the job is not included in the CHFO, the employer has to submit the job offer to the public employment services. If the public employment services certify that no Spanish

Table 4.1 Number of Foreigners Holding Valid Spanish Residence Card, by Residence Scheme and Region of Origin, 2011

	As of December 31, 2011			Annual change since previous year		
Region	Total	General scheme	EU scheme	Total	General scheme	EU scheme
Total	5,251,094	2,696,476	2,554,618	324,486	171,500	152,986
European Union	2,134,375	n.a.	2,134,375	121,837	n.a.	121,837
Rest of Europe	144,409	123,390	21,019	10,741	8,989	1,752
Africa	1,098,599	1,039,238	59,361	70,110	64,398	5,712
Latin America	1,472,897	1,189,521	283,376	83,539	63,534	20,005
Colombia	274,171	224,072	50,099	4,484	2,011	2,473
Ecuador	403,864	372,411	31,453	5,140	2,719	2,421
Peru	140,792	123,116	17,676	2,581	1,458	1,123
North America	21,163	10,812	10,351	974	592	382
Asia	349,240	331,189	18,051	35,512	33,862	1,650
Oceania	1,815	762	1,053	57	16	41
Stateless or unknown	1,138	1,024	114	120	109	11

Source: Ministry of Labor and Immigration various years.
Note: EU = Euorpean Union; n.a. = not applicable.

national can fill the job, the employer can apply for residency and work authorization for a foreign worker.

The annual quota of non–EU foreign workers establishes the number of jobs offered to third-country nationals.[3] The national employment situation, which is approved annually by the Council of Ministers, is a basic criterion for determining the quota. "Visas to search for employment" have been granted through the quota system since 2003.[4] Employment offers are addressed mainly to countries with which Spain has signed bilateral agreements for regulating and planning migration flows (Law 4/2000, in accordance with Law 14/2003, Article 39; table 4.2).[5] However, foreign workers granted permits under the BLA procedures represent a very small proportion of the total permits granted.

The quota establishes a framework for stable job offers (whether generic or specific) and lays down conditions for the employment of temporary workers. The offers may be limited to quotas per territory in Spain or to professions. They reflect the input of autonomous communities, business organizations, and trade unions as well as the report on the employment situation and the social integration of immigrants drafted by the Higher Council for Immigration Policy (Consejo Superior de Política de Inmigración).[6]

The quota includes hard-to-fill jobs that remain unfilled by the Spanish resident population. The quota has three sections. The first is a list of offers of stable (duration greater than one year) or permanent positions. The selection of foreign workers for permanent positions is made in the country of origin of the worker by the Spanish authorities. Business people intending to hire through the quota system may participate directly or indirectly in the selection. The Spanish administration is responsible for managing the system, both in Spain and in the country of origin, and for compiling the job offers from employers through the applicant selection process, in collaboration with local authorities in that country.

The second section is a list of job search visas. The job search visa can be issued to children or grandchildren of Spanish nationals. It grants the beneficiary authorization for a stay not exceeding three months for the purpose of looking for work. This visa may also be granted to foreign workers outside Spain who wish

Table 4.2 Agreements on Migration Signed by Spain

Migratory agreements	Operational cooperation agreements	Cooperation agreements on immigration	Readmission agreements
Bulgaria (2003), Cape Verde (2007), Colombia (2001), Dominican Republic (2001), Ecuador (2001), Guinea Bissau (2003), Mauritania (2007), Morocco (2001), Poland (2002), Romania (2002), Ukraine (2009)	Guinea Bissau (2008), Niger (2008), Peru (2004)	The Gambia (2006), Guinea (2006), Guinea Bissau (2008), Mali (2008)	Algeria (2002); Bulgaria (1996); Estonia (2000); France (1989); Guinea Bissau (2003); Italy (2001); Latvia (2000); Lithuania (2000); Macedonia, FYR (2006); Mauritania (2003); Morocco (1992); Poland (2002); Portugal (1995); Romania (1996); Russian Federation (2006); Slovak Republic (1999); Switzerland (2003)

Source: Ministry of Labor and Immigration n.d.

Let Workers Move • http://dx.doi.org/10.1596/978-0-8213-9915-6

to work in sectors of activity where on-site contact between the employer and the applicant is important (as it is the case for domestic and hotel workers).

The third section is a description of employment mechanisms for seasonal workers. The quota procedure establishes the rules to be followed in contracting seasonal workers but does not specify an annual number of jobs that can be offered, as it does for workers filling permanent positions. In accordance with current legislation, work and residence permits may not exceed nine months for seasonal workers or 12 months for temporary workers. Companies wishing to hire seasonal workers must prove that they have adequate lodging for them, will organize their return trip, and will obtain signed commitments from workers that they will return to their country of origin upon termination of the employment relationship. A dual mechanism is in place that rewards the fulfillment of the commitment to return made by these workers when the season ends: the worker can be hired in successive seasons without going through the selection process, and being hired for four seasons makes it easier for the worker to obtain the authorization to reside in a stable way. Foreign workers who do not return to their country of origin upon the finalization of a contract may not access any other employment offers in Spain for three years.

Figure 4.2 depicts the evolution of permanent and temporary job offers of this system. In 2008, the quota consisted of 15,731 hard-to-fill stable jobs offered. This figure declined to 901 in 2009 and 168 in 2010, an 81 percent decline from the previous year. Seasonal workers were also negatively affected by the economic crisis.

Figure 4.2 Number of Permanent and Temporary Jobs in Spain Offered to and Filled by Foreigners, 2002–10

thousands

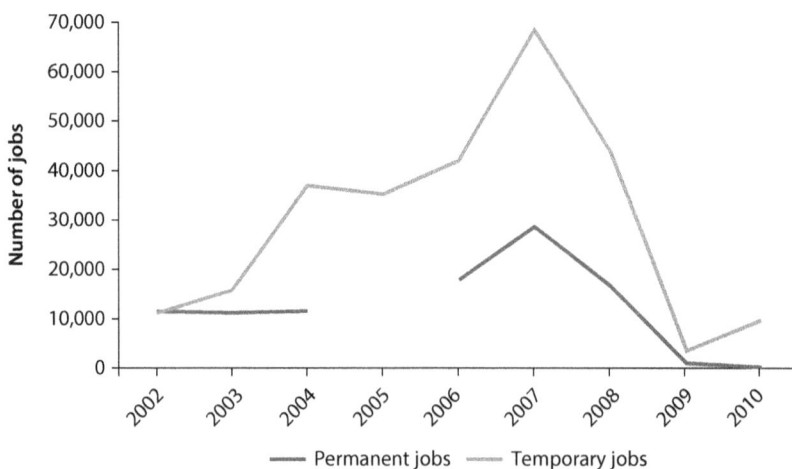

Source: Ministry of Labor and Immigration various years.
Notes: Figures for permanent jobs include only offers for jobs lasting more than a year. The quota was prorogued in 2004; in 2005, no permanent job positions were offered.

In April 2004, the Spanish Economic and Social Council (ESC), a government advisory body, released its diagnostic analysis of quota administration (Consejo Económico y Social 2004). It pointed to several problems.

First, projecting labor needs is difficult. As a result, the number of positions approved by the Instituto Nacional de Empleo (INEM) often differs from the quotas requested by some provinces. Second, a variety of problems with the system has led many companies to reduce their hiring foreign workers. These problems include the unfamiliarity with and complexity and rigidity of the procedure, the difficulty for enterprises to travel abroad to interview potential workers and the mistrust over signing contracts without having done so, and the lack of adequate information provided to businesses and direct contact with the national selection or decision-making bodies. The report suggests that the quota system should be improved by simplifying and streamlining procedures, creating or strengthening "job offer management units" in countries of origin, reinforcing direct and personal contact with businesses, and granting enterprises greater autonomy in the selection process.

Problems with the quota system have led to a significant number of job offered through the quota system going unfilled (table 4.3). More than 276,000 workers entered Spain legally between 2002 and 2009. However, of the 92,911 permanent jobs offered, only 26,912 (29 percent) were filled.

In contrast, the quota appears to be quite successful in filling seasonal or temporary jobs. Since 2002, it has managed access for more than 249,000 temporary foreign workers, mainly in agriculture (table 4.4). Over this period, more than 91 percent of workers who entered Spain through the quota were seasonal workers. The quota is very useful for large companies, which can deploy coaches and trainers to source countries. It is much less convenient for small enterprises, because of the requirement that submitted offers include at

Table 4.3 Quota and Actual Number of Foreign Workers in Spain, 2002–09

Year	Posts offered (based on labor quota system) (a)			Posts actually filled (b)			(b–a)	
	Total	Permanent	Temporary	Total	Permanent	Temporary	Number	Percent
2002	31,979	10,884	21,095	13,914	3,394	10,520	−18,065	−56.5
2003	34,157	10,575	23,582	17,878	2,940	14,938	−16,279	−47.7
2004	30,978	10,908	20,070	38,796	3,864	34,932	7,818	25.2
2005[a]	0	0	0	36,495	3,198	33,297	n.a.	n.a.
2006	16,878	16,878	0	45,995	6,248	39,747	29,117	172.5
2007	27,034	27,034	0	70,444	5,728	64,716	43,410	160.6
2008	15,731	15,731	0	48,693	1,513	47,180	32,962	209.5
2009	901	901	0	4,471	27	4,444	3,570	396.2
Total	157,658	92,911	64,747	276,686	26,912	249,774	119,028	75.5

Sources: Cachón 2009; Ministry of Labor and Immigration various years.
Note: Data for 2007–09 are provisional; n.a. = not applicable.
a. The quota was prorogued in 2004; in 2005, no permanent job positions were offered.

Let Workers Move • http://dx.doi.org/10.1596/978-0-8213-9915-6

Table 4.4 Number of Foreign Workers Entering Spain through the Quota, by Sector of Activity and Type of Authorization, 2006–09

Sector	2006		2007		2008		2009	
	Permanent	Temporary	Permanent	Temporary	Permanent	Temporary	Permanent	Temporary
Agriculture	150	39,024	42	62,938	67	45,681	2	4,050
Commerce	965	91	1,236	90	495	5	—	—
Construction	757	75	369	86	9	14	—	—
Hotel and catering (hotels, restaurants, bars, and related businesses)	2,388	149	1,581	607	430	443	—	4
Food	200	4	67	3	2	208	3	2
Wood	53		121	2	—	2	—	—
Metal	429	5	672	3	72	31	2	4
Textile	1	—	6	—	—	—	—	—
Other industries	2	—	2	110	—	26	—	11
Services	785	—	1,165	504	273	642	20	369
Fisheries	—	—	147	2	23	—	—	—
Transport	518	399	320	371	142	128	—	4
Total	6,248	39,747	5,728	64,716	1,513	47,180	27	4,444

Source: Ministry of Labor and Immigration various years.
Note: — = not available.

least 10 jobs. In this case, business associations can play a role by introducing more flexible requirements or by representing a group of small firms as a consortium.

Exporting Services to Spain through Mode 4 of the GATS

As a member of the European Union, Spain has to adapt its domestic regulations to the agreements signed by the European Union. Under Spanish legislation, a service provider is an employee of a company established outside the European Union or the European Economic Area (Article 63 of Royal Decree 2393/2004). The Authorization for Transnational Provision of Services covers workers who are not nationals of countries belonging to the European Union or the European economic area who will be in a situation of temporary residence and work within the framework of transnational provision of services (Article 63 of Royal Decree 2393/2004).

Spain's commitments under the GATS cover three categories of service providers:

- Contractual service suppliers (the temporary movement of workers that occurs at the risk, and under the direction, of the foreign company as part of a contract between the company and the workers or the temporary movement

of workers who work in Spain within the framework of a transnational provision of services)
- Intracorporate transferees (the temporary movement of workers from working centers of companies established outside Spain to working centers in Spain of the same company or group)
- Essential personnel (the temporary movement of highly qualified workers who supervise or provide advice concerning works of services that companies established in Spain realize outside Spain)

Before these service providers can be granted work authorizations, three conditions must be fulfilled:

- The residence of foreign workers in the company's country of origin must be stable and regular.
- Foreign workers must have worked at least a year in the professional activity they are to undertake and have worked for the company for at least nine months.
- The company temporarily moving its foreign workers to Spain must fulfill the applicable requirements and working conditions in accordance with the provisions of Law 45 of November 29, 1999, on the posting of workers in the framework of transnational services provision. (This law transposes Directive 96/71/EC of the European Parliament and of the Council of December 16, 1996, into the Spanish legal framework.)

The employer must submit an application for residence and a work authorization in the framework of "transnational" services to the government delegation or subdelegation of the place where services will be provided or to the diplomatic mission or consular post of its place of residence. This application must include the employment contract of the foreign worker with the company that transfers him or her. The permits for residence and work are for one year and can be renewed for an additional year if conditions are met. Both permits are limited to a specific geographical area; the work permit is limited to a specific activity.[7]

The number of service providers entering the Spanish market in the framework of Spain's GATS commitments, as measured by total authorizations granted, is very small (table 4.5). The small numbers partly reflect the cumbersome and complex legal procedures required to obtain authorizations. Additionally, labor lawyers and companies may be unfamiliar with these procedures, which are rarely used to obtain temporary work permits.

In 2006, the latest year for which the government separates figures for foreigners working in the service sector and cross-border work authorizations, the number of permits totaled 2,897 (of which 66 percent were issued to cross-border workers), or just 0.35 percent of total authorizations. In 2011, the Spanish government granted 759 permits to service providers, 0.36 percent of total cross-border work authorizations.

Analysis of other statistics suggests that the number of service providers did not actually decline. In 2011, 209,003 permits (66 percent of total work

Table 4.5 Spanish Work Authorizations Granted to Foreign Workers, 2004–11

Item	2004	2005	2006	2007	2008	2009	2010	2011
Total within Spanish quota	38,796	36,495	45,995	70,437	42,719	3,411	11,983	14,615
Total outside Spanish quota[a]	498,280	995,607	822,682	499,408	790,205	370,275	303,933	315,594
Salaried work								
Salaried work authorizations	484,394	984,076	812,979	448,320	690,561	279,330	223,034	212,324
First work authorizations	165,361	661,946	108,410	239,714	119,309	29,522	21,878	68,757
First authorizations	152,514	644,305	101,079	222,561	69,020	26,699	19,310	65,835
Transnational provision of services	1,404	1,091	965	1,396	1,341	881	732	759
Cross-border workers[b]	1,435	2,472	1,920	—	—	—	—	—
Seasonal workers	9,602	13,642	4,032	15,650	46,248	1,927	1,836	2,163
Other fixed-term authorizations	406	436	414	107	2,700	15	—	—
First renewal	110,394	129,082	624,617	108,325	132,689	154,433	86,113	14,305
Second renewal	208,639	193,048	79,952	100,281	438,563	95,375	115,043	129,262
Total renewals	319,033	322,130	704,569	208,606	571,252	249,808	201,156	143,567
Self-employment								
Self-employed work authorizations	13,886	11,531	9,703	8,109	11,370	6,051	5,305	4,798
First work authorizations	2,507	1,134	609	509	465	497	389	1,797
First renewal	3,898	3,046	4,760	4,214	2,489	1,920	2,129	762
Second renewal	7,455	7,246	4,322	3,386	8,416	3,634	2,787	2,239
Total renewals	11,353	10,292	9,082	7,600	10,905	5,554	4,916	3,001
Cross-border workers[c]	26	105	12	c	c	c	c	c
Other								
"Arraigo" and international protection authorizations[c, d]	—	—	—	29,798	65,048	77,875	70,577	68,244
Authorizations to work[c, e]	—	—	—	13,181	23,226	7,019	5,017	30,228

Source: Ministry of Labor and Immigration various years.
Note: — = not available.
a. Work authorizations granted under the quota procedure are not included.
b. Workers resident in France, Portugal, and Morocco who cross into Spain for work on a daily basis.
c. The number of work authorizations for cross-border workers has not been independently available since 2007. It is included within the line "authorizations to work." These work authorizations have been separately accounted and public since 2007.
d. Article 45.1,2,3 and Article 7 of Royal Decree 2393/2004.
e. Authorizations to work include permits granted to foreigners who have residence permits and may be authorized to work in the following situations: family unification of spouse or child, cross-border worker, student visa holders, exceptional circumstances of public interest or national security, collaboration with the administrative and judicial authorities (Articles 41, 84, 90, and 98 and first additional provision of Royal Decree 2393/2004).

Table 4.6 Spanish Work Authorizations Granted, by Activity Sector, 1999–2011

| Year | Total | Agriculture | Nonagricultural sector | | | | Nonclassifiable |
			Subtotal	Industry	Construction	Services	
1999	118,538	28,094	86,846	8,639	11,045	67,162	3,598
2000	292,120	38,164	197,198	17,827	36,846	142,525	56,758
2001	298,676	47,140	220,392	30,276	46,071	144,045	31,144
2002	318,143	53,221	248,941	32,260	58,759	157,922	15,981
2003	284,463	28,541	236,435	26,482	57,103	152,850	19,487
2004	545,208	75,268	345,283	41,088	88,254	215,941	124,657
2005	1,030,944	129,518	752,128	57,774	188,758	505,596	149,298
2006	857,052	103,751	680,911	49,544	177,238	454,129	72,390
2007	499,211	58,677	394,786	32,535	101,719	260,532	45,748
2008	790,205	117,758	605,385	46,662	141,777	416,946	67,062
2009	366,856	35,374	331,482	16,599	43,287	199,597	71,999
2010	303,933	33,235	270,698	16,241	29,147	206,876	18,434
2011	315,594	55,105	260,489	11,135	20,422	209,003	19,929

Source: Ministry of Labor and Immigration various years.
Note: Totals of granted authorizations differ from those in table 4.2, because the statistical procedure is different.

authorizations) were granted to foreign workers employed in service sectors. At the end of 2008, more than 7,800 Colombian, Ecuadorian, and Peruvian nationals were registered as foreign workers in Spain's Social Security system as engineers, university graduates, and technical experts. Many other foreign nationals were linked with the service sector. In fact, in 2008, the number of foreign service providers was larger than the number of permits granted under Spain's GATS commitments (table 4.6).

This large discrepancy between the number of foreign workers in the service sector (table 4.6) and the number of work authorizations granted (table 4.5) suggests that Mode 4 of the GATS, which includes mainly skilled workers, is not the most important mechanism for accessing the Spanish market for foreign engineers, accountants, or lawyers. Authorizations to provide services in Spain are managed primarily through the general immigration scheme.

Spain's BLAs with Colombia and Ecuador

During the past few years, an important aspect of Spanish immigration policy has been cooperation with the countries of origin and transit of immigrants to Spain. The Spanish government believes that in order to control migration flows and fight illegal immigration, it is essential to attack the root causes. Doing so requires encouraging progressive cooperation by formalizing bilateral instruments with countries of origin and transit. One instrument designed for this purpose is the framework agreement on cooperation on immigration.

Main Provisions of the Agreements

The framework agreements on cooperation on immigration include provisions for preventing illegal immigration and promoting readmission as well as measures

Table 4.7 Provisions of Spain's Bilateral Labor Agreements with Colombia and Ecuador

Item	Colombia	Ecuador
Date of signature	May 21, 2001	May 29, 2001
In force since	May 21, 2001	June 28, 2001
Number of provisions	18	22
Aims and scope	Plan and regulate labor migratory flows	
Principles	• Reaffirm special historical and cultural ties	
	• Develop General Treaty of Cooperation and Friendship (1992)	
	• Regulate migratory flows in an orderly manner	
	• Protect foreign workers in Spain	
	• Make migration an enriching social phenomenon	
	• Respect national laws and international conventions	
	• Respect human rights and prevent illegal migration and labor exploitation	
Competent authorities Spain	Ministry of Foreign Affairs and Cooperation, Ministry of Interior, Ministry of Labor and Immigration (now the Ministry of Employment and Social Security)	Ministry of Foreign Affairs and Cooperation, Ministry of Interior, Ministry of Labor and Immigration
Source country	Ministry of External Relations, Ministry of Labor and Social Security, and Administrative Department of Security	Ministry of External Relations
Definition of "migrant worker"	Colombian citizens authorized to exercise a gainful activity as employee in Spain	Ecuadorian citizens authorized to exercise a gainful activity as employee in Spain
Units responsible for determining demand for workers in Spain	Servicio Nacional de Aprendizaje (SENA)	Unidad Técnica de Selección de Trabajadores Migratorios (UTSTM)
Number of migrant workers involved since they are into force	14,626	6,630

for cooperating on employment of workers, integration of immigrants, and contributions to social and economic development in the country of origin. The objectives of these agreements are to tackle migration issues concerning the sending countries in a comprehensive, pragmatic, and cooperative way (table 4.7).

Spain's BLAs include five main areas of cooperation:

• Migratory flows: facilitation of the legal flow of workers
• Voluntary return: assistance in promoting the voluntary return of migrant workers, including support to facilitate the integration of returnees in their country of origin
• Integration: mutual assistance on the integration of nationals of one country residing in the territory of the other
• Migration and economic and social development: creation of employment
• Cooperation in fighting illegal immigration and human trafficking

The main objective of these BLAs is to regulate migratory flows in a coherent way. In addition to managing irregular migration, the BLAs seek to match job offers with the profile of candidates looking for work in Spain, after taking national labor market conditions into account. BLAs state that priority is given to the country of origin in the framework of job offers made through Spain's quota. BLAs also provide a framework for regulating information about job offers, assessing professional requirements, ensuring social and labor rights and conditions, handling specific arrangements for temporary workers (visa applications and voluntary return), communicating about job offers, preselecting workers, facilitating contract hiring, and providing visas for immigrants workers.

These migration agreements are the two first general agreements Spain has signed to manage immigration flows.[8] Before their signing, Spain had signed only an administrative agreement with Morocco on seasonal workers (signed September 30, 1999).

Operation of the Agreements

Once agreements are signed, the Servicio Nacional de Aprendizaje (SENA) in Colombia and the Unidad Técnica de Selección de Trabajadores Migratorios (UTSTM) in Ecuador create specialized units to determine the demands of their nationals wishing to work in Spain (See EMN 2010; Geromini, Cachón, and Texidó 2004).[9] These units launch campaigns to disseminate information in their countries on the possibility of registering in a database for preselection of workers willing to work in Spain.

Job offers for the hiring of foreign workers are submitted by Spanish companies once the yearly quota is approved.[10] They can be generic job offers (offers that include only the characteristics of the workers they wish to contract) or specific job offers (offers that include the name and address of the person the firms wants to hire). Job offers are presented in provincial offices of the Ministry of Labor and Immigration; if approved, they are submitted within 15 days to the Directorate General for Migration (DGM) of the Ministry of Labor and Immigration, to be forwarded, through Spanish embassies, to the units responsible, according to the agreement, for preselection.

In the next stage, if there are workers in their listings that meet the required specifications, the responsible authorities in Colombia or Ecuador provide their lists to the Spanish government. The preselection of candidates is carried out in Ecuador by a commission composed of representatives of the authorities of both Ecuador and Spain; the employers can also participate. In Colombia, the Spanish authorities make the initial selection from the lists provided by SENA.

To select workers, the Spanish authorities and entrepreneurs, with the assistance of the responsible authorities in Colombia and Ecuador, conduct interviews. The final list of selected workers is sent to the Spanish embassies in Colombia and Ecuador as well as to the Ministry of Labor and Immigration. These lists are forwarded to the hiring companies to prepare the employment contracts. SENA and UTSTM receive the contracts through the Spanish embassies and contact the workers for their visa application. They help migrant workers manage flights and other travel-related issues and provide them with information on living in Spain. At the other end, Spanish authorities coordinate the reception of migrant workers and provide them with residence and work permits.

In both agreements, the signatory countries created specialized units (called *Comisión Mixta*), responsible for evaluating and following up on the BLA.[11] In the agreement with Ecuador, the evaluating body must meet once a year; in Colombia, it meets upon request of one of the parties.

Quantitative Results of the Agreements

In 2002, the first year after the signing of the bilateral agreements, the number of nationals from Colombia and Ecuador entering Spain to work reached 2,070 (1,132 Colombians and 938 Ecuadorians).[12] That year, the number of granted authorizations through the quota was 13,914 (3,394 permanent and 10,520 seasonal permits), which implies that only 15 percent of migrants were arriving under ad hoc arrangements with preferential partners.

The number of foreign workers from Colombia and Ecuador increased between 2002 and the year before the global crisis, after which migration declined (figure 4.3). In 2007, the number of foreign workers from Colombia and Ecuador reached its peak of 6,487 (4,336 Colombians and 2,151 Ecuadorians). Only 9.2 percent of the permits granted use the labor quota procedure. Since 2002, about 14,626 Colombians and 6,630 Ecuadorians have entered Spain under the bilateral migratory agreements. These figures represent

Figure 4.3 Entry of Colombian and Ecuadorian Workers into Spain under Bilateral Labor Agreements, 2002–09

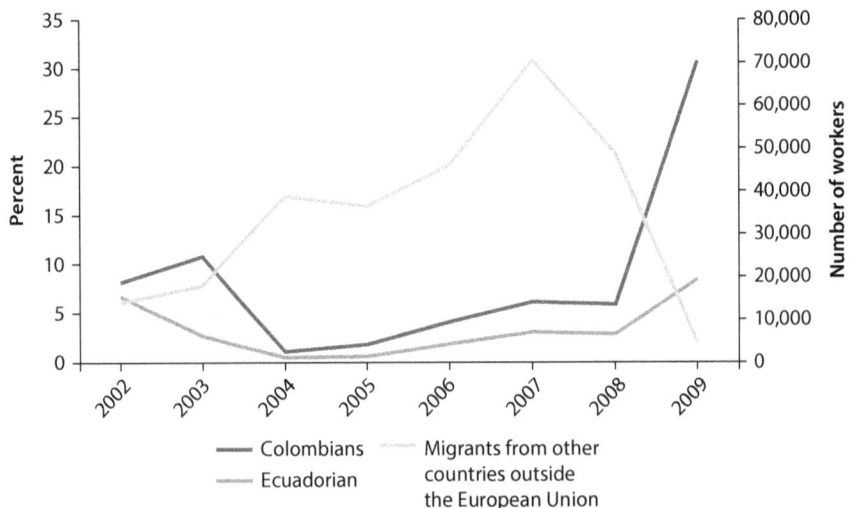

Sources: Cachón 2009; Ministry of Labor and Immigration various years.
Note: Figures for 2004 and 2005 include permanent job offers only.

a small share of the total nationals from the two countries legally residing and working in Spain.

Article 39 of Law 14/2003 states that "the proposal of job offers for the quota will be addressed mainly to countries with which Spain has signed agreements for the Regulation and Management of Migratory Flows." At this stage, however, the main objective of these agreements is to regulate migratory flows to Spain. The agreements do not guarantee a specific number of job offers (either stable or seasonal) or a proportion of the annual quota of migrant workers. Moreover, the annual quota procedure provides no real preferences for countries with which Spain has signed agreements or excludes countries that have not signed them.

In fact, the model works based on "competition between states": the final decision regarding who is offered a job depends on enterprises (Geromini, Cachón, and Texidó 2004). However, the countries that benefit most from the regulating migratory flows instruments, such as the BLAs and the quota, are not necessarily those that have signed bilateral agreements. Although Colombia and Ecuador were the first countries to conclude migratory agreements with Spain, other countries, such as Romania and Poland, receive many more job offers, especially seasonal offers. The number of workers entering Spain through the quota was 5,359 from Poland, 1,164 from Romania, 1,132 from Colombia, and 938 from Ecuador.

This point is confirmed by the evolution in the number of migrant workers by countries of origin. The quota for 2004 (two years after the signing of the agreements with Colombia and Ecuador) included foreign workers from eight countries. Three years later, in 2007 (before the global financial crisis), Spain hosted foreign nationals from 29 countries, most of them not signatories of migration agreements with Spain. A similar pattern is evident in the final volume of job offers: although the government sets the annual quota for permanent jobs, the actual volume depends on the final employment offers presented by the enterprises.

Safeguards to Ensure Temporariness

The agreements with Colombia and Ecuador include specific safeguards to help ensure that migration remains temporary. Migrant workers from Colombia and Ecuador must sign a commitment to return to their countries of origin when their permits expire. They are also required to present themselves at the Spanish consulate that issued the visa within a month after their return. Under the agreement with Ecuador, breach of this commitment disqualifies the worker from all future recruitment in Spain and residence permits submitted to the Spanish authorities. The obligation is less rigorous in the agreement with Colombia, which states that "breach of this commitment will be taken into account in the resolution of any requests for work and residence permits submitted to the Spanish authorities."

Both agreements also include specific provisions dealing with "voluntary return." They state that the contracting parties adopt coordinated measures to develop programs to help migrant workers return voluntarily to their country of origin. The Organic Law 14/2003 (passed two years after the signing of the BLAs) introduced a new provision to the Ley Orgánica de Extranjería (LOE), to provide for "aid for voluntary return." This provision allows the Spanish government to fund programs for the voluntary return for people who request it and to present projects for their resettlement in their countries of origin, provided that such project benefit their communities (EMN 2010).

In September 2008, legislation governing the "plan for voluntary return" was approved. Royal Decree Law 4/2008 allows cumulative contributory unemployment benefits to be paid in advance to non–EU foreign workers who voluntarily return to their countries of origin (developed by Royal Decree 1800/2008 of November 3).

After 2008, when the number of jobs decline as a result of the global economic crisis, the Spanish government offered unemployed foreign workers from third countries with bilateral social security agreements signed with Spain, including Colombia and Ecuador, the opportunity to return to their countries of origin. It made resources available for their labor and professional integration or personal development.

How Well Have the Agreements Worked?

Having a BLA has not yielded significant advantages to Colombia or Ecuador, partly because the general immigration scheme in Spain is liberal: residence permits, and later work permits, are very easy to obtain; relatively few undocumented immigrants are forced to return; and illegal immigrants enjoy free health care and education and other social benefits. A large number of nationals from Colombia and Ecuador provide labor services in Spain outside the specific provisions included in the BLAs.

Spain's BLAs with Colombia and Ecuador introduced a "culture of legal immigration law." The procedures for managing job offers provide some guarantee for migrant workers, and management of the BLAs involves frequent contact between the authorities in the signatory countries. However, only a very small proportion of Colombians and Ecuadorians enter Spain through the agreements. They have only a minor effect on labor migration for a variety of reasons, including the dearth of job offers from Spanish employers (which may reflect the large pool of undocumented immigrants in Spain), the administrative complexities of the system and the fact that offers need to be presented in advance, bureaucratic delays, and the preferences of employers of seasonal migrants to recruit from countries that are geographically closer to Spain (to reduce travel costs). One of the biggest problems is the large pool of irregular immigration to Spain, which serves as a cheap resource for companies and places these workers in a situation of vulnerability that prevents them from demanding decent working conditions. Spanish employers, especially micro and small firms, use undocumented immigrant workers extensively, risking severe penalties by the Spanish authorities in doing so. Firms hire illegal workers in order to avoid paying social security (equivalent to 31 percent of wages), circumvent the rigidities of Spanish labor legislation, and overcome the unwillingness of native Spanish workers to perform many menial jobs. Unless the situation of this very large stock of undocumented migrants is resolved, BLAs are not expected to have much impact (Geromini, Cachón, and Texidó 2004).

Provisions of the agreements that are not directly linked to the recruitment of migrant workers—such as the promotion of the reintegration of return migrants, the development of training projects, and the recognition of foreigner workers' experience in Spain, which would facilitate the creation of enterprises and encourage the transfer of technology—have not been implemented effectively. In contrast, the requirement of visas (for Colombia since January 2001 and Ecuador since August 2003) has considerably reduced the flow of workers from both countries entering Spain as tourists and motivated them to stay illegally beyond the allowed three-month period (Geromini, Cachón, and Texidó 2004).

The agreements provide no effective preference to signatory countries. On the contrary, there appears to have been a decline in the number of workers from Colombia and Ecuador in favor of other countries. The decline may have created frustration, because the signing of the agreements was expected to increase the number of offers from entrepreneurs or channel to the signatory country a greater proportion of the offers approved under the annual quota (Geromini, Cachón, and Texidó 2004).

Nongovernmental organizations in Spain dealing with immigration issues complain about the countries selected for BLAs, the lack of transparency of the processes of screening and selecting migrant workers; the changes between the original job offer submitted and the work contract finally offered to migrant workers; the lack of guidance on important aspects of their life in Spain, such as housing; skills, and noncompliance with provisions of the collective agreements or employment contracts. They argue that BLAs should put more emphasis on promoting economic and social development in sending countries, not only on admitting foreign workers into Spain (see ENM 2010; Geromini, Cachón, and Texidó 2004).

For the Spanish Confederation of Business Organizations (CEOE), the agreements and quota are useful instruments that contribute to legally hiring foreign workers, especially when Spanish workers are not available. It recognizes, however, that smaller firms have no real opportunity to use the quota system because they are not able to travel abroad to select foreign workers and cannot anticipate their labor needs in advance.

GATS Mode 4 and BLAs in Spain

Determining whether BLAs can substitute for or complement GATS Mode 4 is complicated by the fact that the definition of a Mode 4 service provider does not coincide with the Spanish legal definition of parties covered by BLAs. For instance, Mode 4 includes "self-employed" service providers, whereas the Spanish BLAs do not. Thus, any proposal to promote service exports through BLAs would require including special categories relevant to services.

Table 4.8 Work Permits Granted by Spain to Non–European Union Nationals, 2005–11

Item	2005	2006	2007	2008	2009	2010	2011
Total number of work permits granted to non–EU nationals (through general scheme and quota)	1,067,439	903,047	569,665	832,924	370,264	315,916	330,209
Number of permits to cross-border providers of services	1,091	1,920	1,396	1,341	881	732	759
Number of permits to Colombians under bilateral labor agreement	670	1,884	4,336	2,875	1,374	—	—
Number of permits to Ecuadorians under bilateral labor agreement	227	852	2,151	1,398	377	—	—

Source: Ministry of Labor and Immigration various years.
Note: — = not available.

The number of Colombian migrant workers entering the Spanish labor market through the BLA (2,875) was more than twice the total number of non–EU nationals that obtained permission to provide services in Spain in 2008 (1,343). The figures for Ecuador are similar.

However, the numbers of both service providers and work permits under BLAs are dwarfed by the total number of work permits granted by Spain (table 4.8). In 2006, for instance, Spain granted more than 900,000 work permits to non–EU citizens, of which less than 2,000 were for service providers.

Despite the claim of Spanish regulations that countries that have signed BLAs will be given priority when allocating work permits, be it temporary or permanent, in practice no priority has been granted (Geromini, Cachón, and Texidó 2004). Out of almost 250,000 work permits granted by Spain through the annual quota, fewer than 15,000 went to Colombians.

Conclusion

The conclusion of a BLA has not guaranteed a fixed number of job offers or a proportion of the annual quota for migrant workers. This lack of priority could be attributed to characteristics of the Spanish system: although the government determines how many foreign workers are admitted and the skills required, the private sector makes the final selection of specific workers to whom work permits are granted through the annual quota. Private companies may choose workers from countries that have not signed BLAs. However, countries that have signed BLAs have an advantage in that certain provisions of the BLAs facilitate the identification and selection of potential candidates.

BLAs could potentially be used to promote services exports from Colombia and Ecuador, but a different approach both from sending and receiving countries is required. For example, the bilateral memorandums of understanding (MOU) signed by the Philippines with the United Kingdom and Spain seem to provide a positive answer to this question (see chapter 6). Both MOUs are intended primarily to facilitate the movement of Filipino health professionals. By focusing on a specific professional sector (which includes nurses, physiotherapists, radiographers, occupational therapists, biomedical scientists, and other related health professionals regulated by appropriate professional bodies in both countries), the Philippine government has been successful in promoting both the movement of its nationals and the upgrading of their skills.

The BLAs signed by Colombia and Ecuador could also be directed toward improving access for a services provider by focusing on semiskilled workers in specific sectors, such as health or information and communications technology. The existing institutional arrangements are a basis for promoting temporary labor mobility in certain sectors. Implementation could be improved regarding the development of training projects and the recognition of workers' experience in Spain, enabling the creation of enterprises and the transfer of technology. How much can be done depends on factors beyond the control of the parties involved. Spain's bilateral agreements are limited by EU laws and regulations (the EU Schengen visa and border security regulation and EU readmission rules) as well as by other commitments, such as WTO/GATS and bilateral agreements negotiated by the European Union including with Colombia. Colombia and Ecuador could sign BLAs with other countries as a possible means of increasing their service exports, building on the experience and institutions they have created in their agreements with Spain.

Notes

1. As a proportion of the population, Spain now has the second-largest share of immigrants in the developed world after the United States, according to the Fundación BBVA (2009), a Spanish research institute.

2. Geographical regions of Spain are called autonomous communities. They have a large degree of self-government.

3. In December 2009, this quota system was given a new name: *gestión colectiva de contrataciones en origen.*

4. According to LOE 14/2003, the job search visa can be issued to children or grandchildren of Spanish origin. This visa grants the beneficiary authorization for a stay not exceeding three months for the purpose of looking for work. It may also be granted to foreign workers outside Spain who wish to work in sectors where on-site contact between the employer and the worker is important, as is the case with domestic and hotel workers.

5. The LOE states that the "job offer made will preferably be addressed to those countries that signed with Spain agreements focused on the regulation of migration flows."

6. The Higher Council for Immigration Policy is made up of representatives of the state, autonomous communities, and municipalities. It coordinates the actions of public bodies in integrating immigrants into Spanish society.

7. A different work authorization is available to cross-border workers (Article 84 of Royal Decree 2393/2004). These workers reside in countries bordering Spain— countries to which they return every day after carrying out their activities as

self-employed or salaried workers in Spain. The cross-border work authorization is valid only for a specific geographical area. It is issued for five years at most and is renewable on expiration.

8. Spain has extensive experience with bilateral agreements to regulate the outward migration of Spanish citizens. It signed agreements facilitating the migration, recruitment, and placement of Spanish workers with France (1932 and 1961), Belgium (1958), the Federal Republic of Germany (1960), the Netherlands (1961), Switzerland (1961), and Austria (1965). Between 1948 and 1981, Spain also signed several agreements to facilitate the movement of Spanish workers to Latin American countries, including Argentina (1948 and 1960), the Dominican Republic (1956), Brazil (1960), Chile (1961), Paraguay (1965), and República Bolivariana de Venezuela (1979).

9. For information on the Servicio Nacional de Aprendizaje, see http://www.sena.edu .co/portal. UTSTM was the result of an agreement between the government of Ecuador and the International Organization for Migration (IOM). It is now called Unidad de Trabajadores Migratorios (http://www.mmrree.gov.ec/servicios/trab_ migra.asp).

10. Forms to present job offers are available at the website of the Ministry of Labor and Immigration (http://extranjeros.mtin.es/es/ModelosSolicitudes/).

11. The authorities of each country determine their composition.

12. There are no public reports disclosing the results of the agreements or the yearly quotas. There are no statistics on outflows or the nature or motivations of migrant workers.

References

Cachón, L. 2009. *La España inmigrante: Marco discriminatorio, mercado de trabajo y políticas de integración*. Barcelona: Anthropos.

Consejo Económico y Social. 2004. *La inmigración y el mercado de trabajo en España*. Madrid.

EMN (European Migration Network). 2010. *Migración temporal y circular: Evidencia empírica, políticas actuales y opciones futuras en España*. Madrid.

Fundación BBVA. 2009. *Transatlantic Trends: Immigration 2009 Partners*. http://www .fbbva.es/TLFU/dat/key_findings_transatlantic_trends_immigration_09.pdf.

Geromini, E., L. Cachón, and E. Texidó. 2004. *Acuerdos bilaterales de migración de mano de obra: Estudio de casos*. International Labour Organization, Geneva.

Instituto Nacional de Estadística. n.d. *Municipal Register*. Madrid. http://www.ine.es/jaxi/ menu.do?type=pcaxis&path=%2Ft20%2Fe245&file=inebase&L=.

Ministry of Labor and Immigration. 2004–11. *Statistics Yearbooks*. Madrid: Ministry of Labor and Immigration.

———. n.d. *Convenios bilaterales*. http://extranjeros.empleo.gob.es/es/Normativa Jurisprudencia/Internacional/ConveniosBilaterales/.

CHAPTER 5

To What Extent Do Bilateral Migration Agreements Contribute to Development in Source Countries? An Analysis of France's Migration Pacts

Marion Panizzon

Bilateral migration agreements are poorly articulated and understood (Holzmann and Pouget 2010). This chapter attempts to comprehend such agreements by analyzing France's bilateral migration agreements with countries in West and North Africa and Eastern Europe.

The choice of the appropriate agreement template and its sequencing with respect to other types of agreements may have value for temporary migration and trade policy formulation, particularly where labor mobility is conceived of and conceptualized as part of services trade policy. France's recent bilateral migration agreements exemplify contradictory efforts in facilitating labor market admission. Its agreement with Tunisia, for example, contains support mechanisms and structures for facilitating labor migration and improving the employability and skill levels of Tunisian workers. Other French migration pacts are less impressive in terms of formalizing the role of the private sector in host and source countries, but they focus on policy initiatives for increasing unilateral transfers, such as the return migrant entrepreneurship, the circular migration of scientists and academics, the defiscalization of migrants' savings, the co-financing of diaspora investments, and the increases in individual remittances flows.

France's migration pacts vary widely on matters such as the source country's negotiating leverage and access to regional blocs such as the European Neighbourhood Policy (ENP), Mediterranean initiatives, or European Union (EU) preaccession negotiations. In particular, France's bilateral migration agreements with countries falling under the ENP apply a different and more developed

The author thanks Lisa Salcedo Pfeiffer, Ph.D. candidate at the World Trade Institute, University of Bern and University of Montpellier, and Elisa Fornalé, postdoctoral researcher at the World Trade Institute, for their research assistance and constructive comments and Sebastián Sáez, of the World Bank, for valuable comments and an incisive critique.

template than its agreements with countries not considered among the European Union's "closest neighbors." The pacts also vary with respect to the number of issues to be negotiated (including readmission) and the source country's articulation of development priorities. The newest pacts aim to prod the governments of migrant source countries to articulate their own migration policies and to join the fight against irregular migration and document fraud. In contrast to their one-dimensionally focused precursors—seasonal and guest-worker agreements, co-development conventions, fishery agreements, readmission and visa agreements, and exchange agreements for students, young professionals, and trainees—the new pacts are comprehensive agreements for managing migration. Their innovative feature is multifunctionality (Migreurop 2010). They create a common ground for the host and source countries to address the essential challenges of migration management: labor migration; the fight against irregular migration, including readmissions, border securitization, and document fraud; and the nexus between migration and development.

The chapter is organized as follows. The first section illustrates the differences and complementarities between labor mobility liberalized in the context of a preferential trade agreement and labor mobility facilitated in a bilateral, nontrade migration agreement. This section evaluates the viability of emerging, second-generation migration agreements for dealing with temporary labor mobility. In particular, it describes potential limitations of these bilateral agreements with respect to multilateral openings in Mode 4 of the General Agreement on Trade in Services (GATS), including complementarities in terms of regulatory advantages. The second section identifies the motives and determinants of bilateral migration agreements as well as the institutional, regulatory, and administrative features of French migration pacts, which are used to assess the effectiveness of bilateral cooperation as a tool for managing migration. The third section examines French migration agreements for the emerging complementarities with European Union migration and neighborhood policies. The fourth section explores the extent to which France's bilateral migration agreements grant more favorable terms of labor market access to countries of origin concluding such agreements. The last section provides some concluding remarks.

WTO/GATS Commitments versus Bilateral Labor Agreements

Several studies (Chanda 2008; Friedman and Ahmed 2008) find that bilateral migration agreements can have multiple benefits over GATS Mode 4 commitments or preferential trade agreements. Bilateral labor agreements (BLAs) can specify or clarify categories of workers, the scope of work, and the temporariness of stay (through renewal and extension provisions). They can sharpen the focus on a sector or occupation, define conditions imposed on employers and workers, indicate admission numbers (though not admission criteria and determination), and specify administrative mechanisms and institutional frameworks for recruitment and entry. BLAs can give preference to local workers, wages, and working conditions and define the obligations of source and host countries (in the context of bilateral arrangements). They can be flexible in design and implementation to respond to local labor market and sector-specific requirements. They can take a holistic approach to the cross-border movement of labor. They can create mechanisms to protect workers and safeguard their rights and interests in both host and source countries. They can ensure their own coherence with other policies (immigration, taxes, and training); use disincentives (penalties and sanctions) and incentives (for example, return possibilities); reflect broad-based stakeholder participation; facilitate interdepartmental and interagency coordination within and across countries; and regulate intermediaries.

By virtue of being an EU member state, France is a World Trade Organization (WTO) member and thus bound by the most favored nation (MFN) clause of the GATS, which calls on WTO members to multilateralize any preferential market access granted to service-supplying natural persons from another WTO member. For this reason, France cannot introduce a new admission category for select partner countries without granting that preference to all WTO members. French bilateral migration pacts need to comply with the WTO/GATS MFN principle, which precludes them from opening additional channels for labor market admission into France only for citizens of signatory countries as opposed to all WTO members. Thus, with the exception of seasonal (agricultural) workers and young professionals—two categories of migrant workers that most likely fall outside the GATS definition of a service-providing natural person—the French migration pacts do not liberalize admission in channels reserved exclusively for countries partnering with France in the pacts. To the contrary, through quotas, the pacts limit the volume of admissions granted under the French admission categories open on an MFN basis to third-country citizens.

So far, the French migration pacts' only preference—which may be incompatible with the MFN clause—relates to domestic regulation: BLA country partners can attempt to negotiate the addition of occupations to the list of 30 shortage occupations open on an MFN basis to all countries. By widening the skill spectrum and types of jobs for which market access is relaxed, the pacts meet a developmental objective and more broadly comply with demands by developing WTO members that fewer occupations be regulated by economic needs tests (ENTs). The pacts thus contribute to relaxing an important barrier to market access.

This preference, which is based on nationality and thus potentially violates the MFN clause, is less impressive than it appears at first sight for several reasons. First, occupation shortage lists relax rather than eliminate the main market access barrier, which is the requirement that migrants obtain a work authorization. Second, the preference is watered down by the EU preference principle. When selecting jobs to add to the list of 30 shortage occupations, partner countries do not have a free hand; they must first select occupations from the list of 150 occupations applicable to EU countries. Consequently, the French pacts eliminate only the domestic component of the ENT while largely maintaining the EU–wide preference. Nationals from France's BLA partner countries will have to compete with EU nationals as long as the EU preference principle applies (CIMADE 2009).

In terms of matching job offers and demand, French BLAs do not offer much. Although the pacts offer other avenues for lawful labor migration by widening the geographical and occupational scope of shortage occupations and creating a new admission category, young professionals,[1] they do not even contain a negotiating mandate for an agreement on the mutual recognition of qualifications. In this sense, the pacts are like the North American Free Trade Agreement (NAFTA), the United States' free trade agreements with Chile and Singapore, and Asia-Pacific Economic Cooperation (APEC), which also add only one labor market access channel to regular immigration avenues. However, the pacts take back with one hand what they offer with the other, given that numerical benchmarks, which function as quotas, limit the number of nationals to be admitted under certain admission categories.

The level of preferential treatment that can be attributed to the French pacts is low in other areas, too. Most types of favorable treatment—such as the one-stop shop for visa and work permit applications and certain forms of migration-specific development aid (return and reintegration support, co-development savings accounts)—are available to certain migrant source countries without migration pacts with France. Criteria other than a migration pact with France qualify these countries for development aid or facilitated labor market admission.

According to one realistic assessment of the pacts, the "aim of (France's) agreements for the concerted management of migratory flows is to make it easier for employees and temporary workers to obtain residence permits by determining, for each country, a number of occupations for which the employment situation cannot be used to oppose residency" (EMN and MIIINDS 2010, 33). This assessment confirms studies that find that the agreements function as facilitators rather than generators of liberalized labor migration (Amin and Mattoo 2005; Carzaniga 2008; Holzmann and Pouget 2010). Rather than substitute for services trade agreements, the French migration pacts complement these agreements.

One of France's key motivations in getting countries to sign these agreements was to contain certain kinds of labor migration and to secure the readmission of foreign nationals who remain in France illegally. That goal is evidenced by the fact that the largest numbers of labor migrants come from Mali and Morocco, two countries that have refused to sign BLAs with France (EMN and MIIINDS 2010). By obtaining migrant source countries' assurances that they will readmit not only their own nationals but also third-country citizens who are illegally in France, the French pacts temporarily make up for the absence of an EU–wide readmission agreement with third countries.

In this regard, the French pacts could be criticized for not sanctioning employers who hire migrants in irregular stays or tolerate that practice by their subcontractors; not regulating intermediaries; and, most important, lacking mechanisms to protect workers' labor standards and safeguard their rights and interests. Insofar as the French pacts do not expressly cite applicable human rights conventions, they confirm the perspective of "numbers versus rights" (Ruhs 2008), whereby access to a labor market is traded for protection of migrants' rights. France could be criticized for failing to factor in the long- and short-term effects of development aid and for not being sensitive to the fact that return migration is anathema to the positive attitude that source countries harbor toward emigration and the negative attitude they display with respect to return migrants (Olesen 2002). Viewed from an international law perspective, both French BLAs and trade agreements are deficient when it comes to protecting migrants' human rights. This failing disqualifies French BLAs from full compliance with the EU global approach to migration (GAM), at least in theory (see below).

Goals and Policy Objectives of France's Migration Pacts

EU migration and neighborhood policies and Euro-Mediterranean migration policies, and France's desire to actively shape both, have played a key role in determining the design of France's bilateral agreements and its choice of partner countries. France uses its migration pacts as tools for implementing its EU obligations in two ways. First, the pacts temporarily deal with the failure of EU migration policies to reach out to countries in West and North Africa that refused to conclude a readmission agreement with the European Union or to take back their own citizens in unauthorized stays. Second, the pacts directly respond to the new ENP requirement that EU member states match funding granted by the EU Commission to non–EU members covered by the ENP.

The French pacts that attempt to "master migration" (Martin, Abella, and Kuptsch 2006) through a partnership approach—for example, pacts with Spain and Switzerland—remain tilted toward France's interest as a host country. They also reinforce France's immigration law reforms, limiting immigration flows; reversing the ratio between family and professional migration; stimulating international student mobility (attracting skills and talent without granting permanent stays); and more strictly combating irregular migration (Murphy 2006).

One Size Fits All: Eliminating Individualized Preferences

Former French colonies and protectorates individually negotiated labor market access provisions, the terms of which depended in part on geographical proximity to France. Algeria, Morocco, and Tunisia received more favorable treatment than Mali and Senegal.

The new pacts harmonize these provisions (EMN and MIIINDS 2010). In doing so, they lay the groundwork for an EU solution applicable to any migrant source country, whether in Africa, Asia, or the Americas. The pacts specify the categories of lawful stay in France, the procedures for readmitting people who remained unlawfully, the volume of available return aid, and reintegration support.

Although they are based on a uniform template, the new pacts retain some limited flexibility to adapt to the individual demands of migrant source countries. For example, occupations can be added to the list of 30 occupations available to migrants because EU countries cannot fill them. The number of residence and work permits available to young professionals, people with special skills and talents, employees, temporary workers, intracorporate transferees/interns, and seasonal workers can also vary. These maximum benchmarks are set annually, on a country-by-country basis, for each migration pact, taking into account the risk of brain drain from source countries.

Partnership Approach to Managing Migration

The partnership approach to migration management is designed to benefit developing countries, whose large pools of nonformally trained labor were disproportionately disadvantaged by skill-based recruitment schemes. With no outlet for their surplus labor, these countries experienced soaring unemployment, to which irregular migration became the solution. Under pressure, destination countries in Europe—particularly countries with a colonial heritage, such as France—attempted to address this issue with new national immigration laws.

The partnership rhetoric of the French pacts is somewhat removed from the reality. Rather than negotiate its pacts from scratch, France uses a generic template, which it minimally modifies during treaty negotiations with the partner country. It first tested the template with Gabon, which is not a representative country in terms of emigration flows to France. Subsequently, France "sold" the template to other West African countries and Tunisia, imposing on them a package deal of "tactical issue linkages." France's migration pacts are thus not the result of a mutually beneficial exchange of interests in light of the principle of shared responsibility.

Correctives to the Skill Selectivity of French Immigration Law Reform

The 2006 French immigration law reform laid the basis for new pacts on migration management by establishing the Ministry of Immigration, Integration, National Identity and Solidarity Development (MIIINDS) (Gnisci 2008). The new law aims to "redirect French immigration policy toward encouraging economic migration and matching it better to the needs of the French economy" (EMN and MIIINDS 2010, 3) and to reduce family reunification migration, which is perceived as "inflicted" migration (*immigration subie*).

By creating new admission categories—including skills and talents, intracorporate transfer, and student employment—the law of July 2006 sought to attract "professionals" under the concept of "targeted migration" (*immigration choisie*) (Chou and Baygert 2007), limiting entry from non–EU countries to highly skilled, creative, or otherwise talented migrants. As a result of the law, the number of family reunification migrants moving to France declined 10.6 percent in 2007 to 85,800, and the proportion of temporary labor migrants rose 19 percent between 2004 and 2006. During the first five months of 2008, lawful labor migration rose to 16 percent of authorized entries, up from 10 percent in 2007 to 7 percent in 2006 (Van Eeckhout 2009).

In France, BLAs have been effective tools for managing labor flows from third countries. But their added value in terms of liberalizing labor market access may have been overrated. The pacts do facilitate labor market entry for certain categories of workers on a preferential basis by eliminating labor market tests for professions for which a long-term shortage has been established. But these professions are mostly technical in nature and require medium-level rather than low-level skills. Thus, statements that the pacts are a tool for France to "actively solicit low-qualified labor" and that they "complement" the common interests of France and source countries with respect to the management of migratory flows (Gnisci 2008, 31) are somewhat misleading. The statement that "the objective of the agreements is to promote the 'skills and talents' admission card by setting the number of permits that can be issued [under this admission category] for each country, with quotas that range between 100 to 1,500 'skills and talents' permits per year" merely conveys public immigration policy (EMN and MIIINDS 2010, 33).

The extent of labor market liberalization depends largely on whether the partner country has the negotiating skill and bargaining power to extract significant concessions from France. If it does, it can use the pact to export surplus labor to France. If it does not, France will use the pact to strengthen the skill selectivity of its new immigration law, to the detriment of the source country's human capital endowment.

Implementing the European Union's GAM

France's bilateral migration pacts are embedded in the EU GAM (MIIINDS 2009). For the time being, the EU Commission lacks the competency to conclude binding agreements with third countries that would implement all three prongs of the GAM: labor migration, readmissions, and development aid. Thus, EU member states must implement the EU GAM policy through bilateral migration agreements. Recently, multilateral EU mobility partnerships, concluded by interested EU member states together with the EU Commission and the source country, have emerged, but they remain limited in terms of the access they can offer.

The first migration agreements were one-dimensionally focused on labor migration, the exchange of young professionals, or readmission. Co-development conventions moved these agreements to a two-dimensional architecture composed of three "indissolubly" interlinked prongs: securitization, labor migration, and solidarity development (CIMADE 2009).

Rhetoric and reality diverge, however. The resources granted to each of the three components remain inequitably tilted toward securitization. In addition, development aid does not benefit migrants who require assistance reintegrating, going instead to highly skilled migrants who wish to build a business in their country of origin as a subsidiary enterprise to their primary profession (CIMADE 2008).

In terms of thematic coherence, the pacts' main deficiency is the discrepancy between developmental direction and the categories of labor admitted to the French market. If development were truly a concern, the pacts' labor migration component would have to be opened up much more widely to lawful entry of low-skilled workers, including seasonal agricultural labor, domestic workers, cleaners, and waiters/waitresses. To date, these categories are included in only the minority of the pacts.

Complementing EU Migration and the ENP

Migrant source countries linked to France by new migration pacts are often preparing for EU accession or partnering with the European Union in an association/free trade agreement or qualifying for ENP aid. In these cases, EU policies limit the flexibility of the French migration pacts.

The ENP financially and technically determines the direction, scope, and partners of the development assistance foreseen by France's pacts. The EU Commission offers funding (a total of €700 million for 2007–13) for projects of common interest (including migration management), and EU member states are asked to match the EU community contribution.[2] Increases in the scope of the ENP reduce France's flexibility within the development pillar of its pacts. Bilateral discretion is also declining with respect to migration policies that seek to limit irregular migration (readmissions, border securitization) and even labor migration.

In this EU context, France (and Spain) signed bilateral migration agreements in 2005 and 2006 reflecting the political needs of EU members at the southern borders of Europe to address the lack of EU–wide action in the field of migration. The agreements prevent mass regularizations, which France, in particular, opposes.[3] Insofar as readmissions and border securitization are concerned, the bilateralism of the French pacts makes up for the failure to apply a regional EU–wide readmission obligation. Hence, the French pacts strengthen EU migration and neighborhood policies and fill in gaps in EU migration governance.

Selection of Partner Countries and Structure of Pacts

West African countries' reluctance to sign EU–wide readmission agreements gave rise to the new French migration pacts, which contain readmission clauses applicable only to France. Between 2006 and 2010, France concluded 15 BLAs for migration management. Its choice of partner country depended on EU migration and neighborhood policies on the one hand and the reformed French immigration law on the other. Generally speaking, the signatories are among the 28 countries in the French priority solidarity zone (PSZ)—developing countries with postcolonial ties to and thus linguistic, cultural, educational, and historic affinities with, France. Particularly targeted were countries with a significant numbers of citizens residing temporarily or permanently in France, primarily countries in West and North Africa.

Of the 15 pacts, 9 are comprehensive—that is, pacts that link readmission/border securitization, labor migration, and solidarity development, thereby opening the door to negotiation of trade-offs (box 5.1). The innovative feature of these pacts is that they make legal migration a condition of development aid. Migrant source countries are rewarded for combating irregular migration, including signing readmission obligations. Six of the 15 new French migration pacts are not comprehensive. If the partner country is not an African, Caribbean, or Pacific country or is an emerging market economy rather than a developing country, the pact does not address development cooperation. If the partner country has already concluded an EU–wide readmission agreement with France or a bilateral readmission agreement is in force between the two countries, the pact does not address readmission.

Box 5.1 France's BLAs with Tunisia

France's template for BLAs links labor migration, readmission and border securitization, and development cooperation, making its structural terms relatively easy to modify in light of the cyclical nature of labor markets in France. France was eager to make use of this flexibility in negotiating its BLA with Tunisia for three reasons. First, the number of labor migrants from Tunisia is twice the number from West African countries—mainly because France recruits seasonal agricultural labor from Tunisia (and Morocco) but not from West Africa. Unemployment among these migrants would thus impose a significant burden on French social security and welfare services. Second, Tunisia cooperates with French employer unions and industry associations more closely than migrant source countries in West Africa. Third, Tunisia's access to block formation as one of the Maghreb countries, which qualifies it for favorable treatment under the ENP, makes Tunisia's negotiation stance stronger than that of West African countries.

The migration pact with Tunisia is composed of a framework agreement (signed April 28, 2008) that codifies the signatories' obligations and establishes two protocols of application (Article 5). The first protocol, on migration management, contains the modalities for implementing family reunification, circular migration, student mobility and migration for professional reasons, return, and readmission. It is supplemented by a list of shortage occupations. The second protocol refers to solidarity development actions, including social and economic reintegration, vocational training, decentralized cooperation, and projects aimed at fighting unauthorized migration. This treaty architecture allows France to modify the occupational shortage list in response to its labor market demand without revising the entire BLA and to conclude agreements with industrial and professional associations, enterprises, and universities, all key nonstate partners in co-development.

The pact contains three annexes. The first lists professional and vocational training centers that France will establish or modernize and fund in Tunisia. These centers cater to occupations for which Tunisia has stated a development need. A second annex lists projects related to fishery and social integration and bank credits to support young entrepreneurs. A third annex lists other projects of development cooperation undertaken by other French ministries in Tunisia.

The flexibility of the new treaty structure facilitates nonstate actors' implementation of migration control and development strategies listed in the framework agreement as goals or priorities. Protocols can be adjusted quickly and easily to include new actors and new strategies. Protocols are implemented through memorandums of understanding, which are no longer concluded by French ministries but instead by departments, agencies, and other subministerial entities corresponding to Tunisian government entities. These memorandums are often concluded with employer unions, professional associations, and industry associations.

Labor Migration: An Overrated Component of France's Migration Pacts

For third-country citizens, French BLAs offer conditions more favorable for entry into French territory and admission for stay than multilateral migration agreements (CIMADE 2009). Although no data on the flows of citizens from countries that have signed BLAs are available, experts believe that the number of people benefiting from the preferential openings in the pacts will remain low.

The BLAs vary with respect to students, interns, and professionals. The professionals category has three subcategories: skills and talents, salaried/temporary workers, and young professionals. The BLAs specify numerical benchmarks for partner countries on the delivery of admission cards, which function as maximum quotas for the young professionals and salaried/temporary workers cards but as minimum quotas for the skills and talents admission card.

Under French immigration law, an admission card for employment in France is conditional on a work authorization, which in turn relies on a valid employment contract and, in principle, the outcome of the ENT, which must show that no qualified French or EU national is available for the job. The ENT has been eliminated for professionals (MIIINDS 2009); for occupations in which France has an acute labor shortage, the economic means test can be relaxed for students and salaried/temporary workers. In this context, foreign workers admitted under a skills and talents or a young professionals card are free to choose the occupation they take up in France, without competing with French workers. French migration pacts liberalize entry and admissions only for young professionals and interns. However, the pacts preferentially facilitate admission for occupations added to the list of 30 shortage occupations already available to workers from non–EU countries, and they expand the geographical scope of these occupations. In addition, the pacts provide institutional mechanisms to facilitate student employment.

In a very general way, the French BLAs offer four correctives to the French immigration law of July 2006. First, by expanding the list of 30 shortage occupations with respect to third countries, the BLAs offer additional avenues for lawful labor migration. Second, the BLAs reintroduce annual admission quotas, abolished by the 2006 law, for various visa types. Third, the BLAs reintroduce the "first professional experience abroad" admission card, which the 2006 law abolished. France now grants this card not only to citizens of countries that concluded a pact on concerted migration management with France (Benin, Burkina Faso, Cameroon, Cape Verde, Congo, Mauritius, Senegal, and Tunisia) but also to citizens from countries with bilateral agreements with France on the first professional experience abroad (Argentina, Brazil, Bulgaria, Canada, Gabon, Morocco, New Zealand, Romania, Senegal, Tunisia, and the United States). Fourth, the BLAs can be harsher or more lenient than French immigration law on extensions and renewals of admission cards (Panizzon 2011).

Visa Types Created by French Pacts

The French immigration law of 2006 relates to long-term and short-term (Schengen) visas. The Schengen visa is applicable to four admission categories: temporary workers, intracorporate transferees, seasonal workers, and people in France for "temporary stays for scientific reason." For two admission categories, young professionals and "skills and talents," the admission card functions as an entry visa. Students accessing employment or pursuing their first professional experience abroad are covered by either the salaried worker admission card, which in turn justifies a long-term temporary stay visa, or by the skills and talents admission card/visa. Unlike young professionals, students are not automatically exempt from the economic means test. Only students with the skills and talents card and students who work in certain occupations are exempt.

French BLAs affect conditions for entry. Several types of entry visas are available only to citizens originating from countries that have concluded either a migration pact or an agreement on the exchange of young professionals with France. These visas are the circulation visa, the migration and development visa, and the intern visa.

The circulation visa grants the visa holder a three-month residence in France per semester. It qualifies as a short-stay, multiple-entry visa with a validity of one to five years, depending on the BLA. It matches the conditions of the Schengen short-term visa. The categories of people eligible for the circulation visa are the same as the categories for the Schengen short-term visa. In short, the French circulation visa is nothing but a relabeled Schengen short-term visa.

Paradoxically, the categories of migrants eligible for the circulation visa do not include salaried or temporary workers who are in the professions for which the pacts have preferentially relaxed the work authorization requirement by eliminating the economic means test. Rather, the circulation visa is for highly skilled workers in shortage occupations and for two categories of foreigners who do not qualify as labor migrants but who actively strengthen the commercial, economic, academic, research, cultural, and sports-related ties between France and the partner country. These categories are family reunification migrants and medical tourists with sufficient resources and remaining health capacities to travel back and forth between France, where they receive treatment, and their country of origin (CIMADE 2009).

Thus, the French migration pacts create a mismatch between categories of people enjoying preferential entry into French territory (eligibility in terms of the circulation visa) and people benefiting from preferentially relaxed work authorization requirements that facilitate their access to the French labor market. This incongruence puts into question the pacts' much acclaimed internal coherence, comprehensiveness, and government-wide approach. In none of the French pacts have numerical benchmarks been applied to limit entries under the circulation visa. In this respect, the circulation visa is unlike other types of entry visa.

Like the circulation visa, the migration and development visa was created by a French BLA—in this case, a BLA with Mauritius (box 5.2). And like the circulation visa, it is a new label for a preexisting visa. It grants a 15-month stay to Mauritian workers under the employees admission category. Admission as a salaried worker requires a work authorization and an established employment contract. However, the work authorization process under the employees category is relaxed for jobs on the list of shortage occupations. The migration and development visa also constitutes the pathway for legal entry for the admission category of young professionals. Unlike the salaried worker admission category, this category is granted only by BLAs with a maximum quota of 200 young professionals (Commission of Foreign Affairs of the French National Assembly 2010).

The BLA with Mauritius also created the internship visa. It is applicable to students on internships and to intracorporate transferees.

Box 5.2 France's BLA with Mauritius

The pact with Mauritius qualifies as a two-pronged French migration pact, similar to the pacts concluded with the Western Balkan countries. However, it constitutes a unique version of the typical French migration pact for several reasons. First, whereas most French agreements on the joint management of migratory flows (integrate the list of 30 shortage occupations applicable toward third countries and add a few from the list of 150 shortage occupations applicable toward new EU member states, the pact with Mauritius identifies 61 occupations, none of them belonging to either list. Second, it creates an admission category and a visa exclusively for Mauritian citizens. It thereby liberalizes cross-border intracorporate movement, enabling Mauritian students and employees of French firms established in Mauritius or Mauritian firms partnering with French firms to second Mauritians for training and educational purposes in a French subsidiary in France. Third, the pact is the only BLA that follows market-based logic in liberalizing labor migration. It seeks to strengthen Mauritian effort to retrain and upgrade the skills of the Mauritian workforce. It thus responds primarily to Mauritian rather than French concerns (Commission of Foreign Affairs of the French National Assembly 2010).

The pact is harsher in terms of visa renewals than bilateral migration pacts that France concludes with migrant source countries in the French PSZ. It grants only a one-time renewal of the skills and talents admission card, which has a validity of three years (Commission of Foreign Affairs of the French National Assembly 2009).

Preferential Labor Market Access

In addition to facilitating entry into French territory by creating specific visa categories, French BLAs facilitate access to the French labor market by introducing the admission card of young professionals and (for Mauritian citizens only) interns. They set numerical benchmarks, which function as quotas for different admission categories. They expand the geographical scope and sectoral coverage of the list of 30 shortage occupations, eliminating the ENT for some third-country nationals. The BLAs also modify certain criteria within the existing admission categories. For instance, they prolong or cut short the renewal and extension periods of the "skills and talents" admission card and the "access to employment during studies" admission card.

Agreements on Young Professionals

The young professionals admission category is not available on a multilateral basis; it can be established only through a bilateral agreement, either through a young professionals agreement or through a pact on concerted migration management (MIINDS 2009). Countries eligible for such agreements have education systems that are closely aligned to France's. They include former protectorates and colonies (Morocco, Senegal, and Tunisia) as well as Argentina, Bulgaria, Canada, New Zealand, Poland, Romania, the Slovak Republic, and the United States. Pacts with countries without a young professionals agreement in place at the time of signing (Benin, Cameroon, Congo, Gabon, Mauritius, and the Russian Federation) incorporate an admission clause (see annex 5A).

Modifications of Shortage Lists

Like most other migrant host countries, France uses an ENT to give priority in employment to domestic workers (OECD 2009). It has used BLAs to exempt from this test occupations for which France has a critical need. For "shortage occupations," the process of obtaining a work authorization is accelerated, because the requirement to advertise jobs in these occupations in France and to screen French nationals is eliminated.

France maintains two lists of shortage occupations, both of which are biased toward skilled jobs, defined as technicians, installers, retailers, and construction supervisors and foremen (EMN and MIIINDS 2010). One list contains 150 occupations and applies to new EU member states under transitional regimes, citizens of which must obtain authorization to work in other EU countries. Since July 1, 2008, this list has been valid only for Bulgaria and Romania. It is used to ensure the free mobility of workers within the European Union by facilitating the gradual access to the French labor market to European salaried employees (Salcedo 2008).

The other list contains 30 occupations and applies to all third countries. Of these occupations, only 6 are in national shortage; shortages of the other 24 are regionally determined, unless the list is integrated into a migration pact, in which case the economic means test is relaxed for any job opening in the entire French "metropolitan" territory. Only when a French bilateral migration pact incorporates this list into its text (as in the case in 8 of the 9 comprehensive BLAs signed as of June 2011) is the geographical scope of occupations widened to metropolitan French territory. The regional limitation inscribed in the list of 30 is a barrier to labor mobility, because potential migrants benefit only from the list's facilitated entry procedure if they are willing to work in the particular French region where a scarcity for their occupations has been identified.

The list of shortage occupations applies to only two categories of admissions for labor migrants: employees (professionals staying 12 months or longer in France) and temporary workers (professionals staying less than 12 months). For the admission categories of intracorporate transferees, skills and talents, young professionals, and students and trainees, the French job market is irrelevant and a work authorization is granted even if French nationals are available to perform the job (MIIINDS 2009). For seasonal agricultural workers, the French job market is applicable; employers must provide evidence of a failed search for a French national applicant (EMN and MIIINDS 2010).

One-Stop-Shop for Residence and Work Authorization Procedures

The French Bureau for Immigration and Integration (Office Français de l'Immigration et de l'Intégration [OFII]) was founded in 2005 to oversee the arrival procedures of all non–EU legal migrants entering France for employment, study, or family reunification. Its social services section provides immigrants with specialized social services (such as civic and language training courses) on their arrival to France; it also provides reintegration support to return migrants who have received a Request to Leave the Territory. For migrants returning home voluntarily, a stepped-up return aid program is available. It is most extensive for countries with which France has a solidarity development program (Mali, Moldova, Romania, and Senegal). Two of these countries (Mali and Moldova) have not signed a pact on concerted migration management with France.

The OFII has set up satellite offices in 14 migrant source countries—some with and some without BLAs—competing with the traditional functions of French consulates.[4] The OFII satellites facilitate visa, work authorization, and residence permit procedures.

Public-Private Partnerships with Employers and Employer Unions

MIINDS establishes public-private partnerships (PPPs) with employers or employer unions to facilitate "the recruitment of foreign workforce according to business needs" (EMN and MIIINDS 2010, 22). A primary goal of these partnerships is to fast-track the work authorization process for certain economic sectors with recruitment difficulties and thus an acute need for foreign workers. A subsidiary but no less important policy objective is to shorten work access delays by foreign job seekers who have signed a Reception and Integration Contract with the French government, thereby preventing them from remaining unemployed so long that they lapse into informal or illegal work (EMN and MIIINDS 2010).

Encouraging Migrants' Return and Entrepreneurship

At least two prongs of the French solidarity development policies target individual migrants. The first is return and reintegration support. The second is co-development. The original concept, which was to co-finance migrants' collective investments in their countries of origin, met with mixed success; in 2008–09 it was changed to reward the migrant's individual savings through a co-development savings account and bank booklet.

Migrants from countries in France's PSZ are eligible for return and reintegration support, regardless of whether the countries are BLA partners. Reintegration support is defined as "start-up assistance for business or economic activity with the purpose of supporting the economic initiatives of migrants in their countries of origin" (EMN and MIIINDS 2010, 36). The amounts available for individuals (€4,000–€7,000 per project in 2009) are not higher if a country has signed a French pact (Commission on Foreign Affairs, Defense and Armed Forces of the French Senate 2008a).

Migrants, whether irregular or regular, obtain return aid; only individuals with a project plan, regardless of whether they receive return support, qualify for reintegration support, however. They are eligible if they apply for support within six months of their return to their country of origin (which can occur through their own means or through return support), following a stay in France of at least two years (EMN and MIIINDS 2010). The aid envelope contains €1,200 for the development agent who assists the migrant, plus up to €7,000 in financial aid for the migrant's project (the amount can depend on the migrant's country of origin).

Reintegration support has been criticized on several grounds. One is that the migrants who apply for the support are not the ones intended to receive it. Migrants who apply typically moved to France with the skills and talents, migration and development, or young professionals admission card. Because these migrants tend to be highly skilled, they tend not to need financial aid. Migrants who are in France without authorization are not prepared to reveal their illegal status simply to become eligible for return and reintegration support (IOM, ILO and OSCE 2008).

Reintegration support has been criticized on similar grounds. Instead of mobilizing migrants to return to their home countries and open businesses, reintegration support for Malian migrants prompted Malian citizens to migrate to France simply to become eligible for the aid. Individualized return and reintegration support has thus been found to increase rather than decrease migratory pressure (Commission on Foreign Affairs, Defense and Armed Forces of the French Senate 2008a).

The relationship between migration and development is paradoxical: as countries of origin attain higher levels of development, emigration rises. After development improved in Tunisia—thanks in no small part to its free trade agreement with the European Union—its citizens emigrated in greater numbers to France than citizens of Sub-Saharan African countries, particularly Senegal and Congo (Commission on Foreign Affairs, Defense and Armed Forces of the French Senate 2008b). Indeed, a study by the Institute for Public Policy Research and the Global Development Network finds that return and reintegration support was ineffective. It concludes that "compared with other policy tools, specific schemes aiming to motivate return are unlikely to motivate anyone beyond very niche groups of potential returnees" (Chappell and others 2010, 42).

Ironically, the country with the largest number of projects receiving individualized reintegration support (Mali) has not signed a pact on concerted migration management with France. In 2007, France provided reintegration support for 153 projects in Mali. The same year, it funded 28 projects in Senegal and 90 in Romania—two countries that have signed French BLAs. In 2008, France funded 132 projects in Mali but only 85 in Romania and 55 in Senegal. The projects in Mali are in commerce (video games and internet cafes) and transport (taxis and trucks). The projects in Senegal are more diversified and are in the tertiary sector (law, environment, and commerce, especially e-commerce). In Romania, the majority of projects are in pastoral agriculture; the rest are in textiles and production of construction materials (Interministerial Committee on Migration Control 2009).

The economic sector targeted by the project has no direct bearing on the longevity or success of the project. But the lower the qualifications of the migrant, the less the project will contribute to economic growth and productivity in the home country, because it will create fewer jobs and secure less investment. Projects in agriculture, commerce, and transport usually suggest that the project initiators possess low-level skills, which they had no opportunity to upgrade in

France (Interministerial Committee on Migration Control, Report to the French Parliament 2009).

The French pacts could improve the qualifications of migrants in France, which would increase the chance that the return migrants' projects remain viable and generate new employment in their countries of origin. But the shortage occupations listed for preferential access to the French labor market are not occupations that target the majority of migrants emigrating to France. Moreover, reintegration support finances projects of migrants working in occupations not opened by BLAs. These migrants are mainly agricultural workers who move to France under schemes other than BLAs. The occupations in the lists, even those added to the list of 30 professions in the new pacts, continue to respond primarily to French labor market needs rather than the goals of BLAs' solidarity development programs. Remedying this problem would require expanding the list of shortage occupations to include professions for which there is a real need in the country of origin or in which skill upgrading in France could lead to more sustainable reintegration projects.

Beyond its more straightforward financial transmission mechanism, co-development seeks the transfer of skills and know-how of the diaspora for the benefit of origin countries. The new French BLAs establish circular labor migration to encourage migrant elites to contribute to professional education and human capital development of their home countries, thereby increasing those countries' skills bases and productivity. For instance, France's pact on concerted migration management with Senegal seeks the voluntary return of medical doctors and other health professionals by offering research equipment or the prospect of joint university appointments. Its BLA with the Republic of Congo goes farther: it delegates the definition of specific modalities and actions in the field of co-development to a French-Congolese committee tasked with implementing the agreement (Commission on Foreign Affairs, Defense and Armed Forces of the French Senate 2008b).

Skill Spectrum and Selectivity of the French Pacts

It has been suggested that the French pacts have exacerbated skill-selective migration policies (CIMADE 2008, 2009; Salcedo 2008). This finding is true with respect to only some pacts. The pacts concluded with Benin, the Republic of Congo, and Gabon give preferential access to the French labor market to shortage occupations requiring high-level skills. The pacts with Senegal and Tunisia (and potentially Mali) include occupations requiring lower-level skills, perhaps because these countries were better negotiators or had access to EU block formation (CIMADE 2009).

With respect to Mali, Senegal, and Tunisia, the French pacts correct the high-skill bias of France's 2006 immigration law and multilateral market access openings embedded in the EU-15 list of Mode 4 GATS commitments. As Terrot (Commission of Foreign Affairs of the French National Assembly 2009) notes, such correctives defy France's goal of targeted migration, but they hold valuable developmental potential. In the pact with Mauritius, for example, France relaxed the work authorization procedure by giving construction workers and subcategories of such workers preferential access to the French labor market, thereby creating an outlet for a category of workers in surplus supply in Mauritius. France's BLA with Senegal appears to address the brain drain promoted by return and reintegration support. France observed that it was highly educated return migrants, not lower-skilled or unemployed Senegalese migrants, who were returning voluntarily to Senegal and using development funds to set up sustainable enterprises. This realization may have led it to open additional lower-skilled occupations to lawful labor migration. In Senegal and Tunisia, France opened such migration to seasonal migrant workers. None of the other comprehensive labor migration agreements does so.

Another way French pacts can be a corrective to the high-skill selectivity of French immigration law is through the skills and talents admission card. This card is often not issued to highly skilled workers, as the law of 2006 anticipated, because in the pacts, the skills and talents admission category is somewhat watered down in terms of skill levels as a result of the margin of discretion inherent in that category (EMN and MIIINDS 2010). The lowering of the skill level, which basically corrupts the legislative objective of the card, does not follow a developmental rationale. Rather, refraining from insisting on too rigorous a testing of applicants' projects was politically essential in obtaining the migrant source country's cooperation in readmitting migrants in irregular stays.

Table 5.1 shows the range in the allocation of skill levels among third-country migrants in France between 2004 and 2008. It suggests that the 2006 reform of the immigration law achieved its goal of attracting skilled third-country nationals. During this period, the number of low-skilled third-country nationals remained stable, at about 7 percent of the total employed population in France.

Top-Down Administration of Labor Recruitment

In the French pacts, admission to the labor market occurs from the top down. The French government allocates quotas and, together with the source country government, decides which professions to put on the list of shortage occupations.

France invests virtually no resources in the institutional aspects of labor migration, such as training would-be migrant workers before their departure abroad or facilitating the matching of job offers and requests. It continues to rely on its involvement in education and curriculum design in West African countries, which predates its latest-generation BLAs.

French-based educational and professional training facilities have not prepared potential migrant workers for the demands of the global labor market. In fact, the French-based education system is often far removed from labor market needs and employability requirements. Given Spain's positive experience with training migrants for work in Spanish companies (Panizzon 2011). France has replicated

Table 5.1 Skill Levels of Third-Country Migrants in France, 2004–08

Skill level	2004				2006				2008			
	Male	Female	Total	Percentage of total	Male	Female	Total	Percentage of total	Male	Female	Total	Percentage of total
High-skilled	83,340	35,850	119,190	38	86,774	40,173	126,947	20	103,607	59,708	163,315	21
Skilled	261,716	86,393	38,109	12	231,839	96,557	328,396	53	305,172	129,315	434,487	56
Low-skilled	69,929	89,234	159,163	50	65,914	101,938	167,852	27	67,211	106,479	173,690	23
Total	414,985	211,477	316,462	100	384,527	238,668	623,195	100	475,990	295,502	771,492	100

Source: Data from EMN and MIINDS 2010.

some of Spain's institutional structures for facilitating labor mobility, particularly for would-be migrants from Tunisia.

Mobilization of Diaspora by Migrant Source-Country Governments

The best outcome in migration management can be achieved only if the "sending countries also articulate policy objectives and interests" (Holzmann and Pouget 2010, 2). Chanda (2008, 1) points out that "source countries need to invest in creating institutional capacity and frameworks that allow them to address a wide range of economic, social, legal and human development related issues associated with worker mobility, whether or not they have entered into managed bilateral arrangements."

So far, the French pacts have triggered policy actions in source countries with relatively stable governments and a longstanding practice of cooperating with France on migration management. Two of these countries are Senegal and Tunisia, both of which had agreements with France on the exchange of young professionals before the admission channel for these workers was integrated into more comprehensive migration pacts. Tunisia has actively pursued PPPs between its research and training facilities and French multinationals. Senegal has so far not invested in training its workforce for global labor market demands, but it began experimenting with policies to mobilize its diaspora in France before such policies became formalized in the new pacts. That action and its signing of a co-development convention with France in 2001 have put Senegal a step ahead of other West African countries in experimenting with initiatives to engage the diaspora to contribute to source-country development. Senegal has broken new ground in replicating France's initiatives at diaspora-led development. Seeking investment at a distance by the diaspora through various information strategies has become such a popular policy tool of the Senegalese government that ministries and agencies now compete against one another for migrants' private capital inflows.

Even if "modest in numbers and scale" (Katseli and Dalton-Johnson 2008, 349), France's co-development projects have helped improve migration governance structures in source countries, both directly and indirectly. Priority Solidarity Funds directly co-fund diaspora projects incidental to migration. France built institutional capacity for source countries to contact and manage relations with their citizens abroad. The newly established government agencies and (in Mali and Senegal) ministries then designed their own co-development strategies.

Conclusion

France's bilateral agreements emerged in reaction to problematic migrant movements and the desire to manage French-African relations. These motivations are reflected in France's choice of partner countries: countries with the largest numbers of migrants entering France irregularly or remaining there in unauthorized stays as well as countries that have refused to signed a EU–wide readmission agreement or a readmission agreement with France. Because it lacks competencies in the field of labor market access, the European Union was unable to offer the type of rewards that countries of origin requested in return for signing readmission agreements or securitizing their own borders. The French pacts closed a gap in EU migration policy.

Two priorities are evident in the French migration pacts. One is the desire to eliminate the nationality-based preferences in visa and labor market admission policies that France had granted on a differential basis to its former colonies. The pacts harmonize the individualized treatment of former colonies, from which some had benefited at the expense of others. Migrant source countries can realize an advantage from BLAs with France only if they possess sufficient leverage to augment France's list of 30 shortage occupations with occupations in which they have a labor export interest. That bargaining power hinges on the migrant source country's access to a regional block, such as the ENP or the Euro-Mediterranean partnership. The main benefit to signatories of BLAs with France is the young professionals admission category. In contrast, France stands to gain significant advantages from BLAs. By facilitating first professional experiences for students, admitting young professionals, stimulating the return migration of foreign students, and establishing circulation visas for business people, scientists, and artists, the pacts indirectly stimulate French investments in the partner country.

A second priority of the pacts is to combat illegal migration—a goal that France achieves by preparing migrant source countries for EU–wide readmission agreements. France achieves this goal by insisting that migrant source countries take back not only their own citizens who are unlawfully in residence in France but also third-country nationals. By training these countries to enforce a readmission obligation, France prepares them for conclusion of an EU–wide readmission agreement. In return for undertaking this obligation, migrant source countries receive a relaxation of the Schengen visa requirements for business people, artists, and others, who instead receive circular migration (multientry) visas.

French BLAs do not overcome the shortcomings of immigration law. Their function is not only to temporarily substitute for a missing EU readmission agreement. Rather, these agreements are multifunctional, with a clear, if only implicit, objective of mainstreaming into a single template agreement the various preferences of precursor agreements with former colonies. By replacing such preferences with a uniform, EU–compatible solution, France enhances its own bargaining space with respect to the European Union. These bilateral agreements will sensibly reduce the preferences granted to some developing countries in terms of entrance to French territory and admission to the French labor market. For this reason, these countries, including Algeria, Mali, and Morocco, have resisted such agreements most.

Annex 5A: France's Migration-Related Agreements

Table 5A.1 France's Migration-Related Agreements

Country	Young professionals	Securitization (readmission, borders)	Co-development
Brazil (signed September 7, 2009, entered into force September 7, 2009)	X	a	X
Benin (signed November 28, 2007, entered into force March 1, 2010)	✓	✓	✓
Burkina Faso (signed January 10, 2009, ratified by the French National Assembly and transmitted to the Senate April 8, 2010)	X	✓	✓
Cameroon (signed May 23, 2009, transmitted to the French National Assembly July 28, 2010)	✓	✓	✓
Cape Verde (signed November 24, 2008, ratified by the French National Assembly July 28, 2010)	✓	✓[b]	✓
Congo, Rep. (signed October 25, 2007, entered into force August 1, 2009)	✓	✓	✓
Gabon (signed July 5, 2007, entered into force September 1, 2008)	✓[c]	✓	✓
Lebanon (signed June 26, 2010)	✓	—	—
Macedonia, FYR (signed December 1, 2009)	✓	X[e]	✓
Mauritius (signed September 23, 2008, entered into force September 1, 2010)	✓	d	✓
Montenegro (signed December 1, 2009)	✓	X[f]	✓
Serbia (signed December 2, 2009)	✓	X[g]	✓
Senegal (signed September 23, 2006; covenant adopted February 25, 2008, entered into force August 1, 2009)	✓[h]	✓	✓[i]
Russian Federation (signed November 27, 2009)	✓	X[j]	✓
Tunisia (signed April 28, 2008, entered into force July 1, 2009)	✓[k]	✓	✓

Source: An analysis of data from MIIINDS, various years.

Notes: ✓ = young professionals integrated into the pact; X = young professionals not integrated into the pact; — = not available.

a. Readmission agreement of May 28, 1996, entered into force August. 30, 2001. Agreement on public security was of March 12, 1997, entered into force September 1, 2007.

b. EU mobility partnership, June 5, 2008.

c. Young professionals agreement of February 24, 2010, entered into force February 24, 2010.

d. Readmission agreement of April 2, 2007, entered into force December 1, 2007. Agreement on interior security cooperation of June 13, 2008.

e. Readmission agreement of October 8, 1998, entered into force June 17, 1999. EU readmission agreement of September 18, 2007.

f. EU readmission agreement of September 18, 2007.

g. EU readmission agreement, September 18, 2007.

h. Young professionals agreement of June 20, 2001, entered into force June 20, 2001.

i. Co-development convention, May 25, 2000.

j. EU readmission agreement of May 26, 2006, entered into force July 27, 2007.

k. Young professionals agreement of December 4, 2003, entered into force May 10, 2004.

Notes

1. The pacts create a special admission category that is available only to French-speaking citizens originating from countries that have signed migration pacts with France. The young professionals category exists only by authority of a pact, not by national immigration law. By its very nature, it relies on a close affinity with the French culture, language, and education systems.

2. Article 2, Regulation 1638/2006 of the European Parliament and of the Council of 24 October 2006 lays down general provisions establishing a European Neighbourhood and Partnership Instrument. The new ENP builds on preexisting partnerships of the European Union with neighboring countries as the basis for intensified contractual relations. These foundations differ from region to region. The new tool will continue to differentiate according to the region involved. The "Northern Dimension" provides a framework for cooperation between the European Union, Iceland, Norway, and the Russian Federation. Regulation 1638/2006 expressly states that the "relevant elements of the European Union strategy for Africa will be taken into account in the relations with the Mediterranean neighbors from North Africa." Countries like Algeria, Morocco, and Tunisia will thus have leverage in determining EU policy toward Sub-Saharan African countries.

3. France proposed an EU–wide ban on mass regularization during its EU presidency in 2008. It was forced to drop the idea in order to win the support of the Spanish government for a European asylum and immigration pact.

4. The OFII operates satellites in Cameroon, Canada, French Guiana, Guyana, Guadeloupe, Mali, Martinique, Morocco, Réunion, Romania, Saint Martin, Senegal, Tunisia, and Turkey.

References

Amin, M., and A. Mattoo. 2005. "Does Temporary Migration Have to Be Permanent?" Policy Research Working Paper 3582, World Bank, Washington, DC.

Carzaniga, A. 2008. "A Warmer Welcome? Access for Natural Persons under Preferential Trade Agreement." In *Opening Markets for Trade in Services Countries and Sectors in Bilateral and WTO Negotiations*, edited by J. A. Marchetti and M. Roy, 475–502. Cambridge, MA: Cambridge University Press.

Chanda, R. 2008. *Low-Skilled Workers and Bilateral, Regional, and Unilateral Initiatives: Lessons for the GATS Mode 4 Negotiations and Other Agreements.* Geneva, Switzerland: United Nations Development Programme.

Chappell, L., with R. Angelescu-Naqvi, G. Mavrotas, and D. Sriskandarajah. 2010. *Development on the Move: Measuring and Optimising Migration's Economic and Social Impacts.* London: Institute for Public Policy Research and Global Development Network.

Chou, M. H., and N. Baygert. 2007. "The 2006 French Immigration and Integration Law: Europeanisation or Nicolas Sarkozy's Presidential Keystone?" Working Paper 45, Center on Migration Policy and Society, Oxford University, Oxford, U.K.

CIMADE (Comité Inter-Mouvements auprès des Evacués). 2008. "Les Accords Relatifs à la Gestion Concertée des Flux Migratoires et au Co-développment." Document d'Analyse, CIMADE, Paris.

———. 2009. "French Agreements Concerning the Concerted Management of Migration Flows and Co-Development." Briefing Paper, CIMADE, Paris.

Commission of Foreign Affairs of the French National Assembly. 2009. "Concerning the Adoption by the Senate of Draft Laws Authorizing the Ratification of Agreements on Concerted Migration Management and Co-Development between France and the Governments of Benin, Congo, and Senegal," by M. Michel Terrot. Report 1471, Paris.

———. 2010. "Concerning the Adoption by the Senate of Draft Laws Authorizing the Ratification of the Agreement between the French Government and the Republic of

Mauritius Relating to the Stay and Circular Migration of Professionals," by M. Michel Terrot. Report 2343, Paris.

Commission on Foreign Affairs, Defense and Armed Forces of the French Senate. 2008a. "Legal Opinion No. 1201 on Development Aid," by Henriette Martinez, November, Paris.

———. 2008b. *Concerning the Draft Laws to Ratify the Bilateral Agreements for the Concerted Management of Migration Flows between France and Benin, Congo, Senegal, and Tunisia*, by Catherine Tasca. Report No. 129, Paris. http://www.senat.fr/rap/l08-129/l08-129.htm.

EMN (European Migration Network) and MIIINDS (Ministry of Immigration, Integration, National Identity and Solidarity Development). 2010. *Satisfying Labour Demand through Migration*. Brussels: EMN and MIIINDS. http://emn.intrasoft-intl.com/Downloads/download.do;jsessionid=C9454E278D1F46B2FC02ABCCD872C302?fileID=2418.

Friedman, U., and D. Ahmed. 2008. "Ensuring Temporariness: Mechanisms to Incentivise Return Migration in the Context of GATS Mode 4 and Least Developed Country Interests," Global Economic Issues Publication, Quaker United Nations Office, Geneva. http://www.quno.org/economicissues/labour-movement/labourLinks.htm#QUNOPUB.

Gnisci, D. 2008. *West African Mobility and OECD Migration Policies*. Paris: Organisation for Economic Co-operation and Development.

Holzmann, R., and Y. Pouget. 2010. "Toward an Objective-Driven System of Smart Migration Management." Economic Premise 42, World Bank, Washington, DC.

Interministerial Committee on Migration Control. 2009. *Guidelines of the Migration Policy*. Report to the French Parliament. Paris: Interministerial Committee on Migration Control.

IOM (International Organization for Migration), International Labour Organisation (ILO), and Organization for Security and Co-operation in Europe (OSCE). 2008. *Compendium of Good Practice Policy Elements in Bilateral Temporary Labour Arrangements*. Geneva: IOM.

Katseli, L., and J. Dalton-Johnson. 2008. "The Labour Migration and Development Equation." In *World Migration Report 2008: Managing the Labour Mobility in the Evolving Global Economy*, edited by International Organization for Migration, 327–48. Geneva: International Organization for Migration.

Martin, P., M. Abella, and C. Kuptsch. 2006. *Managing Labor Migration in the Twenty-First Century*. New Haven, CT: Yale University Press.

Migreurop. 2010. "European Borders: Controls, Dentention, Deportations." 2009/2010 Report. Migreurop, Paris. http://www.migreurop.org/article1777.html.

MIIINDS (Ministry of Immigration, Integration, National Identity and Solidarity Development). 2009. *The Essentials on Economic Migration*. http://www.immigration.gouv.fr/IMG/pdf/essentiel_immigrprofessionnelle.pdf.

———. various years. *Accords bilatéraux*. http://immigration-professionnelle.gouv.fr/nouveauxdispositifs/accords-bilat%C3%A9raux.

Murphy, K. 2006. "France's New Law: Control Immigration Flows, Court the Highly Skilled." Migration Information Source, Migration Policy Institute, Washington, DC. http://www.migrationinformation.org/feature/display.cfm?ID=486.

OECD (Organisation for Economic Co-operation and Development). 2009. *International Migration Outlook: SOPEMI 2009: Special Focus: Managing Labour Migration beyond the Crisis*. Paris: OECD.

Olesen, H. 2002. "Migration, Return, and Development: An Institutional Perspective." *International Migration* 40 (5): 125–50.

Panizzon, M. 2011. "Franco-African Pacts on Migration: Bilateralism Revisited in Multilayered Migration Governance." In *Multilayered Migration Governance: The Promise of Partnerships*, edited by Rahel Kunz, Sandra Lavenex, and Marion Panizzon, 207–48. London: Routledge.

Ruhs, M. 2008. "Numbers vs. Rights: Trade-offs and Guest Worker Programs." *International Migration Review* 42: 249–65.

Salcedo, P. L. 2008. "Les accords de gestion concertée des flux migratoires et de développement solidaire: Un instrument de la nouvelle politique migratoire de la France au service de l'approche globale des migrations." Mémoire de master en science politique, Université Paris 1.

Van Eeckhout, L. 2009. "Immigration: 29,796 Repatriations at the Border. The Account of M. Hortefeux: Brutal Numbers, but a Complex Reality." *Le Monde*, January 14.

CHAPTER 6

Bilateral Labor Agreements and Trade in Services: The Experience of the Philippines

John Paolo R. Rivera, Denise Jannah D. Serrano, and Tereso S. Tullao Jr.

The Philippines is one of the world's largest labor exporters. In 2009, nearly 10 percent of its 90 million people lived and worked in at least 200 destinations worldwide. Enhancing the positive and mitigating the negative effects of this temporary labor migration requires sound policies and institutions. Over three decades, the Philippines, in cooperation with host countries, has advanced far in this task.

This chapter examines its experience. It is organized into eight sections. The first section describes the substantive provisions of the Philippines' bilateral labor agreements (BLAs) with the United Kingdom; Spain; Qatar; and Taiwan, China, to manage temporary labor migration. The second section analyzes institutional and regulatory arrangements to manage labor inflows and outflows (host country and origin country roles and private sector responsibilities). The third section examines mechanisms for ensuring the protection of overseas Filipino workers (OFWs). The fourth section assesses the development impacts of remittances and knowledge and skills transfers facilitated by BLAs. The fifth section examines several issues raised by the General Agreement on Trade in Services (GATS) and the Framework Agreement on Services of the Association of Southeast Asian Nations (ASEAN). The sixth section compares BLAs and trade in services agreements, showing that BLAs can complement commitments under the GATS. The seventh section highlights best practices of the Philippines in implementing BLAs. The last section summarizes the Philippines' experiences with BLAs. An annex provides statistics on OFWs in selected economies.

Substantive Provisions of the Philippines' BLAs

BLAs are legally binding agreements that are established to facilitate temporary migration flows between labor-sending and labor-receiving countries and sometimes between two labor-sending countries. They are legally binding, because they define terms and conditions of undertakings, violation of which can void the contract or trigger legal repercussions and because they lock in policies through international agreements.

BLAs can take many forms. They can be bilateral social security agreements (box 6.1), whereby migrant workers are required to pay social security taxes to both their home country and the country to which they have temporarily migrated for work. They can be anti-trafficking agreements, which adopt a standard operating procedure for identifying and repatriating victims. They can also take the form of labor treaties, recruitment treaties, and migration agreements, as well as legal instruments presented as protocols, intergovernmental agreements, and memorandums of understanding (MOUs) or agreement (MOAs) (Dela Rosa 2008).

Box 6.1 Social Security Arrangements in BLAs

BLA signatories should make multiple commitments in the area of social security, according to Go (2007):

- Signatories should provide mutual assistance, whereby covered members or beneficiaries may file their claims with the designated liaison agencies of the contracting parties, which will facilitate claims processing. Mutual assistance is becoming ever more critical as the extent and complexity of international trade increases and demands on customs administrations grow.

- The receiving country should treat workers from other countries as they do their own citizens with respect to social security. Thus, these workers should be eligible to benefits under the same conditions as the citizens of the receiving country, and social security coverage should extend to the workers' dependents and survivors.

- Overseas workers should be able to receive their benefits wherever they decide to reside (in their home country, in the receiving country, or in a third country). They should also have additional savings options, such as the Flexi-Fund Program, specifically designed for OFWs who will permanently reside in the Philippines after retirement. This program complements regular social security systems by providing a money savings mechanism for OFWs abroad in addition to existing benefits. According to the 2006 *OFW Guide* (OFWGuide.com 2006), the Flexi-Fund Program helps OFWs prepare for livelihoods once back in the Philippines by encouraging savings while they are employed overseas. The program enables its members to use the accumulated balance in their provident funds to finance housing, education, or a business and to provide a pension. The program promotes the productive use of OFWs' money through partnerships with private sector entities, such as banks, academic institutions, training institutions, and government agencies, a strategy advocated by Calzado (2007).

- Each contracting party should be liable for paying a fraction of the benefit due from its social security system. That fraction should be in proportion to actual contributions or creditable periods.

Since 1974, when its overseas employment program began, the Philippines has established MOUs with 13 countries, most of them in ASEAN (Go 2006). These MOUs are either labor recruitment and special hiring agreements or labor, employment, and manpower development agreements. The labor recruitment agreements focus on the terms and conditions of the employment and mobilization of OFWs or on the exchange of trainees (Go 2007).

Of the four MOUs presented here, the one with Qatar is the most comprehensive, containing detailed provisions and a model employment contract. It facilitates the movement of all types of workers. The MOUs with Spain and the United Kingdom are intended primarily to facilitate the deployment of Filipino health care professionals. The MOU with Taiwan, China, facilitates the deployment of Filipino factory and construction workers (see annex 6A, table 6A.1, for the numbers of OFWs deployed to each economy). In addition to facilitating the flow of labor, these agreements seek to protect deployed workers.

Regulating the Recruitment of Filipino Health Care Workers in the United Kingdom

In 2003, the Philippines concluded a MOU with the United Kingdom that specifies the terms and conditions of recruitment of Filipino health professionals (nurses, physiotherapists, radiographers, occupational therapists, biomedical scientists, and other allied health professionals regulated by appropriate professional bodies in both countries) (Go 2007). The MOU recognizes the importance of exchanging knowledge and expertise through cooperation on health care. Specifically, it aims to give Filipino health care professionals recruited to the National Health Service the opportunity to develop their skills and learn best practices.

The MOU specifies that a recruitment project will be implemented by the Department of Labor (DOLE) and the Department of Health of the Philippines and by the Department of Health of the United Kingdom. The aim of the project is the sustainable recruitment and employment of nurses and other Filipino health care professionals by three means: increasing bilateral exchanges of policy thinking with regard to the development of the nursing workforce and best practice in health care delivery, involving professional staff and health care managers in educating and training Filipino health care professionals, and addressing gaps in the process for recruiting medical professionals.

The Philippine Overseas Employment Administration (POEA) is charged with ensuring that workers deployed in the United Kingdom have a prescribed level of technical qualification and physical, medical, and psychological fitness. Health requirements vary by destination and type of occupation. Technical qualifications are determined at testing centers accredited by the Technical Education and Skills Development Authority (TESDA); physical and medical fitness are determined at medical clinics and facilities accredited by the Department of Health. The Commission on Higher Education (CHED) and the Professional Regulation Commission (PRC) work together to standardize, assess, and certify skills. CHED supervises, monitors, and regulates medical and allied programs; the PRC administers professional examinations for the health programs (Agunias 2008).

For its part, the United Kingdom's labor ministry must ensure that only qualified Filipino health care workers enter U.K. territories. It monitors the hiring of these workers and presents to DOLE and POEA the recruitment applications from U.K. employers. These applications specify required qualifications, experience, and specializations and include the contract span, employment conditions, salary and benefits, probationary period, transportation facilities, accommodation, and other pertinent information regarding employment.

The U.K. labor ministry must work with the U.K. Department of Foreign Affairs, DOLE, and POEA to address disputes. It has the right to repatriate any foreign workers whose presence in the United Kingdom becomes contrary to public interest and national security. It must relay decisions to repatriate to the Philippine embassy.

The United Kingdom and the Philippines must implement their MOU in accordance with legislation in each country and finance the activities with their respective budgets. Any dispute between the two countries that arises from the interpretation or implementation of the MOU must be settled by consultations or negotiation.

Temporary labor migration generates sizable welfare gains for migrants and their countries of origin and destination (Tullao and Rivera 2008). The benefits to the country of origin are realized through remittances, which are vital sources of financing for developing countries (Ratha and Mohapatra 2007). The large number of OFWs in the United Kingdom is partly responsible for the massive flow of remittances to the Philippines, which reached more than $20 billion in 2011, according to the Philippine central bank (BSP 2012). Remittances from the United Kingdom totaled $956 million in 2011.

Strengthening Historic Ties with Spain

The Philippines and Spain signed an MOU June 29, 2006. It reflects a shared desire to reiterate and strengthen the longstanding special friendship between the countries. In addition, it reaffirms both countries' determination to cooperate in the management of migration flows between them. The agreement incorporates a joint position against illegal trafficking of human beings, clandestine migration, and undocumented and illegal recruitment policies. The agreement is governed by the Philippine Department of Labor and the Spanish Ministry of Labor and Social Affairs.

To guarantee that the MOU responds to the needs of their respective labor markets and strengthens their partnership for responsible administration of the management of migration flows, the Philippines and Spain agreed to several tasks, stipulated in the MOU. First, the two countries must develop pilot systems, structures, and processes in the Philippines for Filipinos to accept generic job offers from the health care sector in Spain. Specifically, the agreement calls for a pilot hiring process that will identify procedures to facilitate the selection, documentation, and deployment of selected workers to Spain as well as the social and labor integration of the contracted workers in Spain. Second, the Philippines and Spain will jointly analyze the pilot process for the purpose of establishing long-term collaboration for managing migratory flows of qualified Filipino health care workers to Spain. Third, both countries will undertake the agreement in accordance with their respective legislation, finance activities with their own budgets, and guarantee that no fees are collected from job applicants during the prehiring process.

POEA has the task of ensuring that workers deployed in Spain are technically and medically competent. All workers must possess the prescribed level of technical qualification and physical, medical, and psychological condition as certified by TESDA and the Department of Health. CHED and the PRC provide skills standardization, assessment, and certification (Agunias 2008).

To combat illegal recruitment, a concern that motivated the MOU, regulation of recruitment agencies that deploy Filipino workers to Spain must be enforced. Accreditation is compulsory to verify the existence of the principal employer and identify its labor requirement before any Spanish employer can recruit a Filipino worker (Tullao and Cortez 2004). POEA is responsible for licensing recruitment agencies, regulating and monitoring their performance, and sanctioning illegal recruiters. It also regulates the placement fees charged by recruiting agencies, holds the recruitment agency and the Spanish employer legally responsible for the claims of OFWs, and hears welfare cases and arbitrates contractual conflicts between OFWs and their Spanish employers.

Spain's Ministry of Labor and Social Affairs is responsible for ensuring that only qualified workers enter Spain. It monitors the hiring of OFWs for employment in Spanish territories. It verifies the qualifications, experience, and specializations in the recruitment applications of Spanish employers seeking to employ Filipinos and presents those applications to DOLE and POEA. Recruitment applications must include contract duration, employment conditions, salary and benefits, probationary periods, transportation facilities, accommodations, and other pertinent information regarding employment.

The MOU between the Philippines and Spain carries no specific provision concerning dispute settlement. However, as the official representatives under the MOU, Spain's Ministry of Labor and Social Affairs and the Directorate General of Immigration must work with DOLE and POEA to attempt such settlement. Furthermore, under Spanish immigration law, the ministry has the right to repatriate any Filipino worker whose presence becomes contrary to public interest and national security. Repatriation decisions must be conveyed to the Philippine embassy.

In addition to the BLA, the Philippines and Spain have entered into two other agreements regarding the protection of the rights of OFWs. One is a social security agreement made in 1988 and enforceable since 1991. In accordance with the agreement, benefits are paid to recipients enrolled under both the Spanish and Filipino social security systems. The implication of the agreement is that under the Spanish system, Filipinos receive the same treatment as Spaniards and that Filipinos can receive their pension benefits under the Spanish system even if they retire outside Spain.

The other agreement regarding OFW rights is the Bilateral Tax Treaty for the Prevention of Double Taxation, which states that "taxes paid in one state shall be credited to tax against the tax payable in the other state." This agreement complements the Philippines' MOU with Spain. According to the Philippine central bank, remittances from Spain totaled $73 million in 2011 (BSP 2012). Pe-Pua (2004) argues that the Philippines could increase the benefits of its BLA with Spain in two ways. First, it could pursue additional opportunities, particularly in professional areas, for Filipinos to work in Spain, thereby easing its unemployment. However, the Philippine government should consider the social impact of long-term overseas labor employment and monitor potential effects on the quality of the remaining labor force in the Philippines. Second, the Philippines could increase efforts to ensure Filipinos' settlement in Spain and integration into Spanish society. Lack of Spanish-language proficiency and information about Spanish culture are major hindrances to finding work opportunities in Spain. Pe-Pau recommends that the Philippine and Spanish governments provide scholarships for Spanish language and culture courses, like those offered in the Philippines by the Instituto Cervantes, a worldwide nonprofit organization founded by the Spanish government in 1991.

Safeguarding Worker Rights in Qatar

The Middle East has been the top destination of OFWs, because the region has been engaged in massive development projects since the 1970s (Tullao and Rivera 2008). Reports from various Philippine overseas labor offices of the DOLE and Philippine embassies and consulates abroad suggest that Qatar, together with Kuwait, Oman, Saudi Arabia, and the United Arab Emirates, will continue to have major projects in the construction, energy, industry, petrochemicals, power, water, transport, health, food, tourism, retail, energy, telecommunication, production, distribution and services, banking, education, operations and maintenance, and information technology sectors.

In 1997, the Philippines signed an MOU with Qatar, which was amended in 2008, in part to organize Filipino employment in Qatar. The agreement is governed for the Philippines by the DOLE and for Qatar by the Ministry of Civil Service Affairs and Housing. The Philippines, through the POEA, ensures that only qualified workers are deployed to Qatar and provides them with information on the terms and condition of employment, culture and traditions, and standard of living in Qatar. The Qatari government monitors the hiring of Filipino workers for employment in its territory.

The MOU stipulates that recruitment of Filipino workers and their entry and employment in Qatar must be regulated in accordance with the relevant laws, rules, and procedures of the two countries. The Qatari Ministry of Civil Service Affairs and Housing presents recruitment applications for Filipino workers from Qatari employers to DOLE; through the POEA, DOLE takes measures to fulfill the applications within its available means and resources. POEA licenses recruitment agencies, regulates and monitors their performance, and prosecutes illegal recruiters. In addition, it holds the recruitment agency and the foreign employer liable for the claims of OFWs. POEA also hears welfare cases and adjudicates contractual conflicts between OFWs and their employers. The Qatari Ministry of Civil Service Affairs and Housing is responsible for ensuring that only qualified workers enter Qatar's national territories, in accordance with the agreed terms.

The Philippines and Qatar agreed that the Qatari employer will shoulder the travel expenses of Filipino workers to their workplace in Qatar on entering service as well as the return passage at the end of service. The Qatari employer will also bear the round-trip travel expenses for leave intervals, as agreed with the worker. The employer will be exempt from paying the return passage of the worker to the Philippines if the worker abandons work before the expiration of the contract without lawful cause or commits a breach of contract resulting in dismissal from work without notice and without an end-of-service bonus, in accordance with the provisions of Qatari labor law. Any disagreement over the employment contract will be submitted for settlement to the concerned authority within the Qatari Ministry of Civil Service Affairs and Housing. If settlement fails, the matter will be referred to the judicial authorities in Qatar.

Qatar has the right to repatriate Filipino workers if their presence in Qatar becomes contrary to public interest or national security, provided that wages accruing to the workers under the contract of employment and labor laws are paid before repatriation for the entire unused period of the employment contract. The Philippines also reserves the right to refuse the recruitment of any Filipino if doing so is contrary to the interests of the Filipino employee, the public interest, or the security of the Philippines.

The MOU between the Philippines and Qatar covers documentation, protection, social services, and human resources development. It fosters protection of labor, promotion of full employment, and equality of employment opportunities. More important, it offers timely social, economic, and legal services to OFWs, requiring the Department of Foreign Affairs to protect the rights of migrant workers and other OFWs and to extend immediate assistance, including repatriation of distressed or beleaguered OFWs. The MOU guarantees that, whenever applicable, Qatari labor and social welfare laws, including legal assistance and referral to proper medical centers, be extended to OFWs. The Philippine Overseas Workers Welfare Administration (OWWA) also works with the Department of Foreign Affairs and DOLE to give OFWs and their families the assistance they need to enforce contracts, including representation in settlement conferences or reconciliation meetings.

In what Libo-on (2008) regards as a testament to the Qatari OFW recruitment process and safeguard mechanism, Qatar absorbed about 3,000 OFWs laid off by their firms in the United Arab Emirates by approving allocation of 120,124 visas for Filipinos for 2009. According to Libo-on, these retrenched OFWs will get preference in selection of recruits for jobs in Qatar.

OFWs in Qatar provide a massive volume of remittances to the Philippines. According to the central bank, these remittances amounted to $283 million in 2011(BSP 2012).

Implementing a Special Hiring Facility in Taiwan, China

The Philippines and Taiwan, China, entered into an MOU in 2006, through the Council of Labor Affairs of Taiwan, whose representative is the Taipei Economic and Cultural Office, and the DOLE, whose representative is the Manila Economic and Cultural Office. The MOU recognized the need to continue promoting the welfare of OFWs. Under the MOU, both countries agreed to optimize the benefits of overseas employment for both Filipino workers and Taiwanese employers, in part by establishing a special hiring facility that allows Taiwanese employers to hire Filipino workers directly rather than through agencies (Go 2007).

To implement the special hiring facility, both countries have made several agreements:

- Corporate employers will hire workers in the manufacturing and construction sectors.
- Both countries will regulate and process certain job categories, which will require Taiwanese employers to hire Filipino workers through the special hiring facility.
- The facility will adopt a prescribed employment contract for every skill category—a contract acceptable to both parties and consistent with prevailing rules and regulations.
- The facility will not prevent Taiwanese employers from hiring Filipinos through agencies, but employers will be encouraged to hire workers through the facility.
- The schedule of expenses of workers hired through the facility will be agreed to by both parties without prejudice to the welfare of the workers or the relevant rules and laws of both countries.
- To provide the necessary support for the facility, both countries will establish mutually acceptable guidelines, systems, procedures, and mechanisms to simplify and facilitate the hiring and deployment of foreign workers at the lowest possible cost.

Both entities undertook the MOU in accordance with their respective legislation and finance the activities with their respective budgets. The Philippine government is responsible (through POEA) for ensuring that workers to be deployed to Taiwan, China, are technically and medically qualified and possess the prescribed technical qualifications and physical, medical, and psychological fitness, as certified by TESDA and the Department of Health. CHED and the PRC work together on skills standardization, assessment, and certification (Agunias 2008). The Council of Labor Affairs of Taiwan, China, ensures that only qualified workers enter Taiwanese territories, in accordance with the agreed terms. It also monitors hiring by presenting Taiwanese employers' recruitment applications for Filipino workers to DOLE and POEA.

POEA licenses, regulates, and monitors the performance of agencies recruiting workers to be deployed to Taiwan, China, and prosecutes illegal recruiters. It also regulates the fees charged by recruiting agencies and holds recruitment agencies and Taiwanese employers liable for the claims of OFWs by hearing welfare cases and refereeing contractual conflicts between OFWs and their employers.

The Council of Labor Affairs is responsible for working with POEA and DOLE to address disputes. It has the power to deport any OFWs whose presence is contrary to public interest and national security. Decisions to do so must be communicated to the Philippine embassy.

According to the Philippine central bank, remittances from OFWs in Taiwan, China, amounted to $156 million in 2011 (BSP 2012).

Regulatory Framework for Implementing BLAs

The massive volume of remittances Filipino workers send provides a good source of income for a labor surplus economy. The Philippine government must thus protect the rights of workers to encourage services exports. The government must also regulate relations between workers and employers, local and foreign, recognizing the right of labor to its fair share in total production and the right of enterprises to reasonable returns on investments. To achieve these ends, the government implements a set of rules and regulations regarding the licensing and regulation of recruitment agencies for land-based workers and of manning agencies.

Although the Philippines has some of the best practices in managing labor migration in terms of deployment and protection, it lacks mechanisms for addressing the potential impact of temporary labor migration on education and other sectors in the long run. Tullao and Rivera (2008) find that if the government cannot control migration flows and the propensity of Filipinos to seek external employment, it should increase investments in education and health and make other human capital–enhancing expenditures to increase the competitiveness of Filipino workers abroad.

Labor ministries in Qatar; Spain; Taiwan, China; the United Kingdom; and other labor-receiving countries are concerned with the entry and qualifications of Filipino workers. These ministries work with Philippine government entities to promulgate the rules and regulations for implementing the provisions of their BLAs with the Philippines.

The private sector—sea-based and land-based recruitment and manning agencies—are subject to these rules and regulations. About 350 Philippine manpower agencies deal with sea-based OFWs, placing about 270,000 cruise line service personnel and 10,000 officers annually. About 1,010 agencies place some 350,000 land-based OFWs a year (Soriano 2009).

Unlike sea-based agencies, land-based agencies deal with different countries and therefore with those countries' laws and regulations in addition to Philippine laws and POEA regulations. Some of these agencies are paid by their foreign employer clients and therefore do not charge fees to accepted applicants. Other agencies have a small percentage of job orders that require accepted applicants to pay a legal fee equivalent to one month's salary. A few agencies are nominally

Filipino owned but are actually foreign owned; they charge fees to successful applicants (Soriano 2009).

These agencies tend to specialize in specific occupations. According to Agunias (2008), they represent foreign employers in selecting, registering, and transporting workers. They also ensure the proper implementation of the employment contract. If the employer does not comply with the stipulations of the contract, the agencies can provide legal assistance. Hence, the agencies are liable jointly with and separately from the foreign employer, and the government can exercise pressure on employers through the agencies.

The POEA has been tasked with reducing the growing number of recruitment agencies to avoid cut-throat competition. Policy makers fear that in an over-crowded market, some agencies will not make sufficient profits and rather than leave the market will recover their losses through illegal means (Agunias 2008). This possibility and the fact that Philippine private employment agencies are allowed to continuously participate in the recruitment and placement of OFWs mean that sustained government involvement is required to protect and promote the welfare of OFWs.

Safeguard Mechanisms

Proper implementation of employment contracts can help protect OFWs. Protection of OFWs can be stated in BLAs and advanced through active monitoring of their welfare by government personnel assigned abroad.

Protecting the welfare of illegally deployed and employed OFWs remains difficult. For that reason, the Philippines established the Migrant Workers and Overseas Filipinos Act of 1995 (Republic Act 8042), which addresses documentation, protection, social services, and human resources development. The act seeks to "institute the policies of overseas employment and establish a higher standard of protection and promotion of the welfare of migrant workers, their families, and overseas Filipinos in distress, and for other purposes." Under the act, the Philippines must afford full protection to labor—local and overseas, organized and unorganized—and promote full employment and equality of employment opportunities for all. The Philippine government must also provide sufficient and timely social, economic, and legal services to OFWs.

At one point, the Philippines banned the deployment of female domestic workers to countries where their rights would not be recognized. The ban was eventually lifted because of implementation difficulties and concerns over human and constitutional rights, such as the right to travel, to work, and to seek better opportunities. Instead, POEA paid more attention to improving workers' skills and requiring stricter requirements for entry to other countries for the purpose of employment. In 2006, POEA enforced a policy that requires all deployed domestic workers to be at least 23 years old, have attended a country-specific language and culture course, and have secured a certification on household work from TESDA.

However, POEA needs to address the persistent problems of illegal testing and issuance of forged certificates, passports, and other documents (Agunias 2008).

Tullao (2008) argues that skilled and professional workers should be required to possess an original and a photocopy of their signed employment contract, work permit, visa or equivalent entry permit, and valid passport.

The Philippines' Medium-Term Development Plan for 2004–10 emphasizes the enhancement of productivity for Filipinos seeking overseas employment. To do so, the Philippines established the Labor and Employment Action Plan (LEAP), in part to improve OFWs' competency, productivity, and work values; enhance the worker-employer relationship; improve labor welfare abroad; facilitate Filipino workers' access to overseas labor markets; and promote flexible work and employment arrangements.

Development Impacts of Temporary Labor Migration

Overseas employment can improve development in the source country through the flow of remittances, the transfer of skills and knowledge, and the undertaking of entrepreneurial activities by retired OFWs.

Remittances

Remittances can contribute to the economy of labor-sending countries and improve the welfare of households (Bayangos and Jansen 2009; Chami, Fullenkamp, and Jahjah 2003; Tullao and Rivera 2008). Tullao and Rivera (2008) find that as the income of households with remittances increases, those households increase their expenditures on education, which they attribute to the culture of migration. The success of family members in global employment spurs other family members to seek external employment, and because in the global labor market the favored and highly paid workers are the more educated workers, households tend to invest in education to increase the chances of their family members of acquiring overseas employment. The impact of remittances is not totally positive, however: Chami, Fullenkamp, and Jahjah (2003) find that an increase in remittances has a negative effect on the labor force supply because household members receiving remittances reduce their work effort.

Remittances add to disposable income and then to private consumption expenditure, which strengthens the procyclical impact of remittances, according to Chami, Fullenkamp, and Jahjah (2003). Bayangos and Jansen (2009) find that remittances are positively related to consumption, suggesting that remittances do not even out consumption. Their finding can also be construed as showing that remittances increase when demand for consumption increases.

The benefits of remittances for development are conditional on the receiving country's broad economic and political context, according to Ratha and Mohapatra (2007). Unlike private capital flows, remittances tend to increase when the receiving country experiences an economic slowdown (as a result of a financial crisis, natural disaster, or political conflict), because migrants send more money home during hard times to aid their families (Ratha 2007; World Bank 2005). Yang (2006), for example, finds that remittances as a share of personal consumption expenditure increased in the Philippines following a financial crisis there.

Tullao and Rivera (2008) note that remittances directly augment the income of recipient households. Their analysis suggests that remittances can be effective in reducing poverty and can result in better development outcomes in the Philippines through enhanced educational expenditures. These findings are consistent with those of Ratha and Mohapatra (2007), who also find remittances to be associated with increased household investments in education, entrepreneurship, and health.

Ratha and Mohapatra also find that remittances affect poverty and welfare through indirect multiplier effects and macroeconomic effects. These effects contribute positively in a good policy environment. According to the International Monetary Fund (2005), a good investment climate with well-developed financial systems and sound institutions is likely to imply that a higher share of remittances is invested in physical and human capital. Indeed, remittances promote financial development that can enhance growth, according to Beck, Demirgüç-Kunt, and Levine (2004) and Aggarwal, Demirgüç-Kunt, and Peria (2005). However, according to Taylor (2006, 18), "remittance multipliers outside the migrant household are created when the migrant household spends its new income on goods and services supplied by other households in the migrant-sending economy." The strength of these multipliers depends on how the migrant households spend their income as well as on other households' ability to increase their supplies of goods and services. In the Philippines, households spend their income domestically, expanding the potential for businesses in the migrant-sending area to benefit from remittances.

Skill and Knowledge Transfer
Tullao, Conchada, and Rivera (2009) argue that skill and knowledge transfer from returning OFWs should occur in training centers and educational institutions; permanently returning OFWs should be given employment in TESDA training grounds as instructors. In addition, these OFWs should be involved in redesigning teacher education, certifying soft skills valued by industry, establishing performance-based assessments of skills, promoting ongoing learning through appropriate career guidance, and fostering sound basic and secondary education.

Financial Assistance for Retiring Migrants' Entrepreneurial Activities
Trust funds accumulated by the OWWA are adequate to fund additional reintegration projects for OFWs who want to permanently reside in the Philippines. Some of these funds should be allocated in the form of financial assistance for business ventures and other moneymaking projects undertaken by retiring OFWs. Tullao and Rivera (2008) argue that the OWWA and DOLE must provide more loans to retirees and more educational assistance to their dependents. They should also help OFWs manage their money.

In support of efforts to help returning OFWs resettle in the Philippines, major Philippine banks have cooperated with the National Reintegration Center for

OFWs (NRCO) to develop a more affordable remittance system that will promote savings consciousness and sound investments to help OFWs and their families put their earnings in income-generating projects. Specific plans involve investment by the banks and the sponsoring of seminars on financial literacy, financial planning, and wealth management. Cooperating banks will also assist the NRCO and other stakeholders and service providers in implementing other projects for OFWs.

According to DOLE, the system will help ensure the effective reintegration of OFWs from the time they decide to go abroad until their return to the Philippines. The system will motivate OFWs to transfer funds to the Philippines through formal channels, particularly in the form of savings, loans, and investments. DOLE deems this savings mobilization an essential part of the reintegration program for OFWs.

Addressing Issues Raised by the GATS and the AFAS

GATS Article VII makes mutual recognition agreements an option for accelerating liberalization of trade in services. According to the Philippine Institute of Development Studies (PIDS 2005, 98), a mutual recognition agreement "does not automatically extend the right of professionals to practice in another country, rather it is a formal agreement between two or more countries establishing procedures that assess the manner by which differences between their qualifications systems can be bridged, while considering the mechanisms for the recognition of their respective home country requirements in the host country." PIDS notes the difficulty of conferring mutual recognition agreements and the complexity of the issues that must be addressed in bridging disparities in qualifications, regulations, and requirements for the practice of a profession. It also recognizes that inherent in these reciprocity agreements is the potential for discrimination against third parties.

Another issue, raised by Tullao and Cortez (2006), is the limited impact of the ASEAN Framework Agreement on Services (AFAS) on Movement of Natural Persons and its similarity with the GATS. For instance, commitments on the movement of natural persons are intimately linked to GATS Mode 3 and are viewed simply as a means of facilitating the movement of professionals, managers, and technical staff for intracorporate transfers. Moreover, domestic regulations that restrict the movement of workers across the region—reinforced by domestic regulations governing the practice of professions in most member countries—substantially limit market access for foreign workers.

Tullao and Cortez (2006) believe that the movement of natural persons and the regional flow of workers will proceed despite the inadequacies of institutional drivers. They argue that member countries' management of temporary labor migration is not influenced by regional agreements or by huge flows of foreign direct investments. Instead, that management is a legitimate response to labor market asymmetries in the region.

Hence, under the GATS and AFAS, the Philippines and its labor-receiving partners must simultaneously promote and strengthen cooperation in the areas of labor, employment, and manpower development. In addition, they must foster the exchange of research, technical expertise, and other information that can enhance employment promotion and labor administration in the Philippines and the labor-receiving country and enhance the welfare of Filipino workers in accordance with the labor laws of the receiving country. A committee with representatives from both countries should periodically review agreements and their implementation.

Linkages between BLAs and Agreements on Trade in Services

Unlike the GATS, the Philippines' Temporary Work Program facilitates the transfer of unskilled as well as skilled workers for overseas employment. It supplies workers for all industries for which receiving countries have no labor migration restrictions, particularly agriculture, industry, and services. Industries in Taiwan, China, and the Republic of Korea employ Filipino factory workers; Filipino domestic helpers, caregivers, and nurses are part of the temporary movement of labor in the services sector.

Recruitment agencies in the Philippines are allowed to process applications and deploy workers for overseas employment within the parameters and regulations set by the government to facilitate transfer and protect workers from abuse. Many of these agencies have foreign partners, which are governed by labor recruitment policies and laws in receiving countries. In this sense, labor deployment through the Temporary Work Program differs from deployment through the GATS, under which intracorporate transfers and temporary migration of skilled labor is governed by domestic regulations, including immigration and other preemployment requirements of the host country, or by licensing and recognition requirements of the receiving country.

Return of workers under temporary labor migration in a BLA is governed by the workers' terms of deployment. Some countries require temporary workers in unskilled and semiskilled labor categories to return to their home countries after the completion of their contracts. Once they return, they can apply immediately for deployment in another country. If, however, they want to be deployed by the company or in the country of their previous deployment, they must wait a minimum number of months before reapplying. By contrast, temporary labor migration under the GATS often becomes permanent. For example, a large proportion of skilled workers entering the United States on H1-B visas become permanent residents of the United States.

The Philippines has shown that BLAs can potentially enhance trade in services that may not be limited to the services sector, skilled professionals, or firms establishing a commercial presence overseas (GATS Mode 3). It has designed and implemented these agreements as MOUs, which are nonbinding with respect to the commitments made under a regional trade agreement or the GATS. This flexibility allows receiving countries to engage in dialogue with the Philippines' Temporary Worker Program.

Best Practices of the Philippines in Implementing BLAs

DOLE is aggressive in establishing BLAs with countries receiving OFWs. It has an advantage in convincing receiving countries to undertake these agreements, because the Philippines is one of the major exporters of Mode 4 labor services and can deploy workers with varied levels of skills. Given the huge overseas demand for nurses and other health care professionals and recognition of the quality of Filipino nurses working abroad, Spain and the United Kingdom found it beneficial to enter into MOUs with the Philippines to manage the flow of these professionals.

The BLAs established by the Philippines have helped lower the cost of migration by reducing the risks of that activity and by enhancing intermediation and facilitation processes. The most comprehensive of these agreements, the MOU with Qatar, includes a template for employment contracts and provisions on the deployment and employment of OFWs that are so detailed that they cover the availability of safe and potable water. This specificity implies that problems encountered by OFWs in the past are being addressed—and that the market power of the Philippines to insist on the inclusion of various provisions is increasing. That power may reflect the quality of OFWs deployed in Qatar in the past.

The Philippines has no template for its BLAs. The agreements' contents depend on the economic development and labor needs and on the labor market situation in the Philippines and its labor-receiving countries. If employment and labor protection measures in receiving countries do not meet Philippine requirements, the number and specificity of provisions are relatively large; if the receiving country is highly developed and implements a progressive and proactive labor protection policy, the BLAs focus on recognition requirements.

The Philippines has implemented a strong institutional structure for facilitating the temporary flow of workers. Government agencies, often in partnership with private entities, are involved in prerecruitment, recruitment, preemployment, deployment, and return. POEA manages all aspects of overseas employment; OWWA is in charge of worker protection and benefits. The government has made protection of overseas workers a major pillar of its foreign policy; the Department of Foreign Affairs and DOLE are responsible for ensuring realization of this goal. CHED, TESDA, and the PRC take the lead on OFW qualification requirements.

Conclusion

Over three decades, the Philippines has developed a strong public-private partnership for the management of overseas employment, from recruitment, deployment, and redeployment to return. The government has used this vast experience to push for MOU provisions that promote the interests of OFWs. When worker safeguard measures are absent in the receiving country, the Philippines has insisted on the inclusion of detailed provisions that protect OFWs. It even included a template for an employment contract in its MOU with Qatar.

Despite the importance of worker safeguards, the primary objective of BLAs is to facilitate temporary migration flows from countries with labor surpluses to countries with labor shortages. The Philippines has developed institutions to make the most of the resulting remittances. It has established programs to help returning OFWs manage their wealth, and it has insisted on including provisions for technical assistance to develop the skills of its domestic workforce and for mutual recognition in its MOUs.

As an alternative to multilateral and regional agreements in enhancing trade in services, BLAs can cover the technical and highly skilled professionals under the movement of natural persons in these agreements. They can cover all industries, not just the services sector, as well as workers other than highly skilled professionals. Moreover, they can be used not merely to expand trade in services but to facilitate temporary migration flows in addressing global labor market imbalances.

Annex 6A: Overseas Filipino Workers in Selected Economies

Table 6A.1 Overseas Filipino Workers in the United Kingdom, 2001–08

Year	Professional nurses (new hires)	Caregivers (new hires)	Land-based overseas Filipino workers (new hires and rehires)
2001	5,388	4	10,720
2002	3,105	253	13,655
2003	1,544	481	13,598
2004	800	656	18,347
2005	546	732	16,930
2006	145	1,214	16,926
2007	38	521	9,525
2008	28	31	9,308
2009	165	8	7,701
2010	350	10	5,284

Source: Philippine Overseas Employment Administration (http://www.poea.gov.ph/stats/statistics.html).

Table 6A.2 Overseas Filipino Workers in Spain, 2001–08

Year	Household service workers (new hires)	Caregivers (new hires)	Land-based overseas Filipino workers (new hires and rehires)
2001	619	—	1,783
2002	601	—	1,751
2003	319	2	1,258
2004	527	7	1,452
2005	123	1	907
2006	616	78	1,720
2007	1,542	49	2,619
2008	1,673	70	4,114
2009	573	28	2,826
2010	110	1	3,262

Source: Philippine Overseas Employment Administration (http://www.poea.gov.ph/stats/statistics.html).
Note: — = not available.

Table 6A.3 Overseas Filipino Workers in Qatar, 2001–08

Year	Professional nurses (new hires)	Teachers (new hires)	Information technology–related workers (new hires)	Household service workers (new hires)	Land-based overseas Filipino workers (new hires and rehires)
2001	143	6	2	1,585	10,769
2002	213	2	3	1,899	11,516
2003	243	5	11	1,736	14,344
2004	318	11	4	2,436	21,360
2005	133	6	16	4,998	31,421
2006	141	21	18	6,524	45,795
2007	214	45	29	1,912	56,277
2008	245	68	19	4,682	84,342
2009	133	59	20	6,376	89,290
2010	294	67	28	9,937	87,813

Source: Philippine Overseas Employment Administration (http://www.poea.gov.ph/stats/statistics.html).

Table 6A.4 Overseas Filipino Workers in Taiwan, China, 2001–08

Year	Professional nurses (new hires)	Caregivers (new hires)	Land-based overseas Filipino workers (new hires and rehires)
2001	9	—	38,311
2002	131	—	46,371
2003	200	14,716	45,186
2004	6	13,928	45,059
2005	357	11,604	46,737
2006	273	8,410	39,025
2007	174	6,346	37,136
2008	231	6,251	38,546
2009	202	5,942	33,751
2010	252	6,184	36,866

Source: Philippine Overseas Employment Administration (http://www.poea.gov.ph/stats/statistics.html).
Note: — = not available.

References

Aggarwal, R., A. Demirgüç-Kunt, and M. S. M. Peria. 2005. "Do Remittances Promote Financial Development? Evidence from a Panel of Developing Countries." Policy Research Working Paper 3957, World Bank, Washington, DC.

Agunias, D. R. 2008. *Managing Temporary Labor Migration: Lessons from the Philippine Model.* Program on Migrants, Migration, and Development. Migration Policy Institute, Washington, DC.

Bayangos, V., and K. Jansen. 2009. "The Macroeconomics of Remittances in the Philippines." Working Paper 470, Institute of Social Studies, Manila.

Beck, T., A. Demirgüç-Kunt, and R. Levine. 2004. "Finance, Inequality, and Poverty: Cross-Country Evidence." NBER Working Paper 10979, National Bureau of Economic Research, Cambridge, MA.

BSP (Bangko Sentral ng Pilipinas). 2012. *Overseas Filipinos' Cash Remittances*. http://www.bsp.gov.ph/Statistics/keystat/ofw.htm.

Calzado, R. 2007. "Labor Migration and Development Goals: The Philippine Experience." Paper presented at the International Dialogue on Migration Workshop, Geneva, October 8.

Chami, R., C. Fullenkamp, and S. Jahjah. 2003. "Are Immigrant Remittances Flow a Source of Capital for Development?" Working Paper 03/189, International Monetary Fund, Washington, DC.

Dela Rosa, J. F. 2008. *Migration Management in the Philippines: Development of Bilateral Policies between Sending and Destination Countries*. Manila, Philippines: Institute of Health Policy and Development Studies, National Institutes of Health, University of the Philippines.

Go, S. P. 2006. "Country Report: The Philippines." Paper presented at the Japan Institute of Labour Policy and Training (JILPT) Workshop on International Migration and Labour Market in Asia, Tokyo, February 17.

———. 2007. "Asian Labor Migration: The Role of Bilateral Labor and Similar Agreements." Paper presented at the Regional Informal Workshop on Labor Migration in Southeast Asia "What Role for Parliaments," Philippine Migration Research Network, Manila, September 21–23.

IMF (International Monetary Fund). 2005. *World Economic Outlook*. Washington, DC: IMF.

Libo-on, L. B. 2008. "Qatar Provides Ray of Hope for Retrenched Filipinos." *Khaleej Times Online*, December 18. http://www.khaleejtimes.com/darticlen.asp?xfile=data/theuae/2008/December/theuae_December332.xml&section=theuae.

OFWGuide.com. 2006. "SSS Flexi-Fund Program for OFWs." *OFW Guide*. http://www.ofwguide.com/article_item-330/SSS-Flexi-Fund-Program-for-OFWs.html.

Pe-Pua, R. 2004. "Links with the Philippines: Bilateral Negotiations and Relationships with the Philippines." Paper presented at the workshop on "Migration and International Relations between Asia and Spain: Philippines, China, and Pakistan Case Studies," Barcelona, September 6.

PIDS (Philippine Institute for Development Studies). 2005. *Market Access Issues and the Development of Business Services*. Manila, Philippines; PIDS. http://dirp4.pids.gov.ph/ris/taps/tapspp9817.pdf.

Ratha, D. 2007. "Leveraging Remittances for Development." Policy brief, Migration Policy Institute, Washington, DC. http://www.migrationpolicy.org/pubs/MigDevPB_062507.pdf.

Ratha, D., and S. Mohapatra. 2007. *Increasing the Macroeconomic Impact of Remittances on Development*. Washington, DC: World Bank.

Soriano, L. B. 2009. *The OFW Economic Engine. Philippine Reality and Required Reform Arising from the Global Financial Crisis*. Manila, Philippines. http://xa.yimg.com/kq/groups/23005480/1771765891/name/OFW+Economic+Engine-FINAL.pdf.

Taylor, J. E. 2006. "International Migration and Economic Development." Paper presented at the International Symposium on "International Migration and Development, Population Division, Department of Economic and Social Affairs, United Nations Secretariat," Turin, Italy, June 28–30.

Tullao, T. S. 2008. "Demographic Changes and International Labor Mobility in the Philippines: Implications for Business and Cooperation." Philippine Pacific Economic Cooperation Committee. Makati City, Philippines.

Tullao, T. S., M. I. P. Conchada, and J. P. R. Rivera. 2009. "Trade and Human Resource Development Policies for Inclusive Growth: A Literature Review and a Case Study of the Philippines." Asia-Pacific Research and Training Network on Trade, Bangkok.

Tullao, T. S., and M. A. Cortez. 2004. "Stimulating the Japanese Economy by Promoting the International Flow of Immigrants: A Survey of Policies, Structures, and Issues from the Philippines." Japan External Trade Organization, Tokyo.

———. 2006. "Enhancing the Movement of Natural Persons in the ASEAN Region: Prospects and Constraints." Asia-Pacific Research and Training Network on Trade, Bangkok.

Tullao, T. S., and J. P. R. Rivera. 2008. "The Impact of Temporary Labor Migration on the Demand for Education: Implications on the Human Resource Development in the Philippines." East Asian Development Network, Makati City, Philippines.

World Bank. 2005. *Global Economic Prospects 2006: Economic Implications of Remittances and Migration*. Washington DC: World Bank. http://www.worldbank.org/prospects/migrationandremittances.

Yang, D. 2006. "International Migration, Remittances, and Household Investment: Evidence from Philippine Migrants' Exchange Rate Shocks." NBER Working Paper W12325, National Bureau of Economic Research, Cambridge, MA.

CHAPTER 7

Bilateral Labor Agreements in the Pacific: A Development-Friendly Case Study

Manjula Luthria and Mai Malaulau

Managed labor migration is new in the Pacific region: labor-sending and -receiving countries are still developing familiarity and experience with bilateral labor agreements (BLAs). Australia's Pacific Seasonal Worker Pilot Scheme (PSWPS) concluded in June 2012; the Seasonal Worker Program (SWP) started July 1, 2012. New Zealand's Recognised Seasonal Employer (RSE) Scheme began April 1, 2007. Both schemes involve BLAs with specific Pacific Island countries for the provision of unskilled labor to undertake seasonal work on farms in regions where there are demonstrated labor shortages.[1]

This chapter examines the nature of the BLAs between islands of the Pacific and Australia and New Zealand, the efficacy and experience of BLAs as an instrument for managing temporary labor migration globally, and the potential for expanding trade in services arrangements. The chapter is organized as follows. The first section describes the type of BLAs in effect between individual Pacific Islands and Australia and New Zealand and examines key drivers for the schemes, the implications of BLAs for market access, rule setting and enforcement, and the number of workers employed under the schemes. The second section outlines the scope and structure of BLA. The third section summarizes the development benefits of labor migration in the Pacific and examines the role of the World Bank. The last section discusses the experience of existing BLA elsewhere in the world.

Types of BLAs

BLAs in the Pacific region are not legal agreements. Rather than create a legal relationship between the parties, they document negotiated agreements between Pacific governments and Australia or New Zealand on policy, principles, roles, and relationships necessary for managing labor migration and achieving agreement on practical matters for managing labor migration. Pacific Island countries with

BLAs with Australia or New Zealand include Kiribati, Papua New Guinea, Samoa, the Solomon Islands, Tonga, Tuvalu, and Vanuatu.

The structure and content of Pacific Island country BLAs with Australia and New Zealand are similar, but they allow flexibility for tailoring to reflect issues that are distinctive or of special importance to either the sending or receiving country. The agreements are standardized, however, so that any benefits, responsibilities, and support for Pacific Island countries are applied evenly. The terms of engagement between parties are locked in for all countries. Receiving-country policies and interventions seek to create a level playing field for participating Pacific Island countries (by, for example, adjusting the cost-sharing ratio between employers and workers to improve the competitiveness of Pacific Island countries with higher flight costs).

The BLAs have not yet been tested on the question of what would happen in the event that either party failed to uphold the understandings. Consequences are likely to affect bilateral diplomatic relationships, with the ultimate effect being the nullification of the agreements, potentially closing off access to the RSE or PSWPS. Sanctions are likely to be in the form of political condemnation from within and outside the region. Evidence of corruption or unethical practices that go unaddressed is specifically identified in the BLA as a possible basis for terminating the agreement between the parties.

The power imbalance in this arrangement is obvious; recourse to justice or remedies for Pacific Island countries in the face of a serious breach of the agreement by Australia or New Zealand would be limited largely to regional or international political condemnation. BLAs such as these thus appear adequate as long as the relationship between Pacific Island countries and Australia and New Zealand remain amicable. Fiji's exclusion from both schemes reflects the poor state of the political relationship between Fiji and its Trans-Tasman neighbors.

Australia's PSWPS is an exclusive Pacific scheme; market access is contingent on having a memorandum of understanding (MOU) with Australia. The New Zealand scheme is open to workers from all countries that meet certain criteria—regardless of whether or not the countries have an inter-agency understanding (IAU) with New Zealand—although Pacific Island countries currently enjoy about 75 percent of the 8,000 total places available each year. Once market access is gained, Pacific Island countries can enlist commitment and support from the receiving country for translating market access into market entry. The BLA also provides a vehicle for ongoing dialogue on related issues.

Drivers for Establishing Labor Migration Schemes in the Pacific

Achieving improved access for Pacific Island countries to employment opportunities in Australia and New Zealand has long been a feature of the bilateral and multilateral agendas of Pacific Island heads of government. Excess supply of labor from the Pacific, however, needed to match labor shortages in receiving countries in order to achieve a win-win scenario for all parties.

Industry bodies that historically experienced ongoing severe worker shortages lobbied the governments of Australia and New Zealand intensively, claiming huge losses in productivity and millions of dollars of lost revenue and warning of the threat of collapse of some parts of affected industries. By December 2005, the New Zealand government had collaborated with industry and other partners, producing a seasonal labor strategy that addressed access to labor, including global labor; improved employer practices in their management of seasonal labor; and planning and forecasting of labor demand.

The New Zealand government announced its decision to establish the RSE in October 2006. The scheme was launched in April 2007, providing Pacific Island countries with access to seasonal work as pickers, pruners, and packers in New Zealand farms and packhouses. The scheme's name underscores the focus on New Zealand employers, which is consistent with the objectives of being demand driven and of improving the employer practices of the New Zealand horticultural industry.

Australia's PSWPS commenced in August 2008; the permanent SWP began in July 2012. Its BLA with Pacific Island countries describes the benefits to Australian industries and the economy (demand driven) while safeguarding against displacement and erosion of employment conditions for Australians. The scheme aims to ensure that the potential benefit of the scheme for Pacific Island countries are realized by including more elaborate principles, outcomes, and factors that are critical for success.

Who Achieves Market Access and Why?

Pacific Island country participants in the PSWPS were Kiribati, Papua New Guinea, Tonga, and Vanuatu. Under the SWP, the group of participants was broadened to include Nauru, Samoa, the Solomon Islands, Timor-Leste, and Tuvalu. Australia's approach to granting market access through an MOU were reportedly based on establishing conditions for a tightly managed pilot by selecting one Pacific Island country from each of the Micronesia, Polynesia, and Melanesia regions that have already had some experience of sending workers to New Zealand's RSE. Papua New Guinea's inclusion as the fourth Pacific Island country participant reflects Australia's historical relationship with that country. Although Australia intended to leverage off countries' experience in New Zealand by entering into MOU with many of the same Pacific Islands, the Trans-Tasman neighbors agreed that workers who had recently worked in the RSE would not be eligible for work under the PSWPS.

Pacific Island counties participating with an IAU with New Zealand's RSE include Kiribati, Samoa, the Solomon Islands, Tonga, Tuvalu, and Vanuatu. Most of these countries share a historical relationship with New Zealand, having at some stage been mandated territories of New Zealand or having sizable diaspora populations in New Zealand. New Zealand's limited familiarity (in migration terms) with Melanesia is reflected in the measured approach taken in the initial selection of only a single Melanesian country (Vanuatu) to participate in the scheme. It is possible that New Zealand's decision to include Vanuatu was influenced partly by the successful entry of Vanuatu farm workers under a previous migration policy. In 2010, the Solomon Islands was added.

Rule-Setting and Enforcement

Pacific Island countries' BLAs with Australia and New Zealand set forth the rules determining eligibility to recruit foreign labor; minimum and maximum employment contract (and visa) duration; minimum remuneration for workers; cost-sharing requirements between employer and worker (for example, flight costs and domestic travel costs); responsibility for organizing versus paying for accommodations; and sanctions for noncompliance by employers or workers with policy rules.

The Department of Education, Employment, and Workplace Relations in Australia and the Department of Labor (now the Ministry of Business Innovation and Employment) in New Zealand are responsible for screening and prequalifying employers who wish to recruit workers from the Pacific and then monitoring and enforcing employer compliance with the rules. They investigate and if appropriate apply sanctions on noncomplying employers for breaches in employment contracts or practices. Employers can also be fined if their workers become unauthorized and overstay the term of their visa.

There is a high level of public and political interest in both the Australia and the New Zealand schemes. The schemes strike a good balance of incentives, providing both sending and receiving countries with vested interests in ensuring the scheme's success. Both schemes take breaches of rules by employers seriously, taking care to prequalify employers eligible to participate and recruit workers.

Employment environments in both Australia and New Zealand are generally well regulated; Pacific Island countries thus have a fair degree of confidence that their workers will enjoy the same rights and protections as Australian and New Zealand nationals. In fact, Pacific Island workers are believed to be entitled to greater benefits than receiving country nationals by virtue of close government involvement with and facilitation of their employment. Requirements are placed on employers of Pacific workers to ensure transportation to and from the workplace, reasonable accommodation, and other types of assistance (for example, help in opening bank accounts and establishing connections with local community organizations and churches).

BLAs outlining the responsibilities of the parties are substantially adhered to; regular contact between the parties ensures that issues and the need for practice improvements are dealt with in real time. Receiving-country labor inspectors investigate complaints and issues raised by workers and liaise with sending-country administrations to resolve them and, where possible, prevent them from recurring. Many Pacific Island countries are solely reliant on receiving-country interventions on behalf of their workers, as they lack the capacity to install attachés and tend not to have embassy presence (or adequate resources within embassy offices). Receiving-country administrations and employers may not be the first port of call for workers with grievances or other issues however. Two labor-sending countries (Samoa and Tonga) with long histories and established diaspora presence in New Zealand have installed liaison officers recruited from the resident diaspora to address issues pertaining to migrant worker welfare.

Both Australia and New Zealand have developed specific tax interventions for their scheme's workers with the objective of ensuring the lowest possible tax rate for workers and reducing the paperwork associated with tax returns. To date, there have been no disputes between parties. Any serious issues that cannot be resolved between lead departments are likely to be elevated and resolved through diplomatic channels. It is not uncommon for the Ministry of Foreign Affairs of both sending and receiving countries to sit alongside lead departments in such instances, particularly for the negotiation of BLAs.

Pacific Island workers can raise issues or disputes with the receiving-country administrations responsible for labor and immigration. Labor inspectors in the receiving countries generally manage issues through early and close liaison with sending-country administrations. BLAs specify that the granting of immigration visas or permits—as well as decisions to repatriate noncompliant workers—remains the prerogative of the receiving countries. The unscheduled repatriation of workers occurs only in exceptional circumstances, such as criminal offending or justified dismissal from employment. Where appropriate, worker complaints about employers are also investigated by the Australian and New Zealand administrations. In some instances, employers have been sanctioned, workers transferred to alternative prequalified employers, and issues relating to lost worker remuneration addressed by receiving-country governments.

The BLA with New Zealand for the RSE is supposed to be reviewed regularly (at least annually). In practice, BLAs with Pacific Island countries have been reviewed just once over the last four years, with no substantive changes made.

Demand for Workers from Pacific Island Countries

The RSE and PSWPS are demand-driven schemes; they do not set quotas. However, a maximum number of places available overall each year is stipulated. Both schemes make provision for employers who have been approved and market tested to recruit workers from the Pacific Islands.

Participating countries have distinctive political philosophies with regard to the distribution of opportunities. Some (Tonga) take a propoor approach. Others (Kiribati and Samoa) focus on equitable geographical distribution of opportunities. Yet others (the Solomon Islands and Vanuatu) prefer a less interventionist approach, at least in the short term. These varied philosophical approaches do not seem to have had a direct bearing on performance or market share. However, Vanuatu, Tonga, and Samoa send the most workers to New Zealand under the RSE, and Tonga is an early leader in Australia's PSWPS (table 7.1).

Pacific Island countries currently fill 75 percent of available places. A substantial number of workers return to the same employer each year.

Table 7.1 Number of Workers from Pacific Island Countries Employed through Bilateral Labor Schemes with Australia and New Zealand

Source country	New Zealand 2007/08 (9-month year)	2008/09	2009/10	Total	Australia 2009/10
Kiribati	69	38	48	155	11
Samoa	647	1,228	1,021	2,896	n.a.
Tonga	805	1,355	1,142	3,302	106
Tuvalu	99	49	54	202	n.a.
Vanuatu	1,698	2,342	2,137	6,177	6
Solomon Islands	238	311	256	805	n.a.
Pacific Islands total	3,556	5,323	4,658	13,537	n.a.
Other Asian countries	930	1,498	1,558	3,986	n.a.
Total	4,486	6,821	6,216	17,523	123

Sources: New Zealand Department of Labour 2010 for New Zealand and Australia Department of Education, Employment, and Workplace Relations for Australia.
Note: n.a. = not applicable.

Scope and Structure of BLAs

The BLAs between Pacific Island countries and Australia and New Zealand follow the same basic format, with the Australian MOU closely modeled after the New Zealand IAU. Typically, the BLA contains statements of purpose; principles; objectives and outcomes; critical success factors; facilitative arrangements; immigration; marketing; information collection; review and consultations; variations, amendments, and conditions; and commencement and termination.

Purpose and Principles

The purpose statement in the Australian and New Zealand BLAs is identical. It sets out the arrangements for facilitating access of the citizens of a particular Pacific Island country to seasonal work in either New Zealand or Australia.

The principles of both BLAs are also essentially the same. They include equity of access and opportunity, transparency of process and decision making, accountability, development focus, and the mitigation of risk. A sixth principle relating to the demand-driven nature of employment features only in Australia's MOU.

Outcomes and Objectives

The BLAs record statements of outcomes for all parties involved. Outcome statements for the receiving countries are largely similar, although Australia's agreements provides greater elaboration of Pacific development outcomes (for example, enhanced development through new employment opportunities, increased remittance, options for skilling upgrading, the fostering of economic growth and regional integration, assistance to help Pacific island countries establish robust facilitative arrangements). New Zealand's BLA addresses both potential deal breakers (the risk of migrants' overstaying, the displacement of the domestic workforce, the suppression of wage growth) and deal makers (achievement of development objectives, the spurring of economic growth and

Table 7.2 Policy Objectives of Australia's Pacific Seasonal Worker Pilot Scheme and New Zealand's Recognised Seasonal Employer Scheme

Scheme	Objective
Pacific Seasonal Worker Pilot Scheme (Australia)	• Examine whether a seasonal worker program can help Australian employers (in the horticulture industry) fill seasonal labor shortages.
	• Examine whether a seasonal worker program can contribute to Australia's Pacific region economic development objectives, in particular by enabling workers to contribute to economic development in their home countries through remittances, employment experience, and training gained through participating in the PSWPS.
Recognised Seasonal Employer Scheme (New Zealand)	• Allow horticulture and viticulture businesses to supplement their workforces with foreign workers when labor demand exceeds the stock of available New Zealand workforce and employers have made reasonable attempts to train and recruit New Zealand citizens and residents.
	• Promote best practice in the horticulture and viticulture industries to support economic growth and productivity of the industry while ensuring that the employment conditions of both New Zealand and non–New Zealand workers are protected and supported.
	• Encourage economic development, regional integration, and good governance within the Pacific by allowing preferential access to workers who are citizens of eligible Pacific Island countries.
	• Ensure that workers recruited under this policy are adequately paid and financially benefit from their time in New Zealand.
	• Ensure outcomes that promote the integrity, credibility, and reputation of the New Zealand immigration and employment relations systems.

Note: PSWPS = Pacific Seasonal Worker Pilot Scheme.

regional integration). BLA outcome statements for both Australia and New Zealand refer to the achievement of policy objectives (table 7.2).

The main outcome statements in the BLAs are identical across all Pacific Island countries (table 7.3). Some degree add outcome statements that address specific concerns, however (table 7.4).

Critical Success Factors

Pacific Island countries' BLAs identify factors that are critical to the success of facilitative arrangements. These factors, which are broadly similar across countries, include the following:

- Establishment of effective relationships with employers in Australia and New Zealand
- Enjoyment of fair access to the schemes, fair treatment by employers, successful worker adjustment to conditions in receiving country, worker acquisition of income and skills, successful reintegration upon return, and prospects of employment in subsequent seasons
- Achievement of objectives of the seasonal employment schemes and adherence to the schemes' principles
- Timely sharing of information necessary for effective participation of Pacific Island countries in schemes

Table 7.3 Outcomes Statements of Australia's Pacific Seasonal Worker Pilot Scheme and New Zealand's Recognised Seasonal Employer Scheme

Scheme	Outcome statement
Pacific Seasonal Worker Pilot Scheme (Australia)	• Achieve the key objectives of the PSWPS.
	• Develop the Pacific Islands through new employment opportunities, increased remittance incomes, and options for upgrading the skills of seasonal workers.
	• Contribute to economic development in the Pacific by fostering economic growth and regional integration.
	• Create effective partnerships between Australia and participating Pacific Forum Island Countries (FICs) to support the PSWPS, including through provision by Australian agencies of assistance to specific FICs to help them establish robust and appropriate facilitative arrangements.
	• Match surplus labor resources in partner countries with labor market needs in Australia by providing a reliable and work-ready workforce for areas in rural Australia with a demonstrated shortage of suitable Australian workers.
	• Avoid unethical recruitment practices, application fraud, and overstaying by seasonal workers.
	• Avoid exploitation of seasonal workers or displacement of Australia's workforce.
Recognised Seasonal Employer (RSE) Scheme (New Zealand)	• Achieve the objectives of the RSE policy.
	• Avoid overstaying and exploitation of workers, displacement of New Zealand's workforce, and suppression of wage growth in the horticulture and viticulture industries.
	• During the first five years, secure at least 50 percent of the available places under the RSE policy from eligible FICs. To help achieve this goal specific FICs will be assisted in establishing facilitative arrangements.
	• Contribute to the development objectives of the Pacific by fostering economic growth and regional integration under the RSE policy.

Note: PSWPS = Pacific Seasonal Worker Pilot Scheme.

Table 7.4 Additional Outcome Statements for Papua New Guinea and the Solomon Islands

Country/agreement	Outcome statement
Papua New Guinea for Pacific Seasonal Worker Pilot Scheme (Australia)	• Cooperate effectively with Australia to maintain the integrity of the PSWPS and promote its sustainability.
	• Establish a reputation for providing a reliable labor force for Australia's horticulture industry and other industries as may be determined to fall under the scheme.
	• Comply with all relevant Australian and Papua New Guinea laws and rules of the PSWPS.
	• Secure a satisfactory portion of the seasonal worker demand available under the PSWPS.
Solomon Islands for Recognised Seasonal Employer (RSE) Scheme (New Zealand)	• Cooperate effectively with New Zealand to maintain the integrity of its arrangements to administer the RSE policy.
	• Secure a fair proportion of seasonal work opportunities under the RSE policy.
	• Provide adequate protection for workers and potential workers.
	• Ensure that the cost of transport does not act as a barrier for citizens of the Solomon Islands to access opportunities under the RSE.

Note: PSWPS = Pacific Seasonal Worker Pilot Scheme.

In addition, Australia's BLAs with specific Pacific Island countries specify that workers must not be charged with recruitment costs or subject to excessive up-front charges and that opportunities for employment in the PSWPS should be inclusive of all people, including women and underrepresented groups.

Facilitative Arrangements

All BLAs between Pacific Island countries and Australia and New Zealand include references to facilitative arrangements. Facilitative arrangements are the actions governments, in particular the governments of sending countries, take to inform and engage their populations about opportunities in schemes and the overall management and processes for selection and recruitment. BLAs recognize that facilitative arrangements may evolve. They specify that such arrangements be consistent with the objectives and principles agreed to in the BLAs. In particular, BLAs should ensure that workers are adequately prepared for work and life in receiving countries and understand immigration requirements (for example, passport, health, and character checks) and are not exploited or charged recruiting agency fees other than the expenses associated with visa applications (for example, medical and police checks). The BLA with Australia requires Pacific Island countries to cooperate to ensure the efficient and transparency of recruitment procedures.

Governments vary in their approaches to facilitating the selection, recruitment, and deployment of workers. A few Pacific Island countries operate wholly government-delivered recruitment services, which handle the entire process of selection, recruitment, and predeparture preparation. Others operate a mix of government, private agent, employer, and local representative recruitment.

A key area of support offered by receiving countries' administrations to sending-country administrations is information and training support for government officials to ensure they are knowledgeable about policies, context, and practical implementation of the schemes. Toward this end, New Zealand facilitates orientation secondments for officials from Pacific Island countries covering the role, functions, and connections with service delivery personnel of New Zealand's Department of Labor. It also sponsors regular gatherings of parties involved in the schemes to provide additional opportunities for strengthening Pacific Island country familiarity with receiving-country government personnel and employers and policy contexts.

Private agent recruitment in the Pacific Island countries is extremely limited and constrained by the very limited capacity of private sector agents in these countries. Vanuatu, the most successful labor-sending country, is the only country with legislation regulating private recruiting agents. Its handful of capacity-constrained licensed agents is responsible for only a small share of recruited workers. A further constraint to private agents is the reluctance of employers to pay agent fees, given that scheme rules preclude charging workers for recruitment services. Private recruiting agents can find themselves in direct competition with free government-facilitated recruitment and employers conducting recruitment directly through their local representatives and return team leaders. Some Pacific governments have opted not to support incorporating private agents as a means for delivering recruitment services, wishing instead to maintain tight government control, at least during the early years. After direct government recruitment services, the most common method of recruitment is through employers arriving in person or through their local representatives and return team leaders. Reliance on return team leaders has been growing for the New Zealand scheme. As a result, some Pacific Island governments have been largely excluded from involvement and no longer receive information about workers and local communities.

Several Pacific Island countries seek to achieve tacit objectives, such as equity, in their efforts to spread opportunities for employment to the poorest peoples or across national geographical districts, regions, and outer islands. Attempts by governments to achieve such public good are at times thwarted by private employers' preferences for recruiting in specific areas, such as cities, for convenience and cost, or specific villages from which workers have been recruited in the past. The nature of the work on farms, orchards, and vineyards is such that there are benefits to growers from drawing on workers who are already familiar with one another and have an established social order.

The delivery of predeparture orientation for workers is a top priority. Sending countries endeavor to ensure that all workers receive such orientation as a mandatory requirement. Predeparture seminars in some countries run for two weeks; in others, predeparture orientation lasts just a couple of hours. Orientation is presented by Pacific Island country officials, by employers and their local representatives or agents, or by a mix of these parties. Receiving countries actively support Pacific Island countries in this area, by producing and providing audiovisual material and training to local officials in the language of the sending countries.

Pacific Island countries invest significant time and effort compiling and collating the necessary documentation for workers' visa applications to Australia and New Zealand, in order to ensure that visas are expedited quickly enough to meet flight departure and employment commencement time frames and to ensure harmonious relationships with immigration authorities in Australia or New Zealand. Meeting minimal requirements for character (police clearance) and health (medical tests and x-ray) requirements requires collaboration with other government ministries and departments through service-level agreements or (more typically) the maintenance of positive relationships and communication.

Worker Welfare

Support and advocacy for workers while offshore is approached differently by different countries, with a few countries having established and funded one or two offshore liaison officers tasked with looking after the welfare of workers and addressing issues that arise. Such officers provide on-arrival briefings for workers to varying degrees. Employers are also expected to provide workers with appropriate induction on arrival.

Workers are entitled to join unions in Australia and New Zealand, but the cost of union membership must be met by workers. To date, workers have not elected to pay for the benefits of union representation, relying instead on home country liaison officers or the backing of their governments for advocacy and representation on issues of significance. Most capacity-constrained Pacific Island countries, however, do not have missions in receiving countries and rely substantively on the efforts of labor inspectors and other designated officers of labor and employment departments in Australia and New Zealand for the resolution of worker issues.

Under the BLAs, Pacific workers are not entitled to access social security benefits, such as health and education services. Employers are required to facilitate compulsory worker-funded health insurance.

Australia's pilot scheme engaged a major bank to provide workers with financial literacy training on arrival in Australia. On returning home, the workers do not receive any structured support for reintegrating or investing their repatriated savings. Repatriated or remitted income is spent largely on consumables, education, house building and improvements, and some small business or family enterprises.

Interventions

Table 7.5 sets out the institutional and policy responses and interventions for managing labor migration from the Pacific Islands to Australia and New Zealand. Interventions attributed to individual sending or receiving countries suggest that some degree of activity takes place; however, where sending countries are concerned, the interventions are not always systematized, often occurring on an ad hoc basis. Some interventions are undertaken by employers in receiving countries (for example, negotiating discounts on compulsory health insurance).

Immigration

BLAs outline the prerogative of receiving countries to make and enforce immigration decisions consistent with their own laws and policies. The risk of overstaying is the major immigration risk posed for receiving countries. A mix of incentives and sanctions are in place to manage this risk (table 7.6).

Marketing

BLAs require Pacific Island countries to actively market their workforces. To do so, many countries initially conducted road shows for potential employers. As the New Zealand market is a single-sector market (horticulture and viticulture), there is limited scope for growth, however; the return from investment in repeated road shows is thus marginal. Although some targeted marketing may still yield gains, competition among labor-sending countries centers mainly on the quality of workers, the efficiency of administration, and the overall reputation of the workforce.

Australia's scheme is new; marketing efforts are therefore warranted. However, Pacific Island countries lack the capacity to target and deliver such efforts and

Table 7.5 Policy and Institutional Interventions by Sending and Receiving Countries

Intervention	Receiving countries		Sending countries						
	Australia	New Zealand	Kiribati	Papua New Guinea	Samoa	Solomon Islands	Tonga	Tuvalu	Vanuatu
Rule setting and enforcement									
Prequalification of employers (for example, checking of legal and financial status and viability)	✓	✓							
Labor market test of employers' applications for scheme workers	✓	✓							
Universal entitlements for all workers: employment law monitoring and enforcement, accident compensation insurance, minimum terms and conditions for employment contracts	✓	✓							
Specific tax rates for scheme workers		✓							
Investigation of breaches of scheme rules by employers and apply sanctions on employers for noncompliance	✓	✓							
Investigation of workers' breaches of visa (overstaying) and repatriation of noncompliant workers	✓	✓			✓		✓		
Management and facilitation									
Domestic information and awareness campaign			✓		✓		✓	✓	✓
Marketing strategy, planning, relationships, and tools	✓	✓	✓	✓	✓	✓	✓	✓	✓
Licensing and regulation of private recruiters, including renewal of licenses			✓			✓			✓
Investigation of complaints and enforcement of sanctions on recruitment agencies			✓			✓			✓
Support for direct hiring by employers			✓		✓	✓	✓	✓	✓

table continues next page

Table 7.5 Policy and Institutional Interventions by Sending and Receiving Countries (continued)

Intervention	Receiving countries		Sending countries						
	Australia	New Zealand	Kiribati	Papua New Guinea	Samoa	Solomon Islands	Tonga	Tuvalu	Vanuatu
Government-delivered recruitment service			✓	✓	✓		✓	✓	✓
Leadership training for work group leaders					X		X	✓	✓
Orientation of Pacific Island country government officers[a]		✓							
Monitoring and compliance regime	✓	✓							
Ban on charging workers for fees other than expenses (visa, passports, health checks, and so forth)			✓	✓	✓	✓	✓	✓	✓
Government loan facility for worker expenses			✓	✓	✓	✓	✓		
Delivery of predeparture briefings			✓	✓	✓	✓	✓	✓	✓
Delivery of tools and support for Pacific Island countries' predeparture briefings	✓	✓							
Worker welfare									
Sending country liaison officers, consular support, and pastoral care					✓		✓	✓	✓
Resolution of worker complaints by sending country consul and liaison officers				✓	✓	✓	✓	✓	✓
Worker financed compulsory health insurance			✓		✓	✓	✓	✓	✓
On-arrival briefing (in receiving country)							✓	✓	
Debriefing of workers on return							✓		✓
Training in budgeting and financial literacy	✓						✓		

a. This activity may not be ongoing, as New Zealand's Department of Labor receives support for it through time-limited funding from New Zealand Aid Programme (NZAID).

Table 7.6 Incentives and Sanctions Used to Manage Risk of Overstaying by Temporary Workers from Pacific Island Countries Working in Australia and New Zealand

Country type	Policy and practice
Receiving	• Visas are valid for a maximum of seven months (up to nine months in New Zealand for Kiribati and Tuvalu, to equalize higher cost of travel).
	• Standard requirement for return air travel is relaxed (one-way ticket acceptable).
	• Visa eligibility requirements pertain. For example, workers are not permitted to bring their families with them, visa conditions tie workers to specific employers, and visa holders are not eligible for any other type of visa once they enter New Zealand. Visa may be granted in subsequent seasons if worker receives an invitation to return.
	• Character and police record checks are required.
	• Medical checks including chest x-rays are required and must be updated regularly for return workers.
	• Shared employment arrangements are permitted in order to mitigate financial risk of "short-hours" or premature return home by workers.
	• Employers are fined for workers who must be repatriated (because of overstaying, for example).
	• Visa-processing branches in sending countries liaise with sending-country administrations to ensure that visa applications are known to the lead department in the sending country. Sanctions are imposed on employers whose agents are found to be involved in noncompliant or corrupt practices (such as charging workers recruitment fees).
Sending	• Authorities may seek additional character checks through feedback from village leaders, elders, and district officers.
	• Additional screening checks may be used to discern motivation for seeking overseas work.
	• Village communities may be involved in selection and predeparture processes to leverage traditional authority in order to ensure that workers behave and comply with rules, including visa compliance.
	• Sending country liaison officers (for sending countries that have installed them) in receiving countries are tasked with ensuring the return of all workers at the end of their assignments or the locating overstaying workers and facilitating their return.
	• Some countries level their own sanctions, such as denying the families of overstaying workers the opportunity to participate in the schemes.

sustain ongoing marketing relationships. Information failure on how to identify and connect with potential employers is a key constraint. For most potential employers, the cost of travel within Australia to conduct marketing activities is prohibitive. The Australian government brings Pacific Island country representatives and existing and potential employers together through its regular conference. It also facilitates tours to employer locations.

A (not publicly available) survey of New Zealand employers revealed that the efficiency of administrations and the quality of workers delivered has a strong bearing on employer experience and recruitment preferences. In the early stages of each scheme, however, direct marketing is critical to establishing and maintaining industry linkages. The governments of Australia and New Zealand have assisted Pacific Island countries with marketing efforts. New Zealand continues to facilitate trips by Pacific Island government officials to New Zealand, where it connects them with current and potential employers. It works intensively with countries considered to be disadvantaged by long distance and little organizational capacity (for example, Kiribati and Tuvalu) to increase the number of workers hired under the scheme.

Australia also connects employers with workers. However, the pilot nature of Australia's scheme means that more deliberate and direct brokering of connections between Pacific Island countries and employers occurs.

Institutional Capacity

Responsible ministries in the Pacific Island countries must have capable managers and staff, strong management practices, and effective operational processes, in order to manage labor migration over time. Institutional capacity is key to sustaining market share or scaling operations up and down in meeting the requirements of changing opportunities for supplying labor.

Lessons on the Development Benefits of Labor Migration

Pacific Islands are small, with few avenues for foreign exchange earnings. The World Bank evaluation of development impacts for both the Australian PSWPS pilot (2011) and the New Zealand RSE (2010) schemes found several positive outcomes (McKenzie and Gibson 2010). Table 7.7 summarizes some of the gains and significant impacts for Kiribati, Tonga, and Vanuatu.

The evaluations identify a range of largely positive outcomes for households and communities in Tonga and Vanuatu:

- Per capita incomes of participating households were more than 30 percent higher than incomes of the control group (households with similar characteristics as participating households but which did not participate in the scheme). Household expenditure per capita was also higher (9–10 percent for Tonga and about 28 percent for Vanuatu).
- Rates of home improvement and purchases of durable assets were significantly higher in RSE households than in comparable non–RSE households.

Table 7.7 Impacts of Bilateral Labor Agreements between Australia and New Zealand and Three Pacific Island Countries, 2007–10

Item	Kiribati	Tonga	Vanuatu
Pacific Seasonal Worker Pilot Scheme (Australia)			
Net income gain (A$ thousands)	28.6	343.2	26.0
Percent of aid from the Australian Agency for International Development (AusAid)	0.25	2	0.25
Percent of export earnings	0.3	3.7	0.1
Recognised Seasonal Employer Program (New Zealand)			
Net income gain ($NZ thousands)	189.2	4,336.2	7,898.0
Percent of aid from the New Zealand Aid Programme (NZAID)	4	40	50
Percent of export earnings	2	44	20

Source: Gibson and McKenzie 2011.

- Participating households were more likely to have a bank account, probably reflecting more formal savings.
- RSE households did not make significant business investments.
- On average, migrants from Tonga and Vanuatu contributed $80–$130 per person to community use over the two-year period.
- A significant proportion of Tongan RSE households, non–RSE households, and community leaders reported improved community life and increased job opportunities. Vanuatu households also reported improvement, but to a lesser degree.
- Respondents expressed concerns over family separation, the reduction in labor available for community work, and the impact of alcohol consumption while on the job in New Zealand.
- A positive impact on child education was reported in Tonga: high school participation rates increased 10–14 percentage points. RSE households had higher school attendance rates than non–RSE households, which had higher attendance at the baseline survey. No significant impact on school attendance was reported in Vanuatu.
- In Vanuatu (but not Tonga), a significant reduction in dietary diversity was found among RSE participants.
- No negative health impact was found in RSE households in Tonga. In Vanuatu, the data indicated some negative impact on health.
- There was no significant difference in human capital formation between RSE households and non–RSE households in either country.

The experience of the BLAs between Pacific Islands and Australia and New Zealand provides important guidance for future work. First, analytical work was important in creating create awareness and informing policy makers, stakeholders, and the public about the impacts of facilitating temporary labor mobility. For example, the World Bank (2006) report *At Home and Away* presented the empirical and analytical underpinnings of the claims made about the gains from labor mobility in the Pacific by analyzing household-level data on the impact of remittances on poverty, education, and health. The report proposed a scheme for temporary mobility of labor in horticulture through a case study of the sector in Australia. It also provided some early guidance on how such a scheme could be designed to yield positive outcomes for both sides.

Second, permanent and open dialogue with stakeholders promoted ownership. As a result of frequent and ongoing dialogue with multiple stakeholders throughout the production of *At Home and Away*, the report was well received in Australia, New Zealand, and the Pacific Island countries. It aligned well with the evolution of the policy debate in New Zealand, where the government signaled its readiness to open the horticulture sector to Pacific Islanders starting in May 2007.

Third, initiative was necessary to seize the momentum. To do so, the World Bank initiated a small pilot project between New Zealand and Vanuatu that helped test the potential of a broader arrangement. The pilot tested policy settings so that workable arrangements could be found and scaled up—and disillusionment prevented. Around the world, schemes for the temporary movement of people, including schemes between New Zealand and the Pacific, had resulted in outcomes that left receiving countries wary and sending countries unsatisfied with the development results. If this were to happen again in the Pacific, a rare opportunity for increasing labor market access would have been missed. The pilot helped policy makers understand the mechanisms that resulted in poor outcomes and design and to avoid them.

The pilot helped policy makers identify and avoid design mechanisms that could yield poor outcomes. Experimentation during the pilot allowed the team to:

- Test specific policy settings without preempting policy announcements or raising expectations of beneficiaries in a way that made sound design features emerge, from worker selection to preparation, job matching, and cost-sharing.
- Identify winners and losers and hence public goods, such as training and support services for migrants, which were needed to instill confidence in the new mechanisms.
- Solicit the support of nonstate actors—trade unions, community leaders, banks, educational institutions—in providing selected services in sending and receiving countries.
- Develop a close working relationship with the media, which allowed best practices to be showcased and built wide public support for the program by showcasing the human development potential of such initiatives.

Evidence-based ex post analysis was also critical. The Bank undertook a formal monitoring and evaluation exercise of some of these schemes, gathering data on participants and control groups. Over time, it created a rich panel data, which allowed robust econometric estimates of the development benefits of such programs to be made. These econometric findings also helped fine-tune the schemes so they could meet their commercial and development goals.

Today, the RSE is described as a best practice program. Vanuatu has benefited from its early involving in the program: it is the largest beneficiary in terms of workers placed in New Zealand (more than 8,500 in four years. Their per capital incomes rose more than 30 percent, and their remittances represent about 20 percent of Vanuatu's exports and nearly 50 percent of New Zealand's aid to Vanuatu.

Conclusion

Largely standardized BLAs between Pacific Island countries and Australia and New Zealand achieve a win-win scenario for all participants, because they are based on amicable regional relationships, practical hands-on problem-solving at all levels, respectful historical ties, adequate frameworks for protections and accountability, and a balanced mix of incentives. This mix of incentives enables employers to recruit a substantial proportion of their trained workers for sufficient durations year after year, and it allows workers to raise their incomes and accumulate savings.

Demand-driven BLAs circumvent the problems that stem from the most favored nation principle and the reciprocity rigidities of legally binding trade arrangements on services. Instead of raising fears of opening up labor markets through the liberalization of trade in services, management of labor mobility through BLAs encourages both sending and receiving countries to mitigate risk and enhance benefits. BLAs can provide temporary access to employment in labor-scarce economies for workers from labor-abundant economies without offering them the rights of citizenship or guaranteeing a set number of job opportunities. They also provide flexibility for tailoring understandings within the legislative and policy parameters of receiving-country schemes.

Success depends to a large extent on a set of institutional and policy responses and interventions for managing labor migration. Depending on the objectives, some interventions are the responsibility of the receiving countries and others the responsibility of employers in receiving countries. Sending countries are expected to enforce rules, to manage and facilitate the flows of workers, and safeguard worker welfare. Strengthening the capacity of the relevant authorities to perform these interventions is necessary.

A mix of facilitative recruitment arrangements has been developed to suit the capacity constraints of individual countries and the preferences of employers. Recruiting is handled by government ministries, private agents, and directly by employers through their local representatives and return team leaders. There is some inherent tension, yet to be addressed, between the preference of many employers to draw return and new workers from familiar sources and the public good objectives of sending countries to offer opportunities to the poorest communities or to spread opportunities evenly across the country. This tension can be addressed by sending countries accepting certain due diligence functions and employers respecting the public good objectives and associated information needs of the sending countries for screening and monitoring and evaluation purposes.

Breaches of BLA are likely to affect bilateral diplomatic relations, potentially leading to nullification of the BLA. To prevent this from happening, the Pacific Island countries have maintained amicable ongoing dialogue at government and industry levels to support continued market access and to address issues that emerge.

The case studies reviewed in this chapter reveal that it is indeed possible to design temporary labor schemes that yield win-win consequences for sending and receiving countries. The key is to begin by designing an incentive-compatible program that avoids the mistakes of previous schemes. When followed by hands-on implementation, along with capacity-building and monitoring assistance, a well-designed scheme can offer a real chance for the poor to participate in the benefits of globalization of international labor markets.

Note

1. The PWSPS is based on a memorandum of understanding (MOU). The RSE is based on an inter-agency understanding (IAU).

References

Australia Department of Education, Employment, and Workplace Relations. 2010.

Gibson J., and D. McKenzie. 2011. "Australia's Pacific Seasonal Worker Pilot Scheme: Development Impacts in the First Two Years." Working Paper in Economics 09/11, Department of Economics, University of Waikato, Hamilton, New Zealand.

McKenzie, D., and J. Gibson. 2010. *The Development Impact of a Best Practice Seasonal Worker Policy*. Impact Evaluation Series 48. Washington, DC: World Bank.

New Zealand Department of Labour. 2010. *Final Evaluation Report of the Recognised Seasonal Employer Policy (2007–2009)*. Wellington, New Zealand: Evalue Research and New Zealand Department of Labour. http://dol.govt.nz/publications/research/rse-evaluation-final-report/rse-final-evaluation.pdf.

World Bank. 2006. *At Home and Away: Enhancing Employment Opportunities for Pacific Islanders*. Washington, DC: World Bank. http://siteresources.worldbank.org/INTPACIFICISLANDS/Resources/Executive-Summary-Labour-Mobility-Report.pdf.

CHAPTER 8

Bilateral Labor Agreements: Experience from the Caribbean

Yolanda Strachan

This chapter reviews three bilateral labor agreements (BLAs) and temporary worker programs in Caribbean countries by looking at their scope, objectives, modalities for implementation, and development impact. It examines the demand for workers and trends in flows. It concludes by providing recommendations and distilling lessons that can inform the design of similar labor programs in developing countries.

Caribbean Economies and Trade in Services

The Caribbean region comprises countries of different sizes, levels of income, and economic development. Guyana and Trinidad and Tobago are resource-wealthy, commodity-based economies; Barbados and the countries of the Eastern Caribbean are largely service-driven economies. Most countries in the region have made progress in human development, with indicators on education, life expectancy, and poverty steadily improving in all countries. Per capita incomes range from less than $1,000 in Haiti to $4,000 in Dominica and $21,390 in the Bahamas. There are also large differences in population size.

Countries in the Caribbean Community (CARICOM) are small open economies that rely heavily on international trade.[1] Economic growth has historically been driven by exports of agricultural and natural resource products. In recent years, services exports have also become important.

The region's main trading partners are the United States and the European Union (EU). With the erosion of preferential access to North American and European markets, services trade has become a key driver of growth and development in the Caribbean. On average, services trade accounts for 43 percent of national income, making it the most important component of economic activity in CARICOM countries. Generally, the smaller the economy, the more important is services trade. In Antigua, for example, the share is as high as 67 percent, whereas in Trinidad and Tobago it accounts for only 6 percent (World Bank 2011).

Services exports are dominated by tourism, which is a major source of foreign exchange. International financial services are also a rapidly growing area.

CARICOM Regional Initiatives on Services and the Free Movement of Labor

Services trade is an important aspect of CARICOM's regional integration. The CARICOM Single Market and Economy (CSME) was established in 1989, with the intention of deepening the integration process and accelerating economic growth through the free movement of goods, services, capital, and labor. The CARICOM Treaty provides for services trade in all four modes of supply.

The free movement of skilled workers is a central element of the CSME. One of the main pillars of the single market is to liberalize the movement of labor and abolish the need for work permits for nationals from CSME countries. To date, 11 countries have passed legislation and set up the regulatory and administrative arrangements needed to foster the free movement of university graduates.

CARICOM has taken a gradual approach by liberalizing movement for certain categories of workers. All members have enacted legislation to permit the free movement of university graduates, media workers, athletes, artists and musicians, and certain categories of high-level staff who provide a service or establish a business. Members are discussing whether to expand these categories to include workers in the hospitality industry, artisans, domestic workers, nurses, and teachers who are not university graduates. To facilitate both intraregional and international travel, 10 member states use the CARICOM passport.[2]

Movement of Natural Persons as Area Comparative Advantage

The Caribbean has been exporting both skilled and unskilled workers abroad for more than a century. In the 1880s, a wave of Caribbean laborers (many from Jamaica, Barbados, Martinique, and Guadeloupe) were recruited to work on the Panama Canal. In the 1940s, the United States looked to Caribbean countries as a source of migrant farm laborers. Hundreds of thousands of young Americans were drafted to fight in World War II, creating a critical farm labor shortage. Caribbean farm workers were recruited to grow and harvest crops (Nassau Guardian Online 2005).

The Caribbean is endowed with a well-educated, English-speaking population with strong cultural and historical ties to Canada, the United States, and the United Kingdom. Jamaica and Trinidad and Tobago are already strong exporters of qualified labor, particularly teachers, nurses, and other health professionals. Temporary movement is seen as a mechanism for creating jobs and opportunities abroad, managing domestic unemployment, enhancing professional skills and experience, and encouraging skills transfer to local industries.

Temporary Movement through the Economic Partnership Agreement

The region was able to negotiate market access for certain categories of temporary workers in the European market through the Economic Partnership Agreement (EPA), concluded in December 2007. The agreement provides for the temporary movement for special categories of providers of services, including contractual service suppliers and independent professionals, subject to specific conditions.[3] Contractual service suppliers in 29 sectors can enter the European Union to supply services for up to six months in a calendar year once they get a contract. In addition, the European Union has liberalized 11 sectors for temporary entry by independent professionals and self-employed persons. Although there are some conditions (economic needs tests) in some states, there are no quotas on the number of service suppliers that can enter the EU market (CRNM 2008).

Trends in Temporary Migration, 1998–2011

Demand for foreign labor in Canada and the United States increased strongly over the past decade. North America experienced occupational labor shortages in fast-growing sectors such as construction, agriculture, education, and health care. Although the crisis that began in 2008 reduced demand for foreign workers in some cases, this long-term trend is expected to continue. In the United States, registered nurses, personal care aides, medical secretaries, home health aides, food services workers, and construction laborers are projected to be among the fastest-growing occupations between 2010 and 2020, according to the U.S. Bureau of Labor Statistics (2012). In its 10-year outlook for the Canadian labor market, Canada's Human Resources and Social Development Agency forecasts labor shortages in several occupations at the national level (HRSDC 2006). Canada's aging population and increased government funding for health care has led to a strong increase in demand for health-related services. Labor market pressures are particularly acute for physicians, nurses, pharmacists, medical technologists, and technicians. Shortages are also projected in management occupations, residential construction, information technology, and oil and gas.

Canada and the United States recognize that temporary workers can be an effective way to cope with occupational labor shortages. Both countries have therefore instituted programs to meet temporary labor needs. The Canadian government launched a program to help Canadians hire foreign workers to provide live-in care for children, the elderly, and people with disabilities. In 2011, more than 15,000 foreign worker positions were available for live-in caregivers in Canada (HRSDC 2012). Canadian provinces announced pilot programs to import temporary workers to address shortages in carpentry, machine operations, hotel and hospitality, nursing, dentistry, and pharmacy. In 2011, 190,842 temporary foreign workers entered the country (figure 8.1).

The United States has designated a special visa category (H-visa) to allow firms to employ foreign workers in specialty and seasonal jobs when U.S. workers are not available to fill them (table 8.1). The H1-B visa is an employer-sponsored category available for specialty workers that is open to all countries. It is the most utilized category for college-educated workers, particularly professionals. H-1C is a more specialized category, introduced in 1999 specifically to address the shortage of nurses in the United States. For semi-skilled labor, the H-2A program allows employers to recruit foreign workers for temporary agricultural jobs; the H-2B program is available for nonagricultural temporary workers. In all cases, the

Figure 8.1 Number of Positions for Temporary Foreign Workers in Canada, 2006–11

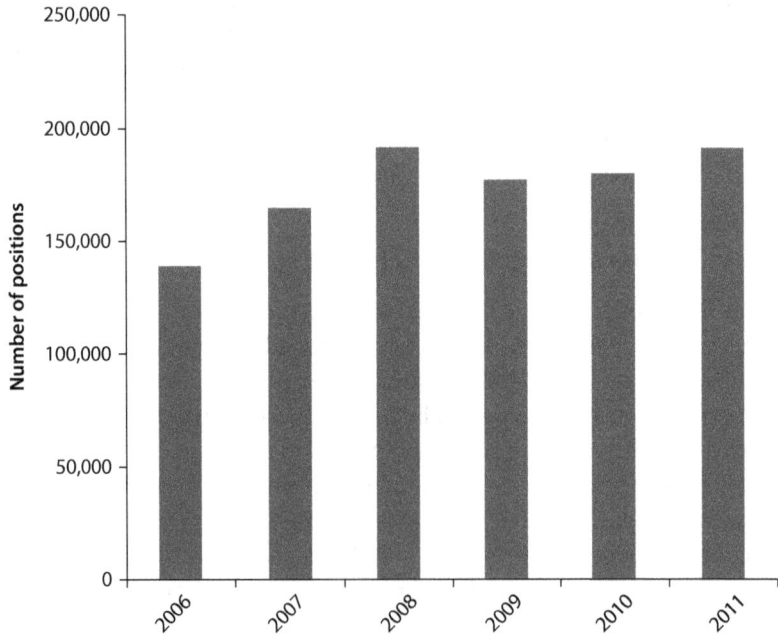

Source: Citizenship and Immigration Canada 2012.

Table 8.1 Main U.S. Visa Categories for Temporary Workers

Visa class	Occupation	Required qualifications	Numerical limits	Maximum duration of stay
H1-B	Specialty occupations	Bachelor's degree	65,000; first 20,000 petitions filed on behalf of beneficiaries with a U.S. master's degree or higher are exempt from the cap	The duration of stay is three years, extendable to six years
H1-C	Registered nurses working in a shortage area (expired December 2009)	U.S. nursing license and international nursing qualification	Only 500 H-1C visas are issued each year; limits by state apply	Three years
H2-A	Temporary agricultural workers	None	None	One year renewable, three years maximum
H2-B	Temporary nonagricultural workers	None	Cap set by Congress is 66,000 per year	One year renewable, three years maximum

Source: Based on information from the U.S. Department of Homeland Security website (https:// www.dhs.gov).

employer must demonstrate that there are not sufficient U.S. workers able, willing, qualified, and available to do the temporary work. H-2 visas are not subject to nationality quotas, but there is a list of (25) designated countries that are eligible to participate. All H-category visas are subject to quantitative limits, and demand invariably exceeds supply.

Between 1998 and 2011, the Caribbean supplied about 400,000 temporary workers to the United States and more than 123,000 to Canada (figure 8.2). Jamaicans accounted for more than 50 percent of all temporary Caribbean workers in the United States. The Dominican Republic and Trinidad and Tobago are also significant source countries (U.S. Department of Homeland Security 2011). For flows to Canada, Jamaica accounted for 68 percent of temporary workers, followed by Trinidad and Tobago and Barbados. Jamaica provides 5 percent of the total foreign labor force in Canada. About 1 percent of the Jamaican labor force is employed in temporary overseas programs in the United States and Canada every year.

The flow of temporary workers from the Caribbean to the United States increased steadily from 1998 to 2007 (figure 8.3). It declined rapidly in 2008,

Figure 8.2 Share of Caribbean Temporary Workers in the United States and Canada, by Source Country, 1999–2011

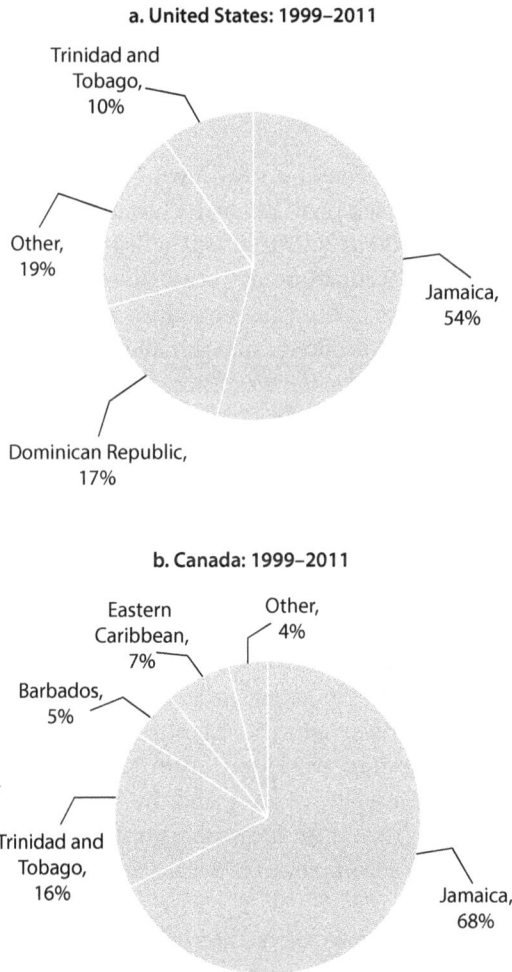

a. United States: 1999–2011

Trinidad and Tobago, 10%

Other, 19%

Jamaica, 54%

Dominican Republic, 17%

b. Canada: 1999–2011

Eastern Caribbean, 7%

Other, 4%

Barbados, 5%

Trinidad and Tobago, 16%

Jamaica, 68%

Sources: Citizenship and Immigration Canada 2012; U.S. Department of Homeland Security 2011.

Figure 8.3 Number of Temporary Workers from Caribbean Countries in the United States, 1998–2011

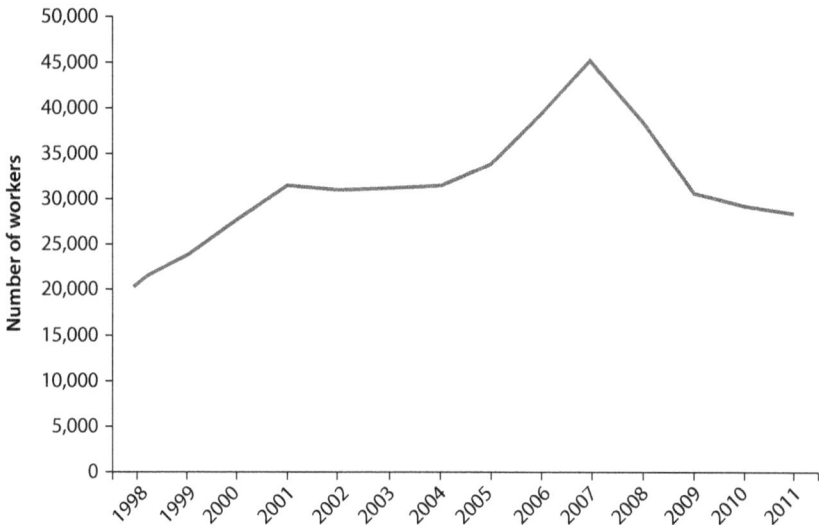

Source: U.S. Department of Homeland Security 2011.

with the onset of the global economic slowdown. The adverse effects of the crisis have been strongest for seasonal nonagricultural workers, whose numbers declined from almost 17,000 in 2007 to 5,000 in 2011, a reduction of 70 percent. Employment in specialty occupations and seasonal agricultural work has proven more resilient to downturns in the U.S. economy.

The downturn in the U.S. economy substantially reduced demand for workers in the hospitality sector. The decline was compounded by changes in the allocation of H2-B visas in 2009. Every year, the United States issues 66,000 H2-B visas worldwide. In the past, returning workers who already held visas were exempt from the 66,000 cap. However, in 2009, the Save Our Seasonal and Small Business Act was not amended to allow for this exemption, as it had been in previous years.

The composition of temporary workers from the Caribbean has shifted over time (figure 8.4). In 1998, 20 percent of temporary workers were seasonal agricultural workers, 17 percent were nonagricultural, 12 percent were in specialty occupations, and 51 percent were in other categories. In 2007, the peak period for labor inflows, nonagricultural seasonal workers accounted for 38 percent of the temporary workforce from the Caribbean. The share of specialty workers was relatively constant, and the share of agricultural workers declined to 9 percent. The shift in workers toward the hospitality sector reflected the Caribbean's comparative advantage in providing tourism and hospitality services.

The number of Caribbean workers entering Canada also increased steadily from 1999 to 2008, slowing thereafter in response to the global financial crisis (table 8.2). Despite the crisis, the number of Jamaican temporary

Figure 8.4 Composition of Temporary Workers from Caribbean Countries in the United States, by Type of Visa, 1998–2011

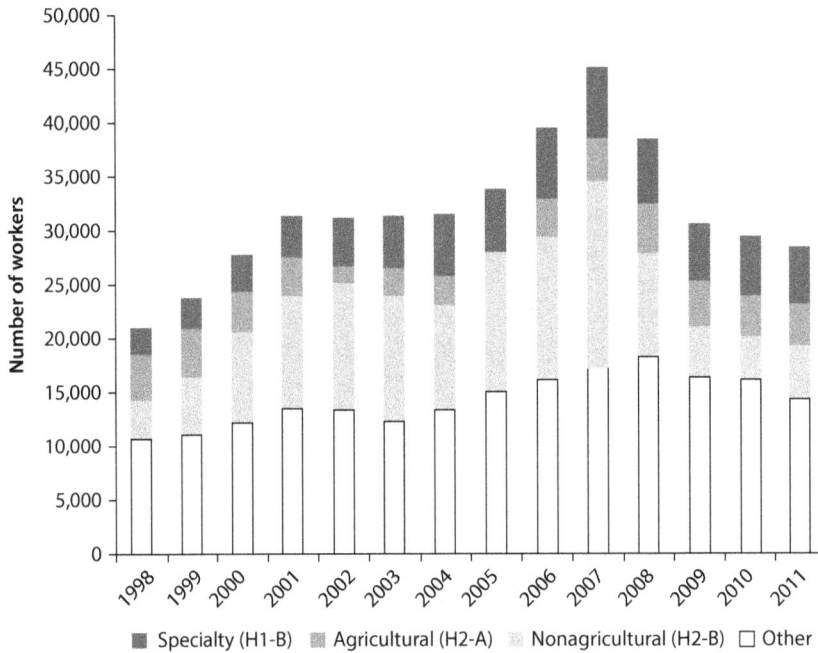

Source: U.S. Department of Homeland Security 2011.

Table 8.2 Number of Temporary Caribbean Workers Entering Canada, by Country, 1999–2011

Country	1999	2000	2001	2002	2003	2004	2005	2006	2007	2008	2009	2010	2011
Jamaica	5,608	5,508	5,959	5,637	5,981	6,008	6,223	6,531	6,745	7,320	7,027	7,546	7,453
Trinidad and Tobago	1,714	1,873	1,875	1,733	1,684	1,719	1,664	1,580	1,407	1,356	1,197	1,179	1,019
Barbados	629	669	702	645	548	582	535	497	473	389	288	286	293
St. Vincent and the Grenadines	220	258	244	215	208	206	246	285	273	299	231	241	243
St. Lucia	115	115	135	99	133	135	179	193	268	295	222	172	179
Dominica	96	116	125	102	111	130	176	102	104	109	96	111	87
Dominican Republic	47	52	50	40	78	29	87	65	60	89	69	111	85
Grenada	123	118	93	83	70	77	90	79	98	89	86	51	79
Cuba	241	290	191	171	95	92	121	104	127	94	80	69	71
Bahamas, The	10	14	9	6	7	7	5	9	10	22	25	21	41
Haiti	89	101	102	105	64	98	103	80	78	49	36	32	30
Guyana	114	143	145	67	45	64	49	29	60	78	37	43	29
St. Kitts and Nevis	29	24	31	28	20	19	33	27	31	29	25	23	24
Total	9,035	9,281	9,661	8,931	9,044	9,166	9,511	9,581	9,734	10,218	9,419	9,885	9,633

Source: Citizenship and Immigration Canada 2012.

Let Workers Move • http://dx.doi.org/10.1596/978-0-8213-9915-6

workers entering Canada continued to grow steadily; there was a gradual decline in participation from most other countries in the region, however.

BLAs in the Caribbean

BLAs and temporary worker programs are two mechanisms for managing labor exports and regulating labor flows into high-income countries. Such programs are frequently established through a memorandum of understanding (MOU) that sets forth the scope, objectives, responsibilities, and modalities of the arrangements agreed upon by the two parties.

An MOU is less official than a treaty or trade agreement, which normally has to be signed by a high-level representative of a government and ratified by a country's legislative body. The legal status of the MOU is defined as an "intergovernmental administrative arrangement." Unlike international treaties, MOUs are not legally binding, and their provisions can be amended at any time with the approval of both parties (Verma 2003). MOUs have emerged as simpler and more flexible mechanism for cooperation.

MOUs for labor mobility are usually between two governments, but there are cases in the Caribbean where they have been signed in partnership with academic institutions, provincial governments, and private sector companies. This section reviews three temporary worker programs being implemented in Caribbean countries: the Seasonal Agricultural Worker Program, the Jamaican Hospitality Worker Program, and the Licensed Practical Nursing Program.

Canada-Commonwealth Caribbean Seasonal Agricultural Workers Program

The Canada-Commonwealth Caribbean Seasonal Agricultural Workers Program (CSAWP) is one of the longest-running temporary worker programs in the Caribbean. It is a government-to-government program of managed migration. The program has been expanded over its 41-year history to include workers from Jamaica (1966), Barbados (1967), Trinidad and Tobago (1967), Mexico (1974), the Eastern Caribbean (1976), and Guatemala (2003).[4] Each participating country has a formal agreement through an MOU with the Canadian government.[5]

The program is a needs-based system that operates on a Canadians first principle: overseas workers are recruited only when qualified Canadian workers are not available. Employers are required to demonstrate that they are unable to recruit Canadian workers before they receive approval to hire workers from abroad.

Jamaican participation in the program increased from 1999 to 2006 and remained steady through the global crisis in 2007 and 2008 (figure 8.5). About 80 percent of CSAWP migrants work on fruit, vegetable, and tobacco farms. Other areas of agricultural production include apiary, ginseng, nurseries, greenhouse vegetables, and sod. Participants are between the ages of 18 and 45 and are overwhelmingly male. The minimum stay is six weeks, although workers are permitted to remain in Canada for up to eight months. The program operates in

Figure 8.5 Number of Jamaican Workers Participating in the Seasonal Agricultural Workers Program, 1999–2011

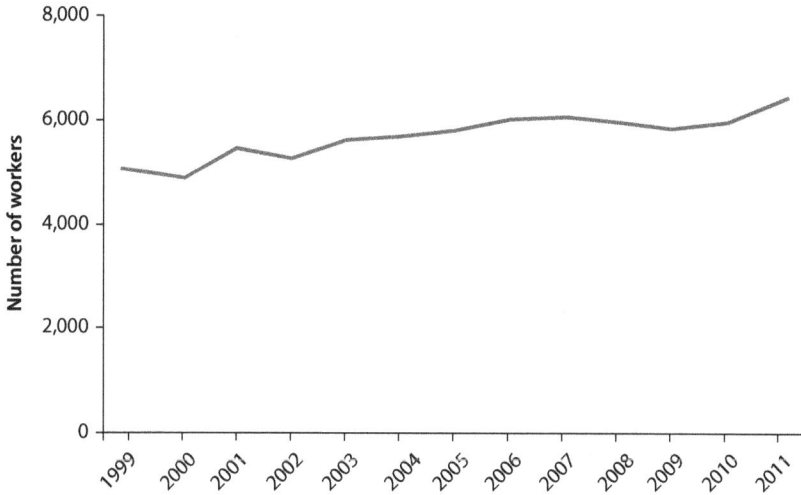

Source: Jamaican Ministry of Labour and Social Security n.d.

nine provinces (Prince Edward Island, Nova Scotia, New Brunswick, Quebec, Ontario, Manitoba, Saskatchewan, Alberta, and British Columbia).

Scope and Objectives

The policy objectives of and rationale for the program are set forth in the MOUs between Canada and the labor-supplying countries. The objective of the program is to alleviate seasonal labor shortages during peak agricultural production periods in Canada while at the same time allowing Caribbean countries to export surplus labor and provide short-term employment opportunities. The MOUs clearly state that the program should be of "mutual benefit to both parties." It also explicity indicates that that the program is dependent on Canada's determination of the need for seasonal agricultural workers to satisfy the requirements of the Canadian agricultural market.

The MOU establishes three guiding principles for the administration of the CSAWP. First, it states that workers should be employed only in the agricultural sector during periods determined by Canada and when Canadian workers are not available for employment. Second, it states that workers under the program are employed at a higher cost than domestic workers, because employers must cover the cost of accommodation and travel. This provision makes it more cost-effective to hire Canadian workers. Third, it states that workers are to receive fair and equitable treatment. The operational guidelines attached to the MOU explain how the program is to be administered, identifying the responsibilities of the parties with respect to monitoring the movement of workers and preventing exploitation.

Roles and Responsibilities of Sending and Receiving Countries

The strength of the CSAWP is its well-defined formal structure, which clearly designates roles and responsibilities. The program is overseen by two Canadian institutions, Citizen and Immigration Canada and the Human Resources and Skills Development Canada (HRSDC). These agencies work in partnership with nonprofit, federally incorporated agencies, which facilitate and coordinate the processing of requests for foreign seasonal agricultural workers. The government regulates private actors and any role they may play in the CSAWP. It has essentially privatized the administration of the CSAWP by delegating certain duties to the Foreign Agricultural Resource Management Services (FARMS) in Ontario, a nonprofit organization charged with transmitting and processing employment orders accepted by human resource centers.

The operational guidelines of the MOU delineate the duties and responsibilities of Canada and the sending counties. Canada is responsible for advising the sending countries on the expected demand for workers during the growing season and ensuring adequate administration of the program and coordination with growers. Caribbean countries are responsible for selecting and maintaining a pool of qualified workers available for deployment, working with Canadian consular offices to facilitate immigration clearances, and appointing liaison officers to oversee welfare and worker compensation issues in Canada.

Recruitment, Entry, and Return

In order to request CSAWP workers, Canadian employers are required to submit an application that clearly demonstrates their inability to find qualified Canadian workers. The application also provides details on the number of workers needed, their expected tasks, and the expected time frame for employment. On the basis of this application, the HRSDC issues a labor market opinion that assesses the likely impact the seasonal foreign worker would have on Canada's labor market. Approved applications are then processed by a coordinating nonprofit agency such as FARMS. Employers can request workers from a specific country; they can even request specific workers by name. Once approved, their requests are sent to the government of the supplying countries chosen by the employer.

In the Caribbean, the process of recruiting and sending workers is coordinated by the ministry of labor in each participating country. Under the agreement, source countries are responsible for assisting in the recruitment, selection, and documentation of bona fide agricultural workers; maintaining a pool of workers who are ready to depart to Canada when requests are received from Canadian employers; and appointing agents at their embassies or consulates in Canada to help the Canadian authorities administer the program and to serve as a contact point for workers.

Caribbean governments have put mechanisms in place to ensure the quality and welfare of workers selected for the program. Workers are recruited by the ministry of labor in the each country, which often works locally with recruiting agencies and training institutes to provide a qualified pool of workers. In Jamaica, the Ministry of Labour and Social Security (henceforth "Ministry of Labour") administers the Canadian seasonal agricultural program. Workers must meet certain basic requirements to apply to the program. They must be between the ages of 21 and 45, have two years of relevant experience, and have no criminal record. Workers can submit applications or be recommended by their member of Parliament. A selection team visits parishes and conducts interviews. Successful candidates undergo a screening process that involves fingerprinting, background checks, and medical clearance. Selected workers are issued travel documents; they receive their work permits upon arrival in Canada.

Foreign agricultural workers in Canada receive the same pay and working conditions as Canadian agricultural workers. Responsibility for ensuring these working conditions rests with the employer, but the Canadian and Caribbean authorities provide regular oversight. Employers are required to provide free housing and ensure that foreign workers are covered by workers' compensation as well as private or provincial and territorial health insurance while in Canada. Payroll taxes and insurance are deducted from workers' pay. Workers and employers share the cost of airfare to and from Canada as well as immigration cost recovery fees in some cases. All workers and employers are required to sign a contract outlining wages, duties, and conditions related to the transportation, accommodation, health, and occupational safety of the foreign worker. Some flexibility allows employers to transfer workers from one farm to another with the worker's consent and prior written approval from HRSDC–Service Canada and the foreign government representative in Canada.

The program has functioned successfully. The vast majority of workers return to their home country as expected. To encourage workers to do so, the sending country government sponsors a compulsory saving scheme. As part of the worker agreement, 25 percent of gross earnings are withheld in savings accounts that can be accessed only when the worker returns as agreed to his or her home country.

Development Benefits
The clear development benefits to Caribbean countries from the CSAWP are employment opportunities and increased remittances. The program provides a predictable source of seasonal employment for unskilled workers. Workers remit a large share of their income, thanks to the 25 percent compulsory savings scheme. In 2012 alone, the Canadian program contributed more than $16 million to the Jamaican economy (Jamaica Information Service 2013). Traditional seasonal agricultural work is mainly unskilled work, with limited potential for skills transfer. However, some high-technology subsectors, such as the greenhouse industry, are employing temporary workers. The industry uses hydroponics and natural gas heat to raise tomatoes and cucumbers, allowing some opportunity for the transfer of knowledge and skills.

For the Canadian economy, the benefits are substantial. Growers receive reliable and experienced agricultural workers. Local communities benefit from expanded employment opportunities for native workers (linked to the growth of agricultural industries staffed by reliable and skilled foreign workers). Foreign workers stimulate demand for local services and goods. They also help the Canadian agricultural industry remain globally competitive, generating exports and foreign exchange for the Canadian economy.

Canadian Licensed Practical Nurses Program for Jamaican Nurses

For decades, Caribbean countries have been losing human capital to a constant flow of outward migration to Canada, the United States, and the United Kingdom. A 2009 World Bank study estimates that the number of English-speaking CARICOM trained nurses working in these countries was roughly three times the number of nurses working in the English-speaking CARICOM (World Bank 2009). Among CARICOM–trained nurses, 750 were living in Canada, 4,750 in the United Kingdom, and 15,500 in the United States, according to the report.[6]

A managed approach to nurse migration seeks to balance the needs and labor demands of developed countries while allowing Caribbean countries to ensure the sustainability and quality of their domestic health and health education sectors. In 2005, Caribbean governments and the Commonwealth Secretariat began outlining a framework for a better approach to ensure managed and moderated migration. Within the region, a number of initiatives are taking shape, although there is no formal region-wide program managing the flow of nurses.

Scope and Objectives

The Licensed Practical Nurses (LPN) program is a partnership between the Jamaican Ministry of Labour and several stakeholders in the Canadian health care industry. The partnership was established in 2008 through a MOU signed by several parties, including the Jamaican Ministry of Labour, Marmicmon Business consulting (a consulting company that specializes in recruiting Canadian health care professionals from the Caribbean), the Canadian Centre for Nursing Studies, and a number of Canadian universities and training colleges. The objective of the program is to increase training and overseas employment opportunities for Jamaican nurses while alleviating the nursing shortage in Canada. The partnership is firmly anchored in the Canadian private sector, which conceptualized the program in response to the high demand for health care professionals in Canada.

This public-private partnership (PPP) operates with the participation of academic institutions, placement agencies, and the Jamaican government. The business model is essentially a work-study program in which Jamaican nurses are trained locally to meet Canadian standards and are subsequently recruited for overseas employment. In addition to nursing, the program covers live-in caregivers and early childhood educators. Training is provided in the Caribbean, with the support of tertiary institutions accredited and approved by Canadian educational institutions and the Jamaican Ministry of Education.

In 2009, the program had about 300 participants, 183 of which were expected to leave the program by the end of 2010. However, in 2011, after just two years of operation, the Jamaican Ministry of Labour suspended the program. The main reason for the suspension was that many trainees were unable to complete the clinical part of the practical nursing program in Canada, without completion of which they cannot work as certified nurses in Canada. Program partners were seeking to put in a place more effective arrangements for completion of clinical experience before enrollment and registration began for new cohorts. By May 2011, some three years after launching the program, most of the nurses trained to work in Canada were still in Jamaica. According to the Jamaican Ministry of Labour, 156 participants completed the academic and practicum requirements, but only 30 had departed for Canada (*Jamaica Gleaner* 2011).

Program Framework

The LPN program operated under the national framework of the Canadian Temporary Foreign Worker Program, which allows employers to hire foreign workers to meet immediate skills and labor shortages. Provisions were introduced in 2006 to allow employers in occupations under pressure to hire foreign workers more easily. Foreign workers who want to work in Canada must first obtain a job offer from a Canadian employer. They then apply to Citizenship and Immigration Canada for a permit to work temporarily in Canada.

As part of the partnership, Canadian colleges partnered with Jamaican community colleges to train nurses using the Canadian curriculum. Admission requirements for the LPN were similar to requirements at training centers in Canada. Upon completion of their studies, nurses would become certified to practice in Canada. In order to be accepted for overseas employment, students are required to maintain a 70 percent grade average, have no criminal record, and pay all educational fees.

Marmicmon was responsible for the placement of successful candidates. The company was expected to play the role of matchmaker and coordinator by working with both employers and graduates to facilitate labor placement. It was to assist employers with the filing of labor market opinions to facilitate the processing of direct hiring of Jamaican graduates. Through Marmicmon and the Jamaican Ministry of Labour, employers would have an opportunity to interview and select candidates two months before they complete their training. Marmicmon and the Jamaican government were responsible for facilitating employers' trips to the Caribbean.

The Jamaican Ministry of Labour played several important roles in the partnership. First, it provided public medical facilities with access to community colleges and Canadian affiliates for training purposes. Second, it coordinated with the Canadian immigration service by screening candidates in accordance with the requirements of the Canadian consular authorities in Jamaica, including medical and criminal background checks. The ministry also helped candidates submit their documents for the visa process. All fees for the processing of visas, background and medical checks, and other requirements are the responsibility of the candidate. Third, the Jamaican Liaison Service in Canada played a coordinating role and supports workers during their employment in Canada.

Box 8.1 Other Managed Migration Programs in the Caribbean

In 2008, Jamaica signed an MOU with Okanagan College in Canada, to launch a work-study program under which skilled and semiskilled Jamaican workers receive training and are placed in jobs in western Canada. The program helps Jamaican students earn Canadian credentials and supplies Canadian employers with much needed staff.

The government of St. Vincent and the Grenadines is establishing bilateral agreements to obtain compensation from health care provider institutions that recruit its nurses. At the time of hiring, U.S. partners will reimburse the government of St. Vincent and the Grenadines with training costs of about $17,000 for each Vincentian nurse employed in the United States. The funds will be reinvested by the government of St. Vincent and the Grenadines to enhance nurse training.

Source: Salmon and others 2007.

Through its training component, the program aims to overcome some of the licensing and mutual recognition barriers foreign nurses can face. Because graduates achieve Canadian certification, it is much easier to place them in accredited Canadian programs.

Without appropriate certification and mutual recognition agreements, barriers to foreign nurses can be significant. For example, foreign nurses who wish to practice in Canada must typically submit academic paperwork and pass the Canadian Registered Nurse Examination to demonstrate that their training meets Canadian standards. Nurses must be licensed by the body in the province in which they hope to work. In the United States, certification is required, with requirements for foreign nurses varying by state. In general, candidates must hold a registration or license in their home country and prove that their foreign education is comparable to that of a U.S.–educated nurse by completing a qualifying exam.

Other temporary worker programs have also been launched in the Caribbean. Box 8.1 describes some of them.

U.S.–Jamaica Hospitality Workers Program

Jamaica has pioneered a hospitality worker program that draws on its comparative advantage in the hospitality industry. The program matches qualified workers with employers, ensures that workers are properly trained, and provides affordable health insurance for workers' stay in the United States.

Jamaica has been a popular source of employees for the U.S. hospitality industry, with many workers returning to the same resorts year after year for decades. Jamaican workers have been in high demand by U.S. resorts because they are considered hard workers, speak English, and have experience in the hospitality sector. Employers of Jamaican hospitality workers are geographically dispersed, representing 22 states. They range from small New England bed and breakfasts to luxury hotels in the Rocky Mountains. Jamaican workers hold positions in food and beverage, housekeeping, and maintenance and grounds keeping.

Scope and Objectives

The hospitality workers program was established in 1989 by the government of Jamaica. It operates within the framework of the U.S. government's H-2B guest worker program. In contrast to the CSAWP, it is not based on a government-to-government MOU but operates under national labor admission program for temporary workers put in place by the U.S. government. Unlike an MOU, a national labor admission program can be revised unilaterally by the receiving country without the agreement of sending countries.

The objective of the program is to provide seasonal overseas employment for qualified Jamaican workers. The workers are allowed entry under the H-2B program to alleviate seasonal labor shortages and manage labor migration in a controlled manner.

The Jamaican government also runs a U.S. farm worker program, which operates within the framework of the H-2A agricultural worker program. It is administered under the same principles as the hospitality worker program. Under both programs, employers must show that there is a labor shortage and that the wages and working conditions will not undercut the job terms of U.S. citizens and immigrants who hold those jobs.

Roles and Responsibilities of Sending and Receiving Countries

The hospitality worker program provides a convenient option for U.S. employers to hire H-2B workers from Jamaica. Under the rules of the H-2B program, employers in the United States must first petition the Department of Labor to hire foreign workers. Once they document the need, employers work with a country of their choice to recruit workers. Visa issuance takes place through the State Department, but clearance must also be received from the Department of Homeland Security.

The Jamaican Ministry of Labour works with local recruiting agencies to ensure that there is a qualified pool of workers to meet employer needs. U.S. employers can also work directly with licensed or unlicensed recruiters or locate the workers themselves.

Thanks to the popularity of the program, a significant number of workers are recruited through unlicensed recruiters. The prevalence of unlicensed recruiters poses some risks to workers and employers, ranging from unreliable service to the possibility of fraud. It also undermines the coordinating function of the Ministry of Labour, as unlicensed workers work outside the official hospitality program. Licensed recruiters submit the number of workers needed and the categories to the Manpower Department in the ministry, who screen applicants.

The Ministry of Labour sets guidelines that selected workers are required to meet and facilitates training for workers where necessary. During the screening process, applications are assessed according to the experience requirements, and background checks are conducted. Workers for the H-2B program are required to have at least three years' experience; if they do not, the government trains them as servers, cooks, housekeeper, or front desk workers through the Human

Figure 8.6 Number of Jamaican Workers Participating in U.S. Hospitality Worker Program, 1999–2011

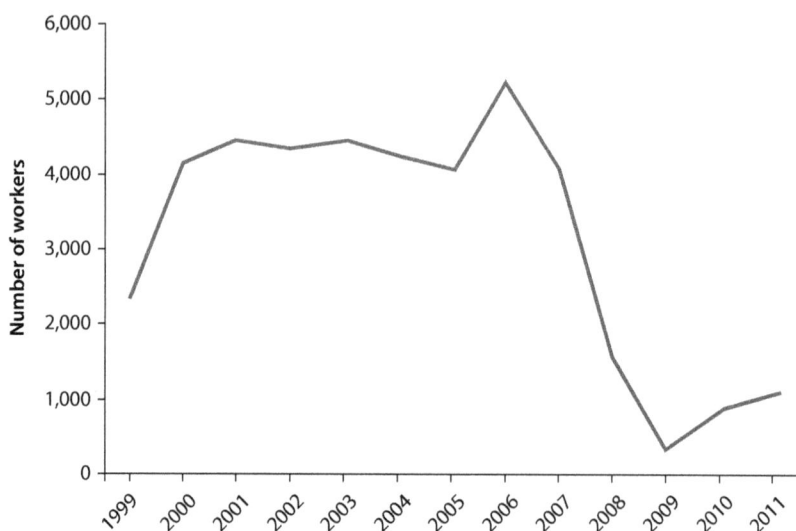

Source: Jamaican Ministry of Labor and Social Security n.d.

Employment and Resource Training (HEART) program.[7] Recruiters then select the workers they want to hire.

To facilitate and regulate the movement of workers, the Ministry of Labour maintains an office in Washington, D.C., that works with the U.S. government in placing temporary unskilled workers. The program provides an orientation for U.S. employers and an orientation for workers when they arrive in the United States. Its liaison officers visit each worker at least four times during the 10-month program.

Participation in the Hospitality Worker Program increased steadily between 1999 and 2006, rising from 2,462 to 5,192 workers (figure 8.6).[8] With the slowdown in the U.S. economy, the number of Jamaican hospitality workers began to decline, falling to their lowest level in 10 years in 2009 (359).

Jamaican workers make up about 20 percent of the annual cap for H-2B visas. A high percentage of the workers (90 percent) return each year (these workers are not included in the cap). In 2009, that cap was 66,000. Jamaicans are the second-largest group of migrants (after Mexicans) entering the United States on both the H-2A program for seasonal agricultural workers and the H-2B program for seasonal nonagricultural workers.

Most of the program's participants come from the hotel industry on the north coast of Jamaica, but workers entering include former teachers, retail workers, office workers, and students. More than half of participants are women.

Developmental Benefits

The hospitality program enables Jamaican workers to gain experience abroad and supplement their personal income. Workers voluntarily save a portion of their

Table 8.3 Remittances from Jamaican Overseas Agricultural and Hotel Worker Programs, 2003–10

thousands of US dollars, except where otherwise indicated

Source of remittances	2003	2004	2005	2006	2007	2008	2009	2010
Total U.S. remittances	11,410	12,611	11,358	13,052	14,832	9,913	6,154	6,391
U.S. farm remittances	3,637	4,296	4,011	4,376	5,721	6,265	4,926	5,630
U.S. hotel worker's remittances	7,773	8,315	7,34	8,677	9,111	3,648	1,228	1,676
Total Canadian remittances (Can $)	6,988	9,466	7,955	10,528	10,715	11,730	11,907	13,970

Source: Jamaican Ministry of Labour and Social Security n.d.

income, which facilitates return migration and increases both savings and remittances (table 8.3).

The success of the program has led to some short-term adverse effects on the local hotel industry, as local hotels are forced to replace workers who leave each year to participate in the program. However, when these employees return, the hotel industry benefits from their improved skills and international experience.

Conclusions and Recommendations

The temporary worker programs described in this chapter demonstrate that BLAs can be a viable mechanism for addressing labor shortages and providing short-term employment and training opportunities for foreign workers. The successes and failures of these programs can provide valuable lessons for establishing new ones.

The success of Caribbean programs can be attributed to the following factors:

- Strong government ownership and oversight of employment programs that are well integrated into the country's labor and employment strategy
- Flexible matching of supply and demand to alleviate seasonal and structural shortages in the labor market
- Good institutional framework for recruiting qualified workers, processing labor market opinions, and securing work permits quickly and efficiently
- Capitalizing on a clear need for workers in destination countries that is well matched to workers' comparative advantage
- Strategic use of PPPs with recruiters, academic institutions, and training institutes
- Combining of skills training with managed migration to strengthen local capacity and produce high-quality workers for overseas employment
- Equitable distribution of roles and responsibilities between sending and receiving countries

- Focus on specialized categories of worker, with clear rules for the length of employment and embedded incentives for return migration, such as compulsory savings schemes

To increase the development impact, governments should encourage more work study programs, which build skills and provide employment opportunities to semiskilled workers. New programs could be established in technical trades, such as mechanics, auto repair, and construction-related occupations.

Although MOUs offer a flexible mechanism for establishing bilateral labor arrangements, Caribbean countries should seek ways to gain preferential access to labor markets in Canada and the United States. A natural way to do so is through preferential trade agreements, which would increase market access for workers and ease the restrictions imposed by H2-A and H2-B quotas. The potential CARICOM–Canada free trade agreement would be a good starting point for locking in market access for Caribbean workers. It is conceivable that Canada could enter into a development-promoting trade agreement with CARICOM that includes a special protocol on labor cooperation (Chaitoo and Weston 2008). Mutual recognition of professional qualifications for services providers should be a key issue in the negotiation in order to facilitate cross-border provision of services. To date, the Canadian government has not offered to include such temporary worker programs in its bilateral free trade agreements.

Notes

1. CARICOM has 15 full members: Antigua and Barbuda, the Bahamas, Barbados, Belize, Bermuda, Dominica, Haiti, Grenada, Guyana, Jamaica, St. Kitts and Nevis, St. Lucia, St. Vincent and the Grenadines, Suriname, and Trinidad and Tobago.

2. The states are Antigua and Barbuda, Barbados, Dominica, Grenada, Guyana, St. Kitts and Nevis, St. Lucia, St. Vincent and the Grenadines, Suriname, and Trinidad and Tobago.

3. These categories include key personnel (managers, specialists); graduate trainees; sellers of business services; suppliers of contractual services; independent professionals; and short-term visitors for business purposes.

4. The economies of the Eastern Caribbean include Anguilla, Antigua and Barbuda, Dominica, Grenada, Montserrat, St. Kitts and Nevis, St. Lucia, and St. Vincent and the Grenadines.

5. The MOUs are not publically available. This information is based on secondary sources (Chanda 2009; Verma 2003).

6. This report points out a number of concerns related to migration of nurses, in particular the impact on nurse shortages and access to health services. A number of policy recommendations were proposed to address these problems, including policies to strengthen nurse education, manage migration, and better monitor and evaluate market developments.

7. The HEART Institute is the official training institute for the Jamaican work force operating under the Ministry of Education, Youth, and Culture.

8. This number is normally supplemented by workers recruited by U.S. employers through other means.

References

Chaitoo, R., and A. Weston. 2008. "Canada and the Caribbean Community: Prospects for an Enhanced Trade Arrangement." Caribbean Regional Negotiating Machinery, Kingston, Jamaica.

Chanda, R. 2009. "Mobility of Less-Skilled Workers under Bilateral Agreements: Lessons for the GATS." *Journal of World Trade* 43(3): 479–506.

Citizenship and Immigration Canada. 2012. *Facts and Figures 2011. Immigration Overview: Permanent and Temporary Residents*. Ottawa. http://www.cic.gc.ca/english/resources/statistics/facts2011/temporary/05.asp.

CRNM (Caribbean Regional Negotiating Machinery). 2008. "The Cariforum–EC Economic Partnership Agreement Treatment of Professional Services in the EPA, Jamaica." EPA Brief 3200.3/EPA-08 [08], CRNM, Kingston, Jamaica. http://www.sice.oas.org/TPD/CAR_EU/Studies/CRNM_professionalservices_e.pdf.

HRSDC (Human Resources and Social Development Canada). 2006. *Looking Ahead: A 10-Year Outlook for the Canadian Labour Market (2006–2015)*. Ottawa. http://www.hrsdc.gc.ca/eng/publications_resources/research/categories/labour_market_e/sp_615_10_06/sp_615_10_06e.pdf.

———. 2012. "Temporary Foreign Worker Program, Labour Market Opinion (LMO) Statistics: Annual Statistics 2008–2011." Ottawa. http://www.hrsdc.gc.ca/eng/workplaceskills/foreign_workers/stats/annual/table8aa.shtml.

Jamaica Gleaner. 2011. "Suspended: Charles Halts Canadian Nurses Training Programme." May 15. http://jamaica-gleaner.com/gleaner/20110515/lead/lead2.html.

Jamaica Information Service. 2013. "Pre-Selection Exercise for Canadian Farm Work Programme." January 16. http://www.jis.gov.jm/news/national/32747-pre-selection-exercise-for-canadian-farm-work-programme.

Jamaican Ministry of Labour and Social Security. n.d. "Labour Market Information System." Kingston. http://www.lmis.gov.jm/lmis.aspx?id=OverseasEmployment,Overseas%20Employment.

———. n.d.b. "Labour Market Information System." Kingston. http://www.lmis.gov.jm/lmis.aspx?id=Remittances,Remittances.

The Nassau Guardian Online. 2005. "The Contract, A Welcome Spinoff from World War II," February 12, 2005.

Salmon, M. E., J. Yan, H. Hewitt, and V. Guisinger. 2007. "Managed Migration: The Caribbean Approach to Addressing Nursing Services Capacity." *Health Services Research* 42(3) Part II: 1354–72.

U.S. Bureau of Labor Statistics. 2012. "Economic News Release. Table 6. The 30 Occupations with the Largest Projected Employment Growth, 2010–20." Washington, DC. http://www.bls.gov/news.release/ecopro.t06.htm.

U.S. Department of Homeland Security. 2009–12. *Yearbook of Immigration Statistics*. Washington, DC: Office of Immigration Statistics.

Verma, V. 2003. "The Mexican and Caribbean Seasonal Agricultural Workers Program." North-South Institute, Ottawa.

World Bank. 2009. "The Nurse Labor and Education Markets in the English-Speaking CARICOM: Issues and Options for Reform." Report 48988-LAC, World Bank, Washington, DC.

———. 2011. World Development Indicators (database), World Bank, Washington, DC, http://data.worldbank.org/data-catalog/world-development-indicators.

www.ingramcontent.com/pod-product-compliance
Lightning Source LLC
Chambersburg PA
CBHW080612270326
41928CB00016B/3025